SECOND EDITION

Reading and Learning in the Content Classroom

DIAGNOSTIC AND INSTRUCTIONAL STRATEGIES

Thomas H. Estes
University of Virginia

Joseph L. Vaughan, Jr.
East Texas State University

ALLYN AND BACON, INC.
Boston   London   Sydney   Toronto

What one knows is, in youth, of little moment;
they know enough who know how to learn.

Henry Brooks Adams

Library of Congress Cataloging in Publication Data

Estes, Thomas H., 1940-
    Reading and learning in the content classroom.

    Bibliography: p.
    Includes index.
    1. Reading comprehension. 2. Study, method of.
3. English language--Composition and exercises.
4. Reading--Ability testing. 5. Curriculum planning.
6. Interdisciplinary approach in education.
I. Vaughan, Joseph L., 1942-   . II. Title.
LB1050.45.E87 1985   428.4   85-3932
ISBN 0-205-08433-8

Printed in the United States of America

10 9 8 7 6 5 4 3 2 1 90 89 88 87 86 85

Contents

Contents

Contents

Contents

Contents

Contents

Contents

Preface to the Second Edition

In the beginning, we assumed that revision of a text already in place would be an easy matter, but how wrong we were! The unanswerable question we faced again and again was whether any change would improve or diminish the quality of what we had done earlier. In some cases, this was easy; for example, there were many places where we needed to update our references or change some detail to reflect more accurately what research and experience have taught us in the six years since the first edition. But in most cases, the problem was worse than that—how could we retain what had made the book so popular before while adding new information and yet stay within the page limitations economy dictated? In every case, any significant addition would result in equally significant deletions. To resolve the dilemma, we decided to cut the number and length of exemplary units of instruction from ten units in 222 pages to four units in 83 pages. The net effect was to give us the room we needed to build on what we'd done before without creating a monolithic tome.

The biggest changes in the second edition are these:

1. The chapter on Sources for Instructional Materials has been expanded into a guide to every major relevant resource likely to be found in a good instructional resource center. To accomplish this, we secured the services of an instructional resource expert, Ms. Betsy Anthony, education librarian at the University of Virginia. Her contributions alone will greatly enhance the value of our book and we are grateful for her help.
2. We have reconceptualized the issue of readability by casting our discussion in more contemporary terms, distinguishing among predictive analysis, measurement analysis, and criterial analysis. No longer will readability be reducible to simplistic formula, a possible danger in the first edition.
3. In both the diagnostic unit, Identifying Reading Needs, and the instructional unit, Diagnostic Instruction, we have added numerous practical suggestions and strategies for classroom use. It has always been our intent to produce a practical book with a strong theoretical base. The theory of what we're doing has not changed, but our work with school children and teachers has resulted in many new ideas for how to implement that the-

ory. (The theory, by the way, remains simple—children will learn best those ideas and information they can relate to what they already know and when given learning tasks they find successful. Reading in content areas *is*, for us, the improvement of learning in subject area study at every grade level.)

4. We have expanded the number of sections composing the book from three to four by setting apart the section on Organizing for Instruction. We hope this will serve to highlight the topics within this important section. At the very least, it has allowed us to incorporate the chapter on instructional resources and the exemplary units of instruction together into the main body of the text.

We are in hopes that the many previous users of the first edition and many new readers will find our work of great help in the important job of teaching students how to learn, how to think in response to text, and how to read what is required of them in schools.

T.H.E.
J.L.V., Jr.

Preface to the First Edition

The philosophy and format of this book are related to two ideas. First, we believe that teaching is not something someone does to someone else. Rather, it is the careful structuring of an environment in such a way as to maximize the possibility that students will learn. Ideally, this structuring results from cooperation between teachers and students. Second, we believe that learning to read is a lifelong process and that the objective of formal education is to help students become learners as well as learned. The *process* of learning, or ability to continue to learn, may well be more important to students than any *product* of learning, or possession of knowledge. In the words of Carl Rogers, "The most socially useful learning in the modern world is the learning of the process of learning, a combining of openness to experience and incorporation into oneself the process of change." (From *Freedom to Learn*, p. 163.)

Reading and Learning in the Content Classroom should provide you with an opportunity to structure the learning environment of students in such a way that they: 1) learn both in light of their abilities and in spite of their problems with reading; and 2) simultaneously develop skills and understandings necessary to their functioning as literate persons in a literate society.

Today, more than ever, subject matter teachers need to understand the relationship between reading and content instruction. They continually face decisions about what to teach and how to teach it. Their job might well be defined as one of maximizing the possibility of learning for students. Very often the learning they seek to effect is tied to students' reading abilities.

However, most content area teachers receive no training in reading instruction and are thus unable to respond to the inability of numerous students to get something from their textbooks. Fortunately, many undergraduate and graduate schools are realizing this and making an effort to correct what they see as a deficiency. Increasing numbers of states are requiring reading courses for secondary certification in an effort to heighten awareness that reading can be—must be—taught concurrently with subject matter. The greatest progress is being made by those teachers and prospective teachers who recognize that reading in content areas means 1) teaching reading and learning skills along with content, and 2) making appropriate instructional provisions for those students who find the reading task interfering with the learning task.

To assist teachers and prospective teachers in becoming more aware of and sensitive to reading in content classrooms, we have designed this book with a dual focus. Our concern is for both *diagnostic* and *instructional* techniques in content area instruction. Content area teachers need the skills with which to diagnose reading and learning difficulties of their pupils. They also need understandings with which to prescribe learning environments and provide learning opportunities for pupils in response to diagnostic information. It is such diagnostic and prescriptive insights that we hope this book will enable you to acquire.

The understandings to which we lead you through this book, however, may extend far beyond that which we may offer directly. In fact, our hope is that each user of this book will come individually to better understandings of the same concepts through different combinations of activities and experiences. In that spirit, we open each unit with a specific statement of conceptual objectives—general understandings toward which the unit is directed. You may consider these objectives a sort of overview of each unit. Think to yourself as you begin each unit: What do I know about these ideas? What might I like to know? Where could I get more information about the ideas? And so forth. It is such questions we want to help you answer.

In education and psychology we often hear that one learns only in proportion to his or her own effort. With that in mind, we have included two additional items immediately after the conceptual objectives for each unit. They are "Selected Readings" and "Suggested Activities." Traditionally, these sections follow chapters or units of books. We want you to view the sections, or units as we call them, as an integral part of your study, a part which you might utilize to at least as great an extent as you do the text of the book per se. These readings and activities may be most important for preservice teachers, as they are intended to stimulate the practice and familiarity with strategies and devices which are so important for "second-nature" application in a classroom.

What we are really trying to do with our suggestions for readings and activities is to help in your search for information and understanding of the concepts related to the topic of the unit. We have keyed the readings and activities to those concepts and have cross-referenced activities within the text. As you come to references to activities and readings in the margins of the text, consider their value *to you*. Certainly, no one will be able or need to recall all we reference, nor do we expect any reader to engage in every activity we suggest. It is certain, however, on the basis of work with our own students, that your learning from this book will be proportional to your active response to it. For this reason, we don't leave your response to chance alone.

As you study any unit, examine the parts and begin to make some decisions. Which concepts are most intriguing to you? Which of the headings are familiar to you, which have you previously thought you might want to explore? Which of the activities do you think would be most helpful to you in developing the skills you feel you need? How do the chapters treat the concepts? In other words, try to get the gist of each unit before you settle in to specific and individualized study. When you do settle in, make your study as purposeful as possible. Direct your effort to the search for understandings and information that you need to have rather than allowing it to be restricted to what we need to say. To the degree this becomes possible, authors and readers both will have accomplished an important purpose with this book.

T.H.E.
J.L.V., Jr.

UNIT 1

Reading in the Content Classroom

Conceptual Objectives

1. Nothing is so unequal as the equal treatment of unequals.

2. What is taught must be determined by what students can learn.

3. The objectives of content area instruction include both the product and the process of study.

4. Reading materials can and should be assessed for difficulty and appropriateness.

Activity and Selected Readings Key

Suggested Activities

	CONCEPTS			
	1	2	3	4
1. Investigate the range of reading abilities of pupils in your classes, using school records of achievements. (p. 9)	X			
2. After responding to the attitude scale (pp. 10–12), discuss your responses and opinions with your colleagues.				X
3. How would you define reading? Write out your definition. (p. 14)		X		
4. Interview persons you know whose reading ability you respect. Ask them why and how they think they read well.		X		
5. Visit a professional library in your school system and survey different authorities' views of reading in content areas. (p. 14)		X		X
6. Systematically skim this text and identify the relationships among the various parts of the book.		X		
7. Read the summary of what you consider to be "key" chapters in this book. Compare the basic ideas inherent in this book with your concept of "higher levels of reading."		X		
8. Determine the readability level of several different chapters in a text or selections in an anthology to see whether the difficulty is consistent throughout. (p. 37)			X	
9. Examine a reading selection that you might use with your class; list the major concepts the author is discussing. Then, conduct a discussion with your students to see how much they seem to know of the concepts. (pp. 40–42)			X	X

	CONCEPTS			
	1	2	3	4
10. Using the information you obtained in activities 1 and 9, compare the results to the difficulty of the book as estimated by the Fry formula.	X		X	
11. Administer a cloze passage to your students. Evaluate the relative appropriateness of the procedure. Compare results obtained with the Fry formula. (p. 38)			X	
12. Check with the librarian of your school to see what information is available on the difficulty of materials related to your subject area. For example, there are various guides to books for young people which might be helpful in selecting materials. (pp. 41–42)	X		X	
13. Among members of your school staff organize a committee for evaluation and collection of supplementary materials to use in your courses. For example, in social studies, consider the wealth of "fictionalized" books and materials. (p. 42)	X	X		X
14. Examine the curriculum guide available for the course you teach. Try to determine whether the objectives of instruction described there are or might be set in conceptual terms. (pp. 23–25)				X
15. Make a list of the reading assignments you have given your students over the last six weeks or so. What kind(s) of reading was required and how satisfactory do you think it was for the students? (pp. 21–22)	X		X	X
16. Consider the curriculum of the course you teach in terms of your own background and ability. Evaluate your perceived success with each topic or chapter to determine whether what you teach best is what you most like to teach. Ask whether the emphasis of your course is appropriate to your strengths and interests.				X

(continued)

	CONCEPTS			
	1	2	3	4
17. Choose a random sample of twenty students from your classes. Investigate their background and interests through cumulative folders and personal knowledge to determine how appropriate what they are expected to learn in your course is to them. (pp. 24–25)	X			X
18. The concept of "Foxfire" is more than a magazine. How could you use the "Foxfire principle" in your classroom?	X			X

Selected Readings*

	CONCEPTS			
	1	2	3	4
1. Wigginton, Eliot. *The Foxfire Book; Foxfire II;* and *Foxfire III.* Specifically, the introductions to each of these. Hitch your wagon to these stars!	X			X
2. Rogers, Carl. *Freedom to Learn.*	X			X
3. Mager, Robert. *Preparing Instructional Objectives.*				X
4. Adler and Van Doren. *How to Read a Book.*		X		X
5. Spache and Spache. *Reading in the Elementary School, 4th edition.* Specifically chapter 1, "Ways of Defining the Reading Process."		X		
6. Klare, George. "Assessing Readability."			X	

*(Full bibliographic information for these items will be found at the and of the book under References.)

CHAPTER 1   Reading and Learning

Nothing is so unequal as the equal treatment of unequals.

What is taught must be determined by what students can learn.

Foxfire: An Experiment in Learning

The Foxfire Book, enjoyed by thousands since its first appearance in 1972, is a testament to the frustrations of one English teacher and, even more importantly, to the way in which he solved those frustrations. In his first six weeks of teaching, Eliot Wigginton had his lectern burned, his chalk stolen, and his chart of the Globe Theatre mutilated. As he pondered his options, he decided that the

> . . . answer was obvious. If I were to finish out the year honorably, it would be necessary to reassert my authority. No teenagers were going to push me around. Besides, my course was too important. First offense would be an "X" in the grade book. Second, a paddling. Third, to the principal. Fourth, out of class for two weeks.
>
> It frightens me to think how close I came to making another stupid mistake. First, I had bored them unmercifully. Now I was about to impose a welcome punishment. Two weeks out of that class would have been more pleasure than pain.

Fortunately, Wigginton had an inspiration; he chose neither to seek greener pastures nor to implement "another stupid mistake." Instead, the

> next day I walked into class and said, "How would you like to start a magazine?" And that's how *Foxfire* began (*The Foxfire Book*, 1972, p. 10).

5

In the next twelve years, Wigginton published seven collections of articles from many editions of *Foxfire*, a magazine produced by his students and distributed through subscriptions in every state and many foreign countries.

In *Moments: The Foxfire Experience*, Wigginton (1975) recounts many of the experiences, thrilling and harrowing, that are etched on the minds and hearts of those who "birthed that baby." As one reads about the organizational nightmares, the unique learning activities, and the English curriculum that emerged from the project, one is struck by the realization that this was almost a project that never was. Wig, as his friends call him, proceeds to share the stories of Suzy, Carlton, Barbara, Claude, Aunt Arie Carpenter, and Bill Lamb, among others. These folks were engaged in learning, for Foxfire, as a project, is rooted in the conviction that students ". . . must have the world outside the classroom as the primary motivation for learning, and at the heart and soul of *what* they learn" (1975, p. 5).

Today, as we read reports that criticize our educational institutions, we can't help but notice the contrast between what Wigginton accomplished and what John Goodlad (1983) observed in classrooms all across the country.

> Students listened; they responded when called on to do so; they read short sections of textbooks; they wrote short responses to questions or chose among alternative responses in quizzes. But they rarely planned or initiated anything, read or wrote anything of some length, or created their own products. And they scarcely ever speculated on meanings, discussed alternative interpretations, or engaged in projects that call for collaborative effort. Most of the time they listened or worked alone. (p. 468)

From what we can tell, Foxfire was born because a teacher decided to design a curriculum around students rather than try to shape students around a subject in school. Wigginton had seen the messages that pervaded his classroom that fall of 1968.

> The kid who had scorched my lectern had been trying to tell me something. He and his classmates, through their boredom and restlessness, were sending out distress signals—signals that I came perilously close to ignoring.
>
> It's the same old story. The answer to student boredom and restlessness (manifested in everything from paper airplanes to dope) maybe—just maybe—is not stricter penalties, innumerable suspensions, and bathroom monitors. How many schools (mine included) have dealt with those students that still have fire and spirit, *not* by channeling that fire in constructive, creative directions, but by pouring water on the very flames that could make them great? (1972, p. 14)

It is easy for most of us to empathize with Mr. Wigginton in his nearly disastrous, first-year experience *and* to envy his courage to accomplish what he knew and felt to be a better way.

Unfortunately, most of us, like him, began our careers teaching as we were taught with our attention focused more on *what* we were to teach than on our students who were to learn. Such ill-directed attention to curriculum at the expense of students can often be attributed to priorities within teacher training programs. Often, the training that teachers receive which prepares them for teaching a content subject concerns primarily the subject and not the students, especially not how the students learn. This is unfortunate because the real job of teaching happens to involve students, not subjects. Eliot Wigginton discovered this secret to teaching, perhaps quicker than others of us, and he also saw fit to remind us that "until we can *inspire* rather than babysit, we're in big trouble" (1972, p. 14).

The Foxfire Principle

For most teachers, the anomaly between students and subjects is soon resolved and a successful career proceeds. You know of Eliot Wigginton's startling awareness. Subsequently, he made several decisions. First, he decided that English could be defined as "communication—reaching out and touching people with words, sounds, and visual images" (*The Foxfire Book*, p. 13). Second, he decided that the lore and legend of Rabun Gap, Georgia, could form the basis of that communication. Thus, he decided that the immediacy of the content would facilitate mastery of the communicative art. In other words, English might be learned as communication if what was communicated was immediate and real to the learners. Accordingly, Mr. Wigginton's success was not so much a function of *Foxfire* (that was evidence of the success) but was a result of defining and teaching his subject matter in a way that it could be learned. This is, we believe, the first principle of instruction:

> Of all that could be taught, what is taught must be determined by what students can learn.

What was true in Rabun Gap—Nacoochee School, grades 9 and 10 English class in 1968—remains everywhere true today. For example, what might be taught in a science class is virtually anything within the domain of natural phenomena. But what tenth grade science students can learn includes only a portion of that domain. This basic principle of instruction holds true for any subject in school. It is ignored when we teach as if what might be learned were synonymous with what might be taught, as if what might be learned included all that might be taught. Figure 1.1 depicts the intersection of two circles. One represents what students can learn; the other represents what might be taught, i.e., the domain of the subject within the course. The intersection of these two circles delimits *what* should be taught. What to teach is only part of the story of diagnosis, as you might guess. It is, however,

7

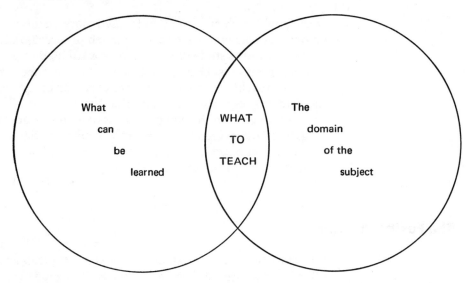

FIGURE 1.1
The Foxfire Principle

so important that much of what we have to say about diagnostic instruction will be directly or indirectly related to determining what to teach. Thus, the intersection of what can be learned and what might be taught is a major focus of our attention.

Literacy and Learning

Determining what to teach from a perspective of what students can learn is half the story of teaching in a subject area classroom; how to teach it is the other half. Eliot Wigginton knew this when he revamped his English curriculum in Rabun Gap. Having defined the curricular domain (communication) and what could be learned (to communicate content of genuine interest), the problem remained of how to involve all the students in the learning. "It hasn't always worked, but we try" is Wigginton's understatement. To involve everyone requires attention to the range of individual abilities and learning styles in the classroom, an educational goal made no easier by the fact that almost every curriculum guide adopts it.

Individual differences in reading ability can be found at all levels of a curriculum, and the nature of this diversity raises an interesting question. What is the relationship between grade level and range of individual differences in reading ability? To delineate the question somewhat more specifically, does the range of reading ability in a classroom decrease, remain constant, or increase with successive grade levels? The answer to this query becomes more evident if one realizes that what pupils learn is directly related to what they already know. The implication of this is that good teaching inevitably leads to increased rather than constant or diminished differences among individuals.

A simple way to approximate the range of differences among students' reading abilities at a specific grade level is to apply the following formula:

$$\text{RANGE} \approx \text{grade level} \pm \frac{\text{grade level} + 1}{2}$$

For example, the range of reading ability in a heterogeneous seventh grade classroom is approximately ($\approx$) 7 $\pm$ 8/2, which is 7 $\pm$ 4, or grades three to eleven. Thus, some students in the typical seventh grade class may be reading on a third grade level, others on an eleventh grade level; and the ability range among these same pupils will increase with successive grade levels! Clearly, if all these students are to be involved in learning in the same classroom, they must be given opportunities to learn as individuals; they should not always be taught as a large group.

Our second principle of instruction, therefore, is this: How to teach is defined by how students learn. By considering individual differences, however, we do not mean to suggest that students should be isolated to progress through programs individually. To pursue the Foxfire story one step further, some students found it possible to write feature articles; for others copying and placing paragraphs in the layout was a challenge. But—all were involved, and all were learning since each was allowed in the setting of that English class to function first as an individual and second as a member of the class.

Can there be any other way for schools to succeed in their mission? Consider the social studies teacher in eleventh grade, for example. In many schools, eleventh grade social studies is United States history, and the domain of study includes the government, geography, history, and sociology of the United States. *What* students can learn of that can be determined by diagnostic instruction. *How* they can learn it is also critical. Some will be able to read in primary sources; others will find the text appropriate; and yet others will learn from simpler material like comics, picture books, magazines, and other media. It is likely each will learn from various sources, but *all* can be involved. *That* is the point and purpose of individualized instruction.

Reading, like attendance and attention, is an assumed prerequisite for academic success. For many pupils, however, reading in content area textbooks is a very real problem. Not uncommonly, up to 50 percent of the students in an upper-grade class cannot read their textbooks. This is not to suggest that these students cannot read; on the contrary, most are quite lit-

9

erate. Literacy, however, does not guarantee success with all types of reading assignments. Because a student can read some material successfully does not ensure that he or she is proficient enough to learn effectively from a content area textbook.

There is a need for reading in content area classrooms. How that is to be effected and what it entails we will examine throughout this book. At this point, however, consider this question: Isn't teaching reading in content area classrooms a reasonable proposition? If taught how to learn and read better, might not students learn more now and in the future? Consider what an affirmative answer to these questions might mean to you. Better yet, reserve a definite answer at this time and give serious consideration to Activity 1.1.

This activity is designed to help you do the following: (1) Examine your opinions regarding a set of statements which are often heard as teachers argue the merits of teaching reading in content areas; and (2) expound on the ideas that you have regarding teaching reading in content areas.

ACTIVITY 1.1

What Do You Think?

Instructions Place a check in the box that best represents your agreement with the corresponding statement.

	7 STRONGLY AGREE	6 AGREE	5 TEND TO AGREE	4 UNDECIDED	3 TEND TO DISAGREE	2 DISAGREE	1 STRONGLY DISAGREE
1. A content area teacher is obliged to help students improve their reading ability.							
2. Technical vocabulary should be introduced to students in content classes before they meet those terms in a reading passage.							

	7	6	5	4	3	2	1
	STRONGLY AGREE	AGREE	TEND TO AGREE	UNDECIDED	TEND TO DISAGREE	DISAGREE	STRONGLY DISAGREE
3. The primary responsibility of a content teacher is to impart subject matter knowledge.							
4. Few students can learn all they need to know about how to read in the first six years of school.							
5. The sole responsibility for teaching students how to study should lie with reading teachers.							
6. Coursework in how to teach reading in content areas should be required for secondary teaching certification.							
7. Only English teachers should be responsible for teaching reading in secondary schools.							
8. A teacher who wants to improve students' interest in reading should show them that he or she likes to read.							
9. Content area teachers should teach content and leave reading instruction to reading teachers.							
10. A content area teacher should be responsible for helping students think on an interpretive level as well as on a literal level when they read.							

(*continued*)

	7	6	5	4	3	2	1
	STRONGLY AGREE	AGREE	TEND TO AGREE	UNDECIDED	TEND TO DISAGREE	DISAGREE	STRONGLY DISAGREE
11. Content area teachers should feel a greater responsibility to the content they teach than to any reading instruction they may be able to provide.							
12. Content area teachers should help students learn to set purposes for reading.							
13. Every content area teacher should teach students how to read material in that teacher's content specialty.							
14. Reading instruction in secondary schools would be unnecessary if elementary schools were successful in their jobs.							
15. Content area teachers should be familiar with theoretical concepts of the reading process.							

We designed this scale (Vaughan, 1977) because we believe that teachers' attitudes are among the most significant determiners of students' learning. Specifically, those teachers who are aware of and sympathetic to any difficulties their students may have reading their textbooks are likely to be those teachers who will do something about it. Resolution of students' difficulties, then, may well begin with the teacher's attitude toward the problem. So, how does your attitude compare to those of other content area teachers? First, you'll have to score your responses, and the scoring of an individual's responses must account for the fact that nine of the items are positive while six are negative in nature. The negative items should be scored in reverse from the positive items, so the following table is provided to assist in the scoring process:

12

TABLE 1.1
Scoring the Vaughan Attitude Scale

		Response Value						
	7	6	5	4	3	2	1	
Response to:								
(Positive items):								
1, 2, 4, 6, 8, 10, 12, 13, 15	7	6	5	4	3	2	1	
(Negative items):								
3, 5, 7, 9, 11, 14	1	2	3	4	5	6	7	

Now compute the total summed score for your responses on the basis of the response values.

Based on a range of summative scores derived from the validation studies for this scale (Vaughan and Sabers, 1977), several broad, descriptive categories have been identified for interpretation purposes. Thus, interpret your score according to the following criteria:

TABLE 1.2
Interpretation Table for Vaughan Attitude Scale

Range	Attitude
91 or higher	High
81 - 90	Above Average
71 - 80	Average
61 - 70	Below Average
60 or lower	Low

Now, then, what do you think? Or, how do you feel? And what does it all mean?

Research related to the teaching of literacy in content area classrooms (e.g., DeWitz, Henning, & Patburg, 1982; Wolf & Greenewald, 1980) suggests that teachers with positive attitudes are more likely to learn about ways to improve students' literacy in their classrooms. Thus, if you are to profit from any ideas in this text, it will be to your advantage to have a positive attitude toward the basic idea that students in content area classrooms may well need help understanding their textbooks. Let us add one caution, however, from the same research. A positive attitude does not necessarily translate into action in the classroom; just because you are positively inclined toward the idea that content area teachers can help students with their reading does not mean that you will do anything about it.

The problem of reading in content areas is not given a solution in the phrase "every teacher is a teacher of reading," which was bandied about several years ago as the nostrum to cure all reading ills. Actually, it is self-defeating to say every teacher is a teacher of reading, just as it is self-defeating to think that a successful English teacher like Eliot Wigginton teaches English. He teaches students. That is the essence of reading and learning in any classroom, and content area teachers cannot be divorced from such a mission.

Reading as Learning

We suspect that your attitude toward teaching reading in content classrooms is largely influenced by your perspective on the issue of teaching students or teaching subject matter. Your attitude is also affected by your perception of reading and what is meant by reading instruction. Therefore, before we discuss issues of diagnosis and instruction, the essence of this book, let's clarify a few things about reading. Let's begin with a definition, yours and ours. So:

Think, and then write out your definition of reading. (Don't cop out by running to the nearest dictionary. Compose *your* ideas here.)

Now, we want you to rely on the definition you just composed to answer two questions. Notice, that in each case, the answer will be either "Yes" or "No".

1. Can you read: "biathlon"? Yes or No?
2. Can you read: "koyaanisqatsi"? Yes or No?

Now, think about your answers especially as *you* have defined reading. WARNING: We are being a bit tricky here! Consider why you have answered each of these questions as you have.

Now let's see where we stand. Our guess about your definition is that you included ideas or terms related to meaning, understanding, and/or comprehension. That is, you probably conceive reading to be something that occurs when one obtains meaningful information from print, much as we hope you are doing now.

What, though, about those two questions? Can you read "biathlon" or "koyaanisqatsi"? Only you will know, but here's the trick we warned you about. If you said that you can read these two words and yet you do *not* know what they mean, you really don't believe meaning is part of reading, not subconsciously anyway. Of course, it is very plausible that you do know that biathlon is a sport that combines skiing and shooting. (You may be interested to know that during the 1984 Winter Olympics, only one person in twenty-seven interviewed by ABC Sports knew the meaning of biathlon.) It is also possible that you know that "life out of balance" is what a Hopi means by koyaanisqatsi. It is also the title of a Francis Ford Coppola film that received rave reviews.

Our point is this: If you do know a meaning for these words and you answered our questions in the affirmative, then you really do believe that meaning is an essential part of reading. The same goes if you responded in the negative if you weren't familiar with a meaning for these words. So, where do you stand? Were your responses consistent with your definition?

If you really believe that reading involves meaning, we agree! Of course, there's more to it than that. Actually we believe that when we speak of reading we are really speaking of learning; reading is a way to learn. What goes on in the mind/brain complex during reading is very much the same activity as when one is thinking about other things. The difference is that the source, or cue, for the thinking is a printed word.

We believe that reading is thinking cued by printed text. This is, of course, our definition and as such we mean only to explain what our thinking is. We cannot cause you to understand all that we mean simply by giving you our definition. We can, however, cause you to think about our definition and thereby think about what we mean. And that is what reading is all about.

An author thinks about ideas and puts those ideas into words, phrases, sentences, paragraphs, and so forth. When the reader sees those words, phrases, sentences, and so forth, they cue the reader to think about experiences, concepts, and feelings. Those experiences somehow come together into what we call comprehension. In that way, reading is thinking cued by printed text. The author provides the cue in the text and the reader interprets the cue based on prior experiences and understandings.

Hence, if you had prior associations with our two words "biathlon" or "koyaanisqatsi" you may have recognized (note: *re* (again) + *cognize* (think) = to think again) a familiar meaning. On the other hand, if we had provided you with a meaningful context for either word, you could have learned the word and its correspondent concept through reading.

Several factors are involved in this communication process besides the author and the publisher. Three are of particular importance: (1) the reader, (2) the text, and (3) the context in which the reading occurs. Of these three, only the text remains constant, though when one reads a text for a second or third time it often appears as though the text has changed. Text, then, is a static element. On the other hand, the reader and the context are never the same. Every second of every day each of us changes in measurable ways and in more ways that are hidden from us. Likewise, the time, place, and circumstance of a reading activity are constantly in flux.

In her book, *The Reader, the Text, the Poem*, Louise Rosenblatt (1976)

15

suggests that reading is an event, something akin to what others (e.g., Iser, 1978; Fish, 1978) refer to as a phenomenological view of reading. The point is that any activity involving reading is unique and can never be exactly the same at any other time. Although the text remains the same, the reader and the contexts will always be different. What the reader brings in the way of experiences and conceptualizations and feelings to any reading event is always changing because readers, as human beings, are always changing.

In the next chapter, we will examine some of the factors that impinge on the contexts of reading and learning in content study. In Chapter 3, we will examine issues related to texts and text selection that make learning through reading easier for students. As we conclude this introduction, however, let us share with you an experience we had recently at a workshop in Louisiana.

A principal participating in the workshop approached us and said that he was perplexed that he could not convey the importance of reading instruction to his high school instructional staff. He had held workshops with local and outside consultants; he had provided them with literature in the form of journal articles and ideas from varied sources. They continued to balk. We asked him what he wanted his teachers to do that they resisted. He replied, "To teach the basic skills of reading once a week in their classes, you know, phonics, main idea skills, and vocabulary drills. If these students can't do these basics, they will not be able to do well in their academic studies."

We were pleased that these teachers had resisted for what they had been asked to do was teach the curriculum of reading, not reading in the context of their own curriculum. By the time this principal left us, he too saw the difference and he has implemented a new approach to the problems he had so correctly identified. Now his teachers have responded favorably. They are teaching reading as a learning activity in the context of content study. How? That is what the rest of this book is all about.

A Summary Comment

With the exception of this chapter, you will find the "summary" at the beginning, not the end of the chapters. Actually, what you will find is not a summary at all, but an "Overview." Our intent is to facilitate your reading by cueing your thinking before you get too far into the chapter. We hope your experiences include enough specific information about each topic so that our overview will focus your thinking as we begin our discussion. This technique of providing an overview, hence focusing a reader's attention, is something we discuss at length in Chapter 9.

Reading is thinking cued by print and the most reasonable context in which to practice thinking and reading is in content area classrooms. After all, when learning to read or when learning to read better, students should read about ideas worth learning about. Too, when learning and reading, students benefit from instruction that guides them to exploration of meaningful content, content that is meaningful to them. After all, that's what the Foxfire project is all about. Eliot Wigginton is one of our favorite teachers, not because he created a magazine or because he recorded the ways of life in north Georgia, but because he teaches students first and English second. The what and the how of teaching must be firmly grounded in that principle: we teach students and our intended outcome is that they learn how to learn.

As for summaries in subsequent chapters, we suggest that you create them for yourself. Among the most prevalent findings from current learning research is the notion that summarizing is an invaluable learning activity. We will provide the overview; you consolidate your own thinking by constructing the summaries.

CHAPTER 2

The Context of Content Study

The objectives of content area instruction include both the product and the process of study.

Overview

Most content teachers think of themselves as experts in a particular field. It is not uncommon for English teachers to have a zealous love of literature and poetry that they want to share with their students; for the chemistry teacher to see students in the classroom as budding young chemists; and for history teachers to dream of creating fellow history buffs. While such fervor for an academic area is admirable in teachers, it is naive to expect such enthusiasm from the average student who is trying to handle five or six different content classes, cope with the same number of content vocabularies, and master hundreds of new concepts. Instead, it is more realistic to see one's students as young people just beginning to acquire a body of knowledge and accompanying skills. We like to see ourselves, therefore, as teaching students how to learn. If we can just make education enjoyable and stimulating enough to create inquiring minds that will keep learning and keep seeking new plateaus after they leave our classrooms, then we can feel satisfied that we have launched them into a lifetime of learning.

You'll recall our first principle of instruction: Of all that could be taught, what is taught must be determined by what students can learn. We have a simple rule of thumb we use to resist the temptation of insisting that students learn everything our content area has to offer. The rule is this: What would I like them to know five years from now? By asking ourselves this question, we steer away from multitudes of dates, details, and definitions. We focus instead on the larger picture of the concepts we are sharing with our students. We find our rule of thumb most helpful in structuring the learning environment. What, though, are the major factors that influence that learning environment? And, for that matter, how do they fit into the overall object of schooling?

Instructional Contexts

Kohlberg and Mayer (1972) make the argument that the most important aim of education is the development of the child. In their view—and ours—schools exist to provide a structured opportunity for children to develop in terms of both what they are and what they know. We must, however, take care that these opportunities fit the developmental plan inherent within the student, thereby avoiding the tragedy that confronts "the hurried child" who is propelled by parents, teachers, and society at large to perform and to achieve at a pace that is contradistinctive to his or her personal developmental timetable. Elkind (1983) encourages parents and teachers alike to be sensitive to children's individual developmental patterns and to create an educational context consistent with the premise that the object of education is to foster intellectual and personal growth among individuals. This goal is best accomplished by allowing the learner the chance to interact with the learning environment while receiving help and guidance of the kind he or she needs. This is the basis for our first principle of instruction: What is taught must be determined by what students can learn.

As we consider the major factors that influence what should be taught, prominent among them are: (1) students' needs, (2) a teacher's goals, and (3) curricular demands. While each of these factors contributes significantly to any instructional context, of greater import is the interaction among them. In fact, an understanding of this interaction is essential if what is to be taught is to be determined judiciously. John Dewey (1902) was speaking of this when he wrote:

> The child is the starting point, the center, and the end. His development, his growth, is the ideal. It alone furnishes the standard. (p. 95) Abandon the notion of subject-matter as something fixed and readymade in itself, outside the child's experience; cease thinking of the child's experience as also something hard and fast; see it as something fluent, embryonic, vital; and we realize that the child and the curriculum are simply two limits which define a single process. Just as two points define a straight line, so the present standpoint of the child and the facts and truths of studies define instruction. It is continuous reconstruction, moving from the child's present experience out into that represented by the organized bodies of truth that we call studies. (pp. 96–97)

19

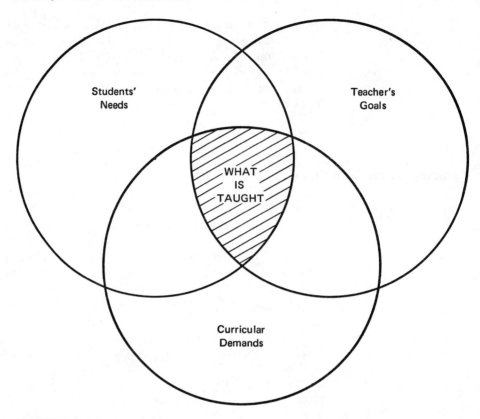

FIGURE 2.1
Factors Affecting Instructional Contexts

Hence, materials and activities that are used in subject matter instruction must be: (1) appropriate to the abilities and interests of pupils; (2) feasible for the teacher to arrange; and (3) honest to the curriculum or domain of study under scrutiny.

We might, then, extend our first principle of instruction to suggest that what is taught must be determined by the appropriate interaction of students' needs, a teacher's goals, and curricular demands. These three elements of an instructional context deserve careful consideration by any content area teacher who wants to create an effective learning environment where the focus is on students, not subjects.

Students' Needs

Given a topic for study and its related concepts which the teacher hopes pupils will come to understand better, the needs of pupils must be considered in light of three categories: (1) personal needs, (2) skill needs, and (3) learning needs. The following kinds of questions are essential to the planning of instructional objectives.

1. *Personal Needs:* What are the possibilities for personal fulfillment in the students' study? Do the information and skills to be explored and taught offer any possibility of personal application *or* fulfillment for the students? For example, career interests might be sparked for some; information and skills that are useful in other courses might be explored. Any unit can offer varied opportunities for application of personal talents (drawing maps, making collages, designing displays, sharing experiences, etc.). The success which is insured by a concern for each student's personal needs may foster more general success and a feeling of personal satisfaction.

2. *Skill Needs:* The specific kinds of skills to be required should be delineated as precisely as possible in the planning of instruction. To what extent are the students adept with the skills required for successful learning? To what extent are you, the teacher, aware of their abilities? For those students who are deficient in requisite skills, what instruction should be provided? What alternative modes of study might be made available? Success in learning may well depend upon appropriate diagnosis and consideration of specific skill needs exhibited by students, followed by appropriate instruction.

3. *Learning Needs:* Of all that might be taught, what can the students learn that will benefit them? What provisions are made for multi-level material? What do the students already know about the subject? What are the basic concepts that they must know? In this aspect, the content teacher must be the authority. Decisions about what to include, as well as what can be omitted, must be made on the basis of what students know and what they will be able to learn.

Teacher's Goals

The teacher's perspective of the breadth and depth of a course largely determines what is taught at a given time. Within any content area there is infinitely more that might be taught than can be taught. Choices must be made. Certain understandings are often necessary for subsequent study of other concepts. This is obviously true in a course such as mathematics, where so much skill work depends on previous understandings, but it is true in other studies also. Learning is itself a preparation for learning; thus, the teacher must orchestrate instruction to simultaneously account for past, present, and future learning. At any moment, a teacher must be able to answer certain critical questions, namely:

1. Why am I teaching this particular lesson or unit?
2. What are the resources which I might use to help students learn? (These

could easily include the teacher's own personal experiences, supplementary reading of all kinds, guests to the classroom, field trips, the librarian and other resource persons, or films and video tapes.)

3. What is my purpose for each part of the overall plan and how much of that purpose and plan will require explanation to the students?

4. How much time will this study require? How much time will be available for diversion?

5. In what ways can I, the teacher, learn along with my students?

Perhaps we can provide some context for the factor of a teacher's goals relative to students' needs with an experience shared by a friend of ours who wrote,

> When my daughter was two years old I decided she was big enough to give up the baby swings and learn to swing in a regular swing, so I helped her up and got her fingers clasped onto the chains. I jumped into the empty swing beside her and took off high into the air while she did nothing but sit there. "Come on, honey, swing!" I called out. "But, Mommy, I don't know how," she replied. I felt like a fool as I stopped my swing and got out to help her. I explained to her how to stretch her legs out and how to bend forward and lean backward to gain momentum. And many times over the years my daughter's words have come back to me. Each time I ask students to take notes and look up at the blank stares, each time I start to ask students to do any task without first explaining it to them, I hear those words, "But, Mommy, I don't know how." And that indignant protest of my two year old many years ago has prevented me from rushing students into new tasks without the proper modeling beforehand. I no longer operate under the assumption that my students already know things. I review it for them anyway.

Indeed, we must keep the needs of our students uppermost in our minds. It is too easy to let our own personal goals and the pressures of curricular demands push us onward with little consideration for whether our students know how to swing.

Curricular Demands

Curricular demands means the content information that is traditionally accepted as what *must* be taught. It represents the third factor on which many instructional decisions must be based. Curricular demands appear in the tertiary position here by no accident; too often they have formed the only foundation for instruction and, yet, they may well be least important after pupils' needs and teacher's goals. We *can* de-emphasize them by minimizing their importance. However, school boards and courts by right can and do say what is to be taught in schools (and, for that matter, what is *not* to be taught).

In planning instructional objectives, therefore, teachers must give attention to curricular demands, all the while keeping students' needs and his or her own goals and resources in mind. A teacher must determine what curricular demands are appropriate for the students. In making such decisions, the teacher outlines the *curriculum*, which we define as "what *is* taught."

An effective way to integrate pupil needs, teacher goals, and curricular demands is to identify and plan each unit around specific concepts. These concepts should be stated and their development fostered at a level appropriate to the needs and abilities of the students. In this way, the teacher can at least partially insure that the abilities and needs of the students are in consonance with the learning demanded by the curriculum.

Effective instruction is the direct outgrowth of careful planning, and careful planning is based on these three curricular foundations. All that takes time, certainly. Nothing is more professionally rewarding, however, than well-planned, smoothly executed instruction, especially since the result is likely to be effective, productive learning.

Instructional Objectives

When Robert Mager published his book, *Preparing Instructional Objectives* (1962), even he probably didn't guess the impact it would have. Educators at every level were literally swept off balance by behavioral objectives. Anything taught in school could be translated into behavioral terms and tested with micrometer-like precision. Curriculum guides were translated with haste; the bandwagon filled quickly. The result is that today many teachers can hardly think of what they teach without relying on behavioral terminology. Where the use of these objectives proves difficult, many begin to question their ability to teach: "Am I doing something wrong? Is what I want to teach wrong?" Probably not. More likely, the trees have eclipsed the view of the forest, and the purpose of teaching is often obscured in the mire of objectives made for purposes of evaluation.

While some objectives lend themselves well to behavioral terms, others that are equally important do not. Though many objectives of education may result in changed behavior, observable behavior does not necessarily provide the most convenient way to view all objectives. Our work with content area teachers has shown us the need to emphasize two kinds of objectives; one that is conceptual, the other process-related.

Conceptual objectives are those objectives that are primarily related to ideas and understandings rather than to behaviors. They can be written in behavioral terms by identifying a behavior that may evidence the learning of them, but the focus of conceptual objectives is on an idea or concept. In other words, conceptual objectives are related to students' understanding of basic, general ideas, for example, "Habitat influences both life forms and life styles of organisms." The emphasis is on the idea or concept to be developed. Another example, one appropriate to social studies, might be, "Man constantly encounters conflict and seeks its resolution." In this case, the basic concept—conflict and its resolution—is identified as the major focus of study. Additional examples of conceptual objectives are identified at the beginning of each chapter within this book.

Process objectives, by comparison, can be related to the development of various processes or skills of learning, such as, "the ability to preread or inspect a selection for the purpose of establishing a set for information acquisition and determining an appropriate reading approach." Of particular importance in the context of reading in a content area classroom is that process objectives are concerned with *how* students learn. The process objectives, then, are those objectives that relate to students' abilities to acquire and develop understanding.

Integration of meaningful conceptual and process objectives is fundamental to reading and learning in a content classroom. The behavior required by mature reading can best be developed in a setting where there is meaningful content to be read. On the other hand, students are most likely to develop meaningful concepts when they are taught how to deal effectively with subject matter. The content teacher who designs instructional objectives with emphasis divided between learning process and learning content, whose instruction reflects the complementary relationship between processes and conceptualizations, will serve both sets of objectives.

Instructional Considerations

How many games, battles, and arguments have been won on paper only to be lost in the heat of the engagement? Likewise, what purpose can be served by discussing instructional objectives without considering how to use them? To be more specific, content area teachers are faced daily with problems in teaching that are the direct result of an inequitable relationship between their students and the material chosen to help those students learn. This book is dedicated to those teachers and their problems.

The units and chapters to follow will delineate specific diagnostic and instructional strategies which can be used to solve or help minimize instructional problems. What we suggest, however, is based on the idea of teaching content and process in consonance. That is the fundamental premise of all that follows, and that premise becomes possible when instruction is characterized by three essential considerations.

First, content area reading can be systematized. That is, it can be approached from the perspective of a clearly-identified framework. This system or framework should be highlighted in any lesson structure used in a content area classroom. Furthermore, the system should be made obvious to students so they can realize that the procedures they are being led through in their study will transfer to other settings. (In Unit 4 we will examine this concept in detail.) The object of such structured lessons is to ensure that in every encounter with reading in a particular content area, students will become better able to deal with similar content in future contacts.

Second, teachers should, where necessary, construct guide materials to accompany students' reading and study. These materials should guide students in their interaction with reading assignments at levels commensurate with their ability, purposes, and background of reference. (This will be the focus of chapter 10.) Both materials and students must be evaluated to determine when such guidance is necessary. (Unit 2 is designed to examine this problem.) Generally speaking, the worth of any guide material is related to the degree to which it fosters conceptualizations and develops increased abilities to read similar materials.

Third, students must be aware that their content area study involves both skills development and content understandings. They should become familiar with and habituated to information acquisition processes that will stand them in good stead in their independent study. Students must learn to ignore the temptation to read everything with precision. We say "temptation." Likely, most of us were taught to do exactly that! The result of such teaching is that most adults, even college graduates, are rather inefficient readers. Too often we've been told (and are telling students ourselves), "Read pages 35 to 47 by Friday." And so we read and they read, word by word, trying to recall every detail in hopes that some of what is remembered might appear on the inevitable and ubiquitous Friday test. For content reading instruction to work, for students to acquire facility in reading content area materials, they must become familiar with a variety of strategies rather than continuing to rely solely on one approach to reading and learning.

CHAPTER 3

Materials in a Content Classroom

Reading materials can and should be assessed
for difficulty and appropriateness.

Overview

Many of the reading problems which interfere with learning in content classes can be traced to the material rather than the students. Before throwing up their hands in despair or charging headlong into a crash remediation program, content teachers should examine carefully the material they have chosen for their classrooms and determine whether the students can realistically be expected to learn effectively from it.

While several devices are available to teachers to analyze reading material, such devices can be considered no better than the person who interprets their results. Any analysis of reading materials must include an examination of their conceptual complexity, vocabulary difficulty, and skills requirements. The various devices currently available provide little more than a place to begin.

The purpose of analyzing reading materials is to determine how well the students will be able to learn from them. If the students are to learn content material effectively, they must be given tasks with which they can succeed, and one of the prime requisites for this success is materials that are at least on their instructional reading level.

The Right Stick

When a little league manager begins batting instruction, he hauls out the canvas bag and empties the contents in the vicinity of home plate. Out spill brown bats, white bats, yellowish bats, and two-toned bats—short bats, long bats, skinny bats, and fat bats. The players eagerly scramble among the bats as the manager helps them find the "stick" that will be best for each of them. When a classroom teacher begins content instruction, the teacher hauls out a briefcase, opens it, and takes out the book for that course. It may be brown, red, green, yellow, or chartreuse—fat, skinny, short, long, easy, or hard. But, there is usually only *one* book. Of all this, one thing is certain. The little leaguers and the readers will not all succeed equally well with their respective tasks, but at least the baseball players will have the best chance of finding the right stick.

Failure to learn in a content classroom is often attributed to a reading deficiency inherent with the learner. Efforts are made to correct such deficiencies because the students could succeed if they could read better. Whenever such a tack is taken, someone is implicitly assuming that the reading material the students have been given is appropriate, but that they are inappropriate for it. That is, they have the right stick; the problem is that they can't use it. Unfortunately, such an assumption is often invalid, because many of the reading difficulties which exist in content classrooms could be eliminated if the material were chosen on the basis of criteria that reflected realistic expectations for students. Frequently, however, the materials are neither adopted on the basis of such criteria nor are they examined as the potential source of learning difficulties in a classroom. If success is to be the goal of education, teachers would benefit from remembering this formula: students + the right task = SUCCESS. The right task must include the right stick.

Basic Components

A reading selection can best be analyzed in terms of three basic factors. These are: (1) the concepts presented in the material, (2) the language used to convey those concepts, and (3) the skills needed by a reader to extract those concepts. If the purpose of analyzing a reading selection is to determine its suitability for a group of students, the analysis should be based on an understanding of the interrelatedness of these components.

The primary function of a reading selection is to convey information, usually in the form of ideas, facts, and inferences. The aggregate of these comprise what may be referred to as the concept load. Basically, the concept load reflects the complexity of the ideas which a reader is to grasp. Therefore, any analysis of a reading selection must include an examination of its conceptual complexity, especially in relation to the experiential background which will be required for readers to understand those concepts.

The ideas or concepts in a reading selection are conveyed by specific words, and the degree of sophistication of those words, taken collectively as language, represents the vocabulary load for that passage. Since words are the outward manifestations of concepts, or verbal labels for concepts, the vocabulary load of a reading selection can provide an index of its conceptual complexity. Unfortunately, the universality of such a premise must be suspect in the face of such sentences as "The Child is father of the Man." The sophistication of the concept in this sentence far exceeds the simplicity and familiarity of the terms used to express that concept. It is evident, therefore, that conceptual complexity is determined by factors other than vocabulary alone; however, that the reader's familiarity with the vocabulary affects his or her ability to understand the concepts cannot be denied. A reader's chances of learning are significantly decreased if the ideas are couched in terminology that isn't recognized. Thus, it should come as no surprise that vocabulary familiarity has long been regarded as a primary variable in determining the difficulty of reading selections.

The skills load represents the reading skills required to extract concepts from a given passage. For a beginning reader, this may be as basic as realizing that the printed symbols on a page represent words; for a mature reader, the necessary skills could include the ability to interpret symbolism successfully. In a sense, the skills load demanded by a reading selection is an index of the author's style. The intricacy of the stylistic conventions which an author employs determines what reading skills will be required to get meaning from a passage. If a reader is to learn from a given selection, he or she must be familiar with the author's mode of presenting the information, be it flashback, dialogue, comparison, contrast, simile, metaphor, or analogy. If an author's style requires skills that a reader does not have, the learner's potential for successful processing will certainly be limited. The ideas and the vocabulary in a passage may be well within a reader's grasp, but to get to the information so it can be learned, a reader must also be sufficiently familiar with the author's stylistic devices.

All three of the components inherent to the composition of a reading passage are usually considered by an author, especially when the author is preparing materials to be used in a classroom. Certain things are assumed about the readers' conceptual and linguistic abilities, and the author adjusts the ideas, choices of language, and stylistic conventions to accommodate these assumptions. Once the material is introduced into the classroom, the author's assumptions become inconsequential because of the reality represented by the students. If the students' abilities are in fact equivalent to the author's assumptions, the material can be used appropriately in that classroom. It is the teacher's responsibility to ensure this match and by so doing to enhance the probability of successful learning. If a teacher is to make decisions about the appropriateness of specific materials for students, he or she must first understand what relationships can exist between those materials and students.

Reading Levels

Most readers of any age experience varying degrees of understanding every day when they read the daily newspaper. The comics and sports pages offer little or no difficulty; the front page can be perplexing; the editorials and comments are often enigmatic.

Success in reading is determined by such variables as prior knowledge of the topic, conceptual complexity, vocabulary familiarity, and author's style. In the jargon of the reading specialist, three levels of understanding have been delineated and identified as: (1) the independent reading level, (2) the instructional reading level, and (3) the frustration level. Each of these levels predicts a varying degree of success which a person will have with a specific reading task.

The *independent reading level* is the level at which a reader can completely understand material without outside help. That is, the reader can virtually learn everything the author has to offer and can do so with ease. In such situations, the reader is familiar with the vocabulary, has the necessary skills to extract the ideas, and can understand the concepts being conveyed. Thus,

What the author assumed		*What the reader has*
vocabulary load	=	vocabulary
skills load	=	skills
concept load	=	conceptual awareness

Unfortunately, such an exact match between the author's assumptions and the reader's abilities rarely occurs, especially in a classroom situation. Perfect congruence, however, is not necessary for students to learn from a reading selection. When students' abilities in skills, vocabulary, or conceptual awareness fall slightly below an author's expectations, they may not learn with the thoroughness or ease associated with a perfect match, but they will be able to learn. In fact, this is what usually happens in academic situations; students struggle with assignments and learn what they can. If students can learn from material in a limited way, often a teacher can provide instruction which will help them read with greater ease and understanding. Thus, when

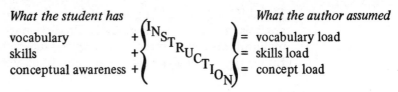

What the student has			*What the author assumed*
vocabulary	+		= vocabulary load
skills	+	INSTRUCTION	= skills load
conceptual awareness	+		= concept load

the material is said to be on the student's *instructional reading level*. In essence, instruction can bridge the gap between the student's abilities and those necessary to read with satisfactory understanding.

Sometimes material which is used in classrooms is so difficult for students that a reasonable amount of instructional assistance will not be sufficient to bridge the gap between the students' abilities and an author's assumptions. In such cases the learning potential is notably limited because of the frustration and anxiety which often accompany the students' efforts. This reaction frequently produces negative results because the student associates failure and frustration with reading. The *frustration level* therefore reflects material where

What the student has		*What the author assumed*
vocabulary	+	≠ vocabulary load
skills	+ INSTRUCTION	≠ skills load
conceptual awareness	+	≠ concept load

All readers perform with varying degrees of proficiency, depending on the demands of the particular task. Some general guidelines suggested by the aforementioned reading levels might be:

Reading Level	*Appropriate Use*
Independent	Homework; extended learning activities; basis for discussion of concepts
Instructional	Discussion in class with directed help through instruction; homework *after* appropriate "bridging of the gap" instruction
Frustration	NONE

A teacher's awareness of the relationship between students' abilities and the reading materials in the classroom should enable the teacher to realize maximum utility from those materials. Furthermore, it should suggest to a teacher the kinds of materials that will be necessary as a supplement to the basic text(s) of a course.

Analyzing Reading Materials

The difficulty of reading material can be determined by either predictive analysis or measurement analysis. Predictive techniques are restricted to the material; measurement analysis requires interaction of readers with material. Either type of analysis can be accomplished with both formal and informal procedures, and the objective is almost always the same—to determine whether the designated readers can learn from the material.

Predictive Analysis

The most common method of predictive analysis requires the use of readability formulas. Readability is a term which is applied to "the question of what makes the language in materials easy or difficult to read" (Bormuth, 1968, p. v). Readability formulas generally tap linguistic variables within a passage and these variables are used as indices of its complexity. Primary among these variables are: (1) sentence length and (2) vocabulary difficulty.

Underlying the application of readability formulas is the premise that material consisting of short, simple sentences and familiar vocabulary is more easily understood by readers than material written with complex sentences that include difficult or unfamiliar words. Consider the following sentence:

> Sally ran down the street.

The familiar vocabulary and the simple sentence structure suggest that few readers would have difficulty understanding that sentence. However, many young readers and even some older ones, would not learn much from the sentence:

> The only aim now is to hurt the enemy, in any way possible and, with every available weapon, to destroy not only his will to resist but also to eliminate every ability to implement that will effectively.

Analyses of materials with readability formulas enable a teacher to make reasonably accurate predictions about the success students will have in learning from a particular book or passage. They can further serve as the basis for a more complete estimate of that selection's overall difficulty.

Historically, classroom teachers have not used readability formulas because most of the reputable ones have been very time consuming and complex to administer. These formulas, such as the Dale-Chall (1948) and Spache (1960), have been widely used in reading research and textbook preparation, however, and their complexity lies primarily in the process of determining vocabulary difficulty. Both formulas require that each word in a passage be compared to a graded list of familiar words. Thus an adequate administration of these formulas may require as much as an hour per book or passage. This demands time which few teachers are able to devote.

Fortunately, several short-cut formulas are available which give just about the same accuracy as the longer, more complicated procedures from which they are derived. Two of these formulas, the Fry Readability Estimate (Fry, 1977) and McLaughlin's SMOG formula (McLaughlin, 1969), will be discussed here. You are also encouraged to read the excellent review of readability measures by Klare (1982).

Fry Readability Graph

Fry's formula is actually a graph. Several simple calculations must be applied to a selection and the results then interpolated by plotting them on an accompanying graph. This analysis begins by determining the average sentence length of three 100-word samples and continues with an estimate of vocabulary familiarity by a count of the syllables in each sample. The specific steps suggested by Fry are:

1. Randomly select three sample passages and count out exactly 100 words each, beginning with the beginning of a sentence. Do count proper nouns, initializations, and numerals.
2. Count the total number of sentences in each hundred word passage (estimating to the nearest tenth of a sentence). Average these three numbers.
3. Count the total number of syllables in each 100-word sample. There is a syllable for each vowel sound. For example: cat (1), blackbird (2), continental (4). Don't be fooled by word size. For example: *polio* has three syllables, *through* has one. Endings such as -y, -ed, -el, or -le usually make a syllable. For example: ready (2), bottle (2). When counting syllables, Fry suggests that you put a mark above every syllable over one in each word and add 100 to your total count of marks. This simplifies the syllable count since one-syllable words would be included in the adding of 100, as would the first syllable in each word with one or more marks. Average the total number of syllables for the three 100-word samples.
4. Plot on the accompanying graph the *average* number of sentences per 100 words and the *average* number of syllables per 100 words. The perpendicular lines mark off approximate grade level areas.
5. If a great deal of variability is found, more samples to determine an average should be used.
6. A word is defined as a group of symbols with a space on either side; thus, *Joe, USA, 1945,* and *%* are each one word.
7. When counting syllables for numerals and initializations, count one syllable for each symbol. For example, *1980* is one word with *four* syllables, *USA* is three syllables, and *$* is one syllable.

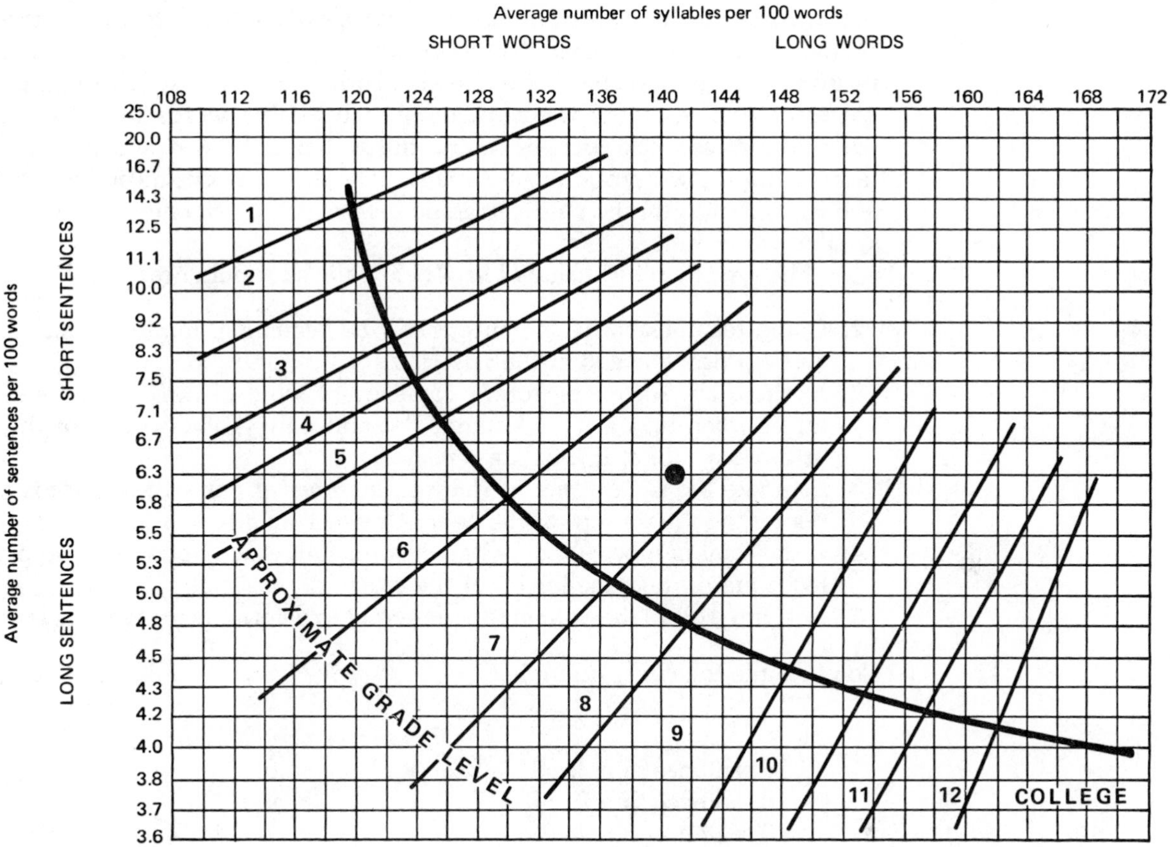

Average number of syllables per 100 words

SHORT WORDS   LONG WORDS

FIGURE 3.1
Fry Graph for Estimating Readability—Extended

EXAMPLE:	SYLLABLES	SENTENCES
1st Hundred Words	124	6.6
2nd Hundred Words	141	5.5
3rd Hundred Words	158	6.8
AVERAGE	141	6.3

READABILITY 7th GRADE (see dot plotted on graph)

McLaughlin's SMOG Formula

This formula is probably the least complicated of all those available and its efficiency has made it widely attractive for many content teachers. It is based on the interrelationship of sentence length and vocabulary difficulty, though the inclusion of these two variables is not clearly evident at first glance. McLaughlin has approached these two variables from a slightly different direction than other designers of readability formulas. The SMOG formula requires determination of the number of polysyllabic words in three ten-sentence samples. The premise behind this is that if the sentences are short, there is diminished possibility for many polysyllabic words to be included, and the difficulty of the passage can be determined by the number of polysyllabic words in it.

The specific steps included in McLaughlin's formula are:

1. Count ten consecutive sentences near the beginning, ten in the middle, and ten near the end of the selection.
2. In the thirty sentences (total), count every word of three or more syllables when they are read aloud. Recount polysyllabic words (of three or more syllables) if they are repeated.
3. Estimate the square root of the total number of polysyllabic words by taking the square root of the nearest perfect square.
4. If the total number of polysyllabic words falls exactly between two perfect squares, take the lowest of the two.
5. Add three (3) to the estimated square root to determine the reading level.

Consider the following example.

	Number of polysyllabic words
10 sentence sample #1	6
10 sentence sample #2	9
10 sentence sample #3	7
Total	22

The nearest perfect square to 22 is 25 (5 × 5). Add 5 + 3 and the reading level by the SMOG formula is 8. The simplicity of this formula and its slight deviation from the procedures of other formulas more highly regarded through time and research has caused this formula to be somewhat suspect among some reading professionals. However, it can serve some vital purposes for content teachers, and the real value of such formulas comes not in the specific grade level they reveal, but in the interpretation of their results.

ACTIVITY 3.1

Directions   Before proceeding to a discussion of an interpretation of readability formulas results, try this short activity. Assume that the following passage is one of the sample selections which you would use to try out the Fry and the SMOG formulas. Determine the results with both formulas and insert your results into the other data provided in the table following the selection.

It was a cold winter morning in 1925. Everywhere, the Arctic was covered with ice and snow. Beside a frozen sea, the little town of Nome, Alaska lay hundreds of miles away from the nearest railroad.

Suddenly came a radio call for help—sickness in Nome. Twenty-five people lay sick with diphtheria! Four people were dead. The lives of all were in danger—the townspeople of Nome and the Eskimos of the region. Only shots of antitoxin would keep the diphtheria from spreading. The need was desperate.

In the south of Alaska, a doctor heard the call for help. At once he packed up a twenty-pound supply of the antitoxin and sent it by rail as far as the train could go. He telegraphed Doctor Welsh in Nome that the antitoxin was on its way.

Fry		
	Sentences per 100 words	Syllables per 100 words
100-word sample # 1	?	?
100-word sample # 2	7.7	139
100-word sample # 3	8.9	135
Average	3 ⟌	3 ⟌

SMOG	
	Number of polysyllabic words
10-sentence sample # 1	?
10-sentence sample # 2	8
10-sentence sample # 3	9
Total	

Table of results for readability activity.

Using the Fry procedures, the 100th word is "At" in the third paragraph. In this sample, there are 10.0 sentences and 148 syllables. (If you're close, don't worry about minor discrepancies.) Adding these results to those already provided, you can determine average counts of 8.9 and 141. Plotting these scores on the graph indicates that this is sixth grade material, but since the mark is not very close to the curved line for typical material, something may be awry.

Using the SMOG formula, twelve polysyllabic words can be found including "twenty-five." "Twenty-five" is *a* word, even though hyphenated, and numbers are not words, *per se*, unless written out, and are not included by the SMOG.

The total number of polysyllabic words, then, as determined by the SMOG formula, is 29. The nearest perfect square is 5, thus the reading level is (5 + 3) or 8. Had the sample results of the SMOG administration been widely inconsistent, for example, 4, 10, and 16, further samples would need to be taken to provide greater accuracy.

Interpreting Readability Formulas

Since the results of the preceding activity indicate different grade levels for this material, a natural assumption may be to consider one or both formulas to be inaccurate. In fact, however, both are accurate. Herein lies the importance of accurate interpretation.

An examination of the validation procedures for each formula provides an explanation for the discrepancy. The Fry formula estimates the reading ability a reader will need to understand the material with 50 to 75 percent accuracy. On the other hand, the SMOG formula predicts the reading ability required for 90 to 100 percent comprehension. Thus, these two formulas are each providing valuable information, but information that cannot be applied appropriately without an understanding of the underlying criteria.

To relate this discussion to the reading levels presented earlier, the SMOG formula predicts an appropriate reading ability equivalent to reading on an independent level while the Fry graph suggests a level somewhere between the frustration and instructional reading levels.

Because of the variance which exists in the validation criteria of these two formulas, it would be inappropriate for a teacher to assume that the average sixth-grade reader would be able to understand this material, on his or her own, with 90 percent accuracy. Such assumptions have been made in the past with consequences that have been unfair to students. Thus, if teachers intend to use readability formulas, they must assume responsibility for interpreting their findings accurately.

Once a readability score is determined, a further examination of the results is required if a teacher wants to use the material appropriately. As has been implied, these formulas tap *only* linguistic variables. Concept and skills factors are only tangentially related to formula results. To assess reading materials thoroughly, readability formula results must be accompanied by informal examinations of the conceptual complexity within the material to determine whether the difficulty level indicated by a formula is also a reasonable representation of the concept load. If not, further adjustments must be made of the expectations that can reasonably be established for a reader's success. Likewise, if the author's style is such that it will pose difficulties undetermined by an analysis of the linguistic variables through a formula, this factor must be accounted for when determining the applicability of the material for particular readers.

While readability formulas can provide a basis for examining the difficulty of reading materials, they must not be considered infallible or definitive. Properly used, they can be very helpful aids in instructional planning, but when realistically examined, they provide only a rough estimate of the difficulty of a reading selection, and not much more. Thus, as teachers use readability formulas and other predictive techniques, they would be admonished to consider these cautions:

1. The predictive criteria for comprehension does vary among some of the formulas, and users should be aware of what they are determining when they use a particular device.
2. Readability formulas directly tap some linguistic variables, but not concept load; they provide only a basis from which to extend an analysis of the difficulty of reading material to a consideration of its conceptual difficulty.
3. The scores derived by such devices are only estimates and cannot be assumed definitive.
4. Readability formulas are not very helpful when used with poetry or other forms of material that do not conform to the basic characteristics of regular prose.
5. The true value of such devices can be derived only in tandem with knowledge of the reading skills of the students who will use the material.

It may seem that predictive analysis through readability formulas is subject to so many restraints that they are of little value. Consider, however, these realistic and valuable uses:

1. As the basis for analysis of the difficulty of a particular reading selection.
2. As a means of evaluating materials for adoption without having to rely blindly on a publisher's analysis.
3. As a comparison of books to be used within a course to determine which would be more appropriate for certain times or certain students.
4. As a comparison of stories, chapters, or sections within a required text.
5. As empirical data to indicate whether adopted material is appropriate to the reading abilities of students with whom it is to be used.

Measurement Analysis

As described earlier in this chapter, measurement analysis is based on an interaction between the reader and the material being examined. There are times when the readers are not available, and it is then that predictive procedures are most useful. However, when analyzing material for use in a classroom, the pertinent issue is how well specific students will be able to learn from it. Thus, an analysis based on an interaction between the readers and the material will prove more fruitful than one based on prediction.

Cloze Procedure

In 1953, Wilson Taylor introduced to reading specialists a technique of measuring how well students could read a particular text or reading selection. He called it the cloze procedure. It is based on the psychological percept of closure (hence, cloze) and the linguistic concept of redundancy within the English language. Since then, the cloze procedure has been intensively researched and applied in many ways. One of its most frequent uses has been as a method of determining the appropriateness of reading material for a particular group of students. The cloze procedure may be defined as a "method of systematically deleting words from a prose selection and then evaluating the success a reader has in accurately supplying the words deleted" (Robinson, 1971, p. 2).

Consider the following sentences. As you read, try to replace the words which have been omitted:

> Their accounts may be _____, but many consumers write _____ anyway during periods of _____ and inflation. Their intention is to try to _____ to the bank with _____ before a merchant turns _____ the check.

The degree to which you were successful in replacing the exact words deleted from the sentences can be considered an index of your ability to read the material from which it was taken. (The words deleted were *empty, checks, recession, often, get, money,* and *in.*)

The following steps are recommended in the construction of a cloze passage:

1. Select a reading passage that your students have not yet read. It should be approximately 300 words in length.
2. Type the first sentence intact. Starting with the fifth word in the second sentence, delete every fifth word until you have fifty deletions. Replace each deletion with an underlined blank fifteen spaces long.
3. Finish the sentence in which the fiftieth deletion occurs. Type one more sentence intact.

Once a cloze test has been constructed, it is a simple matter to administer it in a classroom. To guide you in this, follow these steps:

1. Provide directions which might read: "You are to fill in the blanks in the following selection with the word that has been left out. Try to supply the exact word the author used. Only one word has been deleted from each blank. You will have as much time as necessary to complete this exercise."
2. If the students are unfamiliar with the task, show them some examples prior to handing out the test.
3. The students are not to use any books or materials when completing the test.
4. Let students know that they should try to use context clues to determine what word fits each blank.
5. Allow them as much time as necessary to complete the test.

While a cloze test can be administered easily in a classroom, several cautions should be observed if the results are to be meaningful. Often the task itself interferes with obtaining valid scores. If the students have never taken a test like this, they may become very frustrated and not apply themselves in a way that is essential to obtaining valid scores. Thus, teachers should familiarize their students with the task prior to administering a passage from which meaningful results are to be determined. Initially, let them work on short passages and even let them work in pairs or teams. Try to make the task a challenging game and help them become involved in the process. Cloze passages are often used as instructional devices to improve the use of context clues, so introducing the task in an instructional setting may be the most productive method of familiarizing students with the procedures.

The scoring procedure can also cause unforeseen problems. While the scoring process will be discussed later, it is not unusual for students to get only 30, 40, or 50 percent correct, and few students are accustomed to being only 30 percent successful with a task. Thus, an anxiety factor can interfere with their production, and teachers need to be prepared to lend support and encouragement during the testing, especially for students with limited language awareness. Finally, the real purpose of a cloze test is to "test" an author's assumptions in relation to a particular group of readers. Many reluctant students respond to an opportunity to test an author, and such an approach often relieves them of feelings of anxiety.

Scoring a cloze test is the easiest part of the procedure, though interpretation of results requires experience. The most widely researched aspect of the cloze procedure has been in scoring and interpretation. Ruddell (1964), Bormuth (1966), and Miller and Coleman (1967) have shown that the most valid scoring system with cloze tests is to accept only the *exact replacement* as correct. That is, do not give credit for synonyms. (One should, however, count misspellings correct if it is clear that the intent was to provide the exact word deleted.) Once the total number of correct replacements is determined, compute the percentage score for each student.

The value of accepting only exact replacements is twofold. First, it does not require a subjective evaluation of the subtle connotations of synonyms, and thus retains objectivity. Second, it allows a set of stable criterion scores to be used in interpreting the results. Teachers and students often express scorn, disdain, and a few four-letter words for such seemingly arbitrary procedures. However, if synonyms were allowed to be correct, valid interpretations of the results would be all but impossible. It may help to mention that the rank order of scores rarely changes appreciably when synonyms are included as correct responses. However, as a person interprets the results he or she must consider the possibility that the responses may in fact be better than the words used by the author. When a person consistently includes more sophisticated or more expressive words than the author, the results for that individual may not be valid. Because of such possibilities, individuals' scores are often uninterpretable without a careful examination of the relationship among the various types of miscues they have inserted in the blanks. (This is facilitated by an understanding of the syntactic and semantic relationships suggested by Goodman and Burke (1972) in the *Reading Miscue Inventory.*)

Once percentages of exact replacement scores have been determined for each student, record them all and *compute the average for the class.* To our knowledge, no research has found cloze to be valid for an individual's score. Hence, it is the *group's average score that is compared to the criteria.* It may be advantageous to chart individual results in a format like the one that follows. This will allow comparison to criteria modified from the research of Bormuth (1968).

Cloze Test Results

Material _____

Class _____   *Date* _____

Above 60%	Between 40% and 60%	Below 40%

The difficulty of the material can then be determined by comparing the class average to the following set of criteria.

If the mean score is:	*The material is probably:*
60% or higher	Easy for this group and will be on their *independent* reading level.
between 40% and 60%	Suitable for this group and is within their *instructional* reading level.
below 40%	Difficult for this group and will be on their *frustration* level.

To summarize, the following guidelines may be helpful:

1. Count only exact replacements. Do not include synonyms.
2. Determine the percentage scores for each individual.
3. *Compute the class average and compare it to the criterion scores.*
4. Use the material appropriately or discard it as being unsuitable for that group of students.

Analysis by Judgment

In this age of scientific investigation, the older, more subjective methods of determining the appropriateness of materials for a group of students seem to have been shoved in a closet. Whatever happened to the idea of giving students a book, asking them to read from it (silently), and then having them explain what they learned? Such an uncomplicated, unobjective method may seem to be out of tune with today's computerized, technological world. But the time-proven validity of assessments based on informal procedures and teachers' intuitions makes it unwise to abandon such methods. In fact, such assessments may at times be more valid and practical than any scientific, objective analysis such as those based on readability formulas and the cloze procedure (Klare, 1982).

If you would like guidance in measuring a reading selection informally, try this procedure, a combination of measurement analysis and analysis by judgment.

1. Select a passage from material that the students have not previously read. Choose a length that is complete in itself and will approximate the length that they might be expected to read as an assignment.
2. Ask the students to read it.
3. Administer a ten-question test based on:
   a. main idea
   b. factual information
   c. inferences
   d. vocabulary.
4. Go over the test with them. Discuss the answers and determine through intuition and their opinions how well they will be able to learn from this material.

Informal assessments of reading material can be extended beyond these suggestions and can become rather complex, depending upon the ability of the teacher to interpret the results of the testing. Rather than deal with some of the more advanced methods of classroom diagnosis here, it will be more appropriate to treat them at length in two later chapters: *Standardized Testing* and *Analyzing Reading Comprehension*. It should be noted, however, that the criteria for determining whether or not to use a book, as measured by an informal assessment, must remain the responsibility of the individual teacher. This relates to the various purposes for specific materials that a teacher might want or expect within the classroom. Thus, while 80 percent comprehension might be needed in one situation, 40 percent comprehension might be acceptable in another. Rather than suggest criteria that may not be appropriate in certain situations, it is preferable that teachers realize and accept the responsibility of modifying criteria based on individual purposes and expectations. To do otherwise would, in effect, violate the inherent attractiveness and utility of informal assessments.

Criteria for Evaluating Materials

When examining materials for adoption or use with groups of students, teachers should be alert to other elements of the material which extend beyond the limitations of "the right stick" concept. Materials should be chosen for their maximum utility in helping children learn. The following suggestions might be considered.

1. Does the material include sufficient directions to the user so that it does not require students to have the very skills and understandings it purports to develop?
2. If a teacher's edition or manual accompanies the material, does it provide sufficient examples and suggestions for instruction?
3. Do the skills to which the material is directed relate to problems confronted in more realistic reading tasks?
4. Is the material appropriate to students' abilities, interests, and needs?
5. Does the material seem to lend itself to flexible, individual application in the classroom setting?
6. Will the content and format of the material promote interaction among pupils and between pupils and teachers?
7. Is the purpose of the material apparent to students, and will they be able to use it independently, given sufficient reading and study skills?
8. Is the appearance of the material attractive?
9. Does the material include a bibliography or additional resource material?
10. Is the material conducive to divergent, creative thinking, or is it convergent and dogmatic?

While this list is not all-inclusive, it may suggest other criteria which deserve examination to meet the needs of a specific classroom—YOURS! The overriding question, of course, has to be, "Does this material provide the students with the maximum opportunity to learn, and does it do it as well or better than anything else?" If the answer is "No," keep looking.

Textbook Selection by Teacher Judgment

A teacher acquaintance of ours recounted the following account of serving on a committee to choose new history textbooks for a junior high school. In the fall, four history teachers were reminded by their department chairman that this was the year of textbook adoption in their area and that they should be thinking about what book they wanted. Numerous sample volumes were tucked away in a far corner of the department office for their examination, but with all the demands of getting a new school year underway, the sample texts went unnoticed. In January the four teachers each received an urgent message to bring their lunches to the departmental conference room for a lunch-hour meeting. One by one the teachers casually ambled in and took their seats. The department chairman rushed in with an armload of textbooks and dumped them onto the table. With a grand gesture he looked at his watch and announced, "You have exactly 22 minutes to choose a textbook for next year. I just learned this morning that the decision has to be on the superintendent's desk by 2:00 this afternoon."

Needless to say, this is not the way to choose textbooks. The best approach is for the textbook selection committee to adopt a systematic approach to examining each text. This orderly review of books will insure that each text is examined on the same criteria rather than teachers haphazardly thumbing through volumes with no clear idea of what to look for.

Fortunately, several sets of criteria have been developed with which to conduct rather detailed textbook analysis with relatively little complication or time investment. The best of these, we believe, has been formulated by Judith Irwin and Carol Davis at Purdue University. Their checklist, reproduced here with their permission, appears in the November, 1980, issue of *Journal of Reading*. It defines readability in specific terms of understandability and learnability. As you will see when you examine the scale closely, "understandability" is defined in relation to prior knowledge, concept development, syntax, relevance of detail, complex relations, resources, and readability score. "Learnability" is defined in relation to organization, reinforcement, and motivation quality. These qualities of text either cause problems or facilitate learning, and textbook selection can validly rest on these. Irwin and Davis have shown that when two raters analyzed the same textbooks, they were in very high agreement on the strongest and weakest features. It is the likelihood of such interrater consistency that led Klare (1982) to recommend analysis by judgment as a viable approach.

A question which must always arise is, "What if I have to use a book which is too difficult or inappropriate?" Our inclination is to say, "Don't!" and we mean it. No unit of study can work if it includes only one thing to read, the single textbook. Yet a more reasonable answer is this: "Try to identify what it is about the book which makes it difficult or inappropriate and then ask what you can do in teaching with the book to compensate for its weaknesses." The Irwin-Davis checklist will help to pinpoint shortcomings in textbooks which good teaching can sometimes alleviate.

So, the following checklist has two uses which we think you will find valuable. It can be used in selecting textbooks and it can be used in identifying specific strengths and weaknesses of textbooks already in use. It is a welcome addition to the literature and we are grateful to its authors for permission to share it with you.

IRWIN-DAVIS
READABILITY CHECKLIST

This checklist is designed to help you evaluate the readability of your classroom texts. It can best be used if you rate your text while you are thinking of a specific class. Be sure to compare the textbook to a fictional ideal rather than to another text. Your goal is to find out what aspects of the text are or are not less than ideal. Finally, consider supplementary workbooks as part of the textbook and rate them together. Have fun!!

Rate the questions below using the following rating system:

5 - *Excellent*
4 - *Good*
3 - *Adequate*
2 - *Poor*
1 - *Unacceptable*
NA - *Not applicable*

Textbook title: _____

Publisher: _____

Copyright date: _____

Understandability

A. _____ Are the assumptions about students' vocabularv knowledge appropriate?

B. _____ Are the assumptions about students' prior knowledge of this content area appropriate?

C. _____ Are the assumptions about students' general experiential backgrounds appropriate?

D. _____ Does the teacher's manual provide the teacher with ways to develop and review the students' conceptual and experiential backgrounds?

E. _____ Are new concepts explicitly linked to the students' prior knowledge or to their experiential backgrounds?

F. _____ Does the text introduce abstract concepts by accompanying them with many concrete examples?

G. _____ Does the text introduce new concepts one at a time with a sufficient number of examples for each one?

H. _____ Are definitions understandable and at a lower level of abstraction than the concept being defined?

I. _____ Is the level of sentence complexity appropriate for the students?

J. _____ Are the main ideas of paragraphs, chapters, and subsections clearly stated?

K. _____ Does the text avoid irrelevant details?

Understandability (*continued*)

L. _____ Does the text explicitly state important complex relationships (e.g., causality, conditionality, etc.) rather than always expecting the reader to infer them from the context?

M. _____ Does the teacher's manual provide lists of accessible resources containing alternative readings for the very poor or very advanced readers?

N. _____ Is the readability level appropriate (according to a readability formula)?

Learnability

Organization

A. _____ Is an introduction provided for in each chapter?

B. _____ Is there a clear and simple organizational pattern relating the chapters to each other?

C. _____ Does each chapter have a clear, explicit, and simple organizational structure?

D. _____ Does the text include resources such as an index, glossary, and table of contents?

E. _____ Do questions and activities draw attention to the organizational pattern of the material (e.g., chronological, cause and effect, spatial, topical, etc.)?

F. _____ Do consumable materials inter-relate well with the textbook?

Reinforcement

A. _____ Does the text provide opportunities for students to practice using new concepts?

B. _____ Are there summaries at appropriate intervals in the text?

C. _____ Does the text provide adequate iconic aids such as maps, graphs, illustrations, etc., to reinforce concepts?

D. _____ Are there adequate suggestions for usable supplementary activities?

E. _____ Do these activities provide for a broad range of ability levels?

F. _____ Are there literal recall questions provided for the students' self review?

G. _____ Do some of the questions encourage the students to draw inferences?

H. _____ Are there discussion questions which encourage creative thinking?

I. _____ Are questions clearly worded?

Motivation

A. _____ Does the teacher's manual provide introductory activities that will capture students' interest?

Learnability (continued)

B. _____ Are chapter titles and subheadings concrete, meaningful, or interesting?

C. _____ Is the written style of the text appealing to the students?

D. _____ Are the activities motivating? Will they make the student want to pursue the topic further?

E. _____ Does the book clearly show how the knowledge being learned might be used by the learner in the future?

F. _____ Are the cover, format, print size, and pictures appealing to the students?

G. _____ Does the text provide positive and motivating models for both sexes as well as for other racial, ethnic, and socio-economic groups?

Readability Analysis

Weaknesses

1) On which items was the book rated the lowest?

2) Did these items tend to fall in certain categories?

3) Summarize the weaknesses of this text.

4) What can you do in class to compensate for the weaknesses of this text?

Assets

1) On which items was the book rated the highest?

2) Did these items fall in certain categories?

3) Summarize the assets of this text.

4) What can you do in class to take advantage of the assets of this text?

UNIT 2 Identifying Reading Needs in a Content Classroom

The skilled teacher sees diagnosis as a first step in planning appropriate instruction and materials for his students.

Mary Austin

Conceptual Objectives

1. Standardized reading tests can be useful to the classroom teacher when their results are interpreted within certain limitations.

2. Analyzing students' study skills is an important aspect of diagnosis for a content teacher interested in improving students' ability to learn.

3. Reading comprehension is the best window through which to observe reading ability.

4. Attitudes are a measurable outcome of learning.

5. Vocabulary and conceptual development are essentially related.

A Thesis

The cornerstone of effective instruction is accurate diagnosis. Instruction in any classroom can only approach maximum effectiveness when it is designed to bridge the gap between what a student knows and what he or she needs to know. The first step of teaching, therefore, is to determine what students can learn. Diagnosis is that aspect of instruction that enables a teacher to identify what the student knows. Without diagnosis, instruction is likely to be based on conjecture, and the extent of the "gap" tends to be veiled by uncertainty. Even worse, the presence of the "gap" may not be realized.

If instruction is to bridge this gap, it must be based on a definite awareness of what the student knows, in terms of both content and abilities; it cannot be based on suppositions and conjecture.

Our purposes in this second unit—*Identifying reading needs in a content classroom*—are two: (1) to suggest various ways by which content teachers can identify what students know about reading and learning; and (2) to lay the groundwork for unifying diagnosis and instruction in a content classroom. We are isolating diagnosis in this unit as a convenience; our ultimate objective remains that of fostering unified diagnostic reading instruction in content classrooms. In examining diagnosis by itself, we are paving the way for a discussion of literacy instruction in the context of content study.

As you proceed through this unit, we hope you recognize that we treat reading diagnosis from the perspective of the content teacher, not the specialist. Furthermore, consider one overriding concern: *instruction is more likely to be effective when a teacher can discover what students are trying to do and when the teacher can then provide the students with appropriate activities to help them succeed.* Thus, while it may be valuable for you to become familiar with basic diagnostic strategies, it is more important that you become diagnostically aware.

To become diagnostically aware, you need to become a kidwatcher (Goodman, 1978). Through their behavior and their attitudes, students reveal much about what they learn and how they learn. As a "kidwatcher" a teacher becomes sensitive and responsive to the clues that students provide. To develop kidwatching skills, you might learn to carry a small notebook or a clipboard with you (as any good coach does) to record your observations about students and their learning (or their frustrations). Many experienced teachers are instinctively kidwatchers; it comes with "becoming *real*", as Marjorie Williams expresses it in her story, *The Velveteen Rabbit.* In the long run, becoming diagnostically aware will serve you and your students far better than if you seek only to develop skills of assessment. Effective diagnosis that affects instruction is not something that happens apart from instruction; it emerges from various instructional activities.

On this point, let us be clear: *diagnosis is not testing!* We hope this distinction can become clear for you. Testing involves assessment through the administration of tests or specified tasks, formal or informal. The results of testing are presumably made evident in the data, the numbers. Diagnosis involves perceptiveness and an awareness that extends well beyond any test instrument, or task.

Effective use of the concepts set forth in the preceding chapters may well depend upon how diagnostically aware you can become rather than on how many devices and strategies you may come to know. Familiarizing yourself with specific aspects of diagnosis may lead you into the trap of "Diagnosis . . . then what?" To be diagnostically aware means simply that one can approach the students with the intent of being responsive to their needs rather than feeling an overriding responsibility to a given body of knowledge or a predetermined curriculum. The teacher who understands the interrelationship between diagnosis and instruction is the one who will become diagnostically aware, hence the most responsive and the most effective.

Activity and Selected Readings Key

Suggested Activities

	CONCEPTS				
	1	2	3	4	5
1. Propose an antithesis to the preceding thesis. (See pp. 48–49.) Which do current educational practices exemplify?	X				
2. Collect standardized test data on the reading ability of your students from their cumulative files and analyze them for any value you think they might have to you in your own teaching.	X				
3. Make a point of going by the guidance or testing office in your school or central offices to discuss the standardized testing program they employ. Find out what sources are available to teachers as aids to test data use and interpretation. (If not currently teaching, you might visit a school for this purpose.)	X				
4. Devise a study skills program for your class by the steps we suggest in Chapter 8.		X			
5. List your objectives for a content reading inventory as we suggest on pp. 74–75, Chapter 6.			X		
6. Conduct analyses of students' responses to the sample IRI we provide on pp. 82–100.			X		
7. Using the suggestions provided in chapter 6, devise a group inventory of your students' comprehension of material required of them to read in your course. Analyze the results and continue to more careful diagnosis of students who would seem to need it. (See p. 100.)			X		
8. Using data of the sort you collected in Activity 2 pick out the half-dozen or so students in each of your classes who are probably in deepest trouble in reading. Either on your own, or, preferably, in cooperation with a reading specialist, conduct an individual, in-depth assessment of these students.			X		

	CONCEPTS				
	1	2	3	4	5
9. As preface to Chapter 5, identify achievement tests and attitude scales of which you know. (See p. 63.)				X	
10. Analyze the study skill requirements of the course you teach, as suggested in Chapter 8, pp. 121–122.		X			
11. Following the guidelines suggested in chapter 5, design an attitude scale for your class. (See pp. 66–67.)				X	
12. Select a passage from material you would use with your class. Identify the key concepts and the key concept words for that selection. Then describe how you would assess your students' knowledge of the concepts and the terms that reflect those concepts. (See pp. 112–114.)			X		X

Selected Readings*

	CONCEPTS				
	1	2	3	4	5
1. Lyman, Howard B. *Test Scores and What They Mean.*	X				
2. Thomas, E. L., and Robinson, H. S. *Improving Reading in Every Classroom.*		X			
3. Shepherd, David. *Comprehensive High School Reading Methods.*		X			
4. Valmont, William J. "Creating Questions for Informal Reading Inventories."			X		
5. Vaughan, Joseph & Gaus, Paula. "Secondary Reading Inventory: A Modest Proposal."			X		
6. Sanders, Norris M. *Classroom Questions: What Kinds?*			X		

(*continued*)

*Full bibliographic information for these items will be found at the end of the book under References.

	CONCEPTS				
	1	2	3	4	5
7. Edwards, S. L. *Techniques of Attitude Scale Construction.*				X	
8. Vaughan, Joseph L. "Affective Measurement Instruments: An Issue of Validity."				X	
9. Hoffmann, Banesh. *The Tyranny of Testing.*	X				
10. Rakes, Thomas A. & McWilliams, Lana. "Assessing Reading Skills in the Content Areas."			X		X

CHAPTER 4

Standardized Tests and Reading Diagnosis

Standardized reading tests can be useful to the classroom teacher only when their results are interpreted within certain limitations.

Overview

Diagnosis is a matter of making qualitative judgments. Testing is a matter of quantification. While it is true that diagnosis and evaluation may overlap in purpose, it is good to keep the differences between the two activities in mind and never to try to substitute the administration of tests for the conduct of diagnosis.

Several basic references on testing are to be recommended. Some are standbys like Buros' *Mental Measurements Yearbook* which provides scholarly reviews of most tests in print. Other references, equally creditable, take a much less charitable view of the whole business of testing, and with just cause, we think. The very idea of standardized testing is suspect and is being questioned on several fronts. The matter boils down to validity and use of tests. Do the tests we administer to students serve us or them as evidence of achievement of either our goals or theirs? One could even go so far as to say that not only do tests fail to test what we teach but, worse still, schools have fallen into a trap of trying to teach what they test.

It is possible that standardized tests have a purpose to serve. They may indicate the range of ability among groups of students. They may serve to indicate which students should be looked at more closely to see what may be special problems or special talent. In any case, we will borrow a phrase from an article by David Harman (1975) that should well set the tone for what we want to say about standardized testing. *Si duo idem faciunt, non est idem* or "If two people do the same thing, it is not the same thing."

A Mini-Review of Some Pertinent Literature

Standardized testing in this country is very big business today, and there are more tests of reading achievement available than of any other dimension of the curriculum. Their pervasiveness alone should cause an interest in standardized reading tests. Here is a brief review of several references which you might find it helpful to know.

The exemplar of reference sources for standardized tests is *The Mental Measurements Yearbook*, by O. K. Buros. It is not a yearbook in the strict sense; there have been eight editions published since 1938 when the first one appeared. Virtually all tests available are reviewed in M.M.Y., in one or more of the editions, with basic information and authoritative reviews included, usually both pro and con.

Buros also published *Tests in Print*, a simple listing of tests, and offers a collection entitled *Reading: Tests and Reviews* amassed from various editions of M.M.Y. These two additions to the line of service provided by Gryphon Press, the publisher, makes the service invaluable to the intelligent consumer of tests and related services. Chances are that any adequate professional library associated with a public school or college of education would have copies available.

The Educational Resources Information Center (ERIC) also has available good information on testing. The *Guide to Tests and Measuring Instruments for Reading*, for example, is straightforward and helpful. It is available from the ERIC clearinghouse on reading, NCTE (National Council of Teachers of English).

Educational Testing Service (ETS) serves as a base for the ERIC clearinghouse on testing. A treasurehouse of free or inexpensive material and information is available from either the company or the clearinghouse. The best way to get to resources in the clearinghouse is through the ERIC references, and again this source will be found in most sizeable professional libraries in education.

The references we have mentioned thus far are all more or less neutral in treatment of the topic of testing. Many other sources do not take nearly so neutral a stance. Neither do we, for reasons which we hope will become apparent. Much of the ammunition one would need to argue against the use of standardized tests, or to argue for more discretion and caution in interpretation as we will do, is available in a few sources.

The classic attack on standardized tests is *The Tyranny of Testing*, by Banesh Hoffmann (1964). In similar tone, and a little more up to date, is *Uses and Abuses of Standardized Tests*, by George Weber (1974). These two books are imperative for the serious critic. It is our opinion that school officials who haven't done so, should take a closer look at the warnings and recommendations in these books. In fact, the National Association of Elementary School Principals once devoted two issues of *Principal* to attack the wrongs perpetrated by standardized tests. Volume 54, No. 4, March/April, 1975, dealt with "the great I.Q. myth." Volume 54, No. 6, July/August, 1975, was devoted to "The scoring of children: standardized tests in America." The issues are available from NAESP or are likely in the professional collections of many school principals.

Even commercial television has had its say in recent years, and many educators watched with no small pleasure as CBS aired its "special" on I.Q. They called it a great myth, and their criticisms gave the industry no quarter. With so many people up in arms over the issue, can the problem be summarized fairly? What good can be said about testing? What guidelines can be offered the teacher who may want to make the best use of standardized tests? These are the concerns we hope to address in what follows of the present chapter.

The Wolf in Sheep's Clothing

Let us begin by saying that the most serious problem with standardized reading tests is that they are not what they seem. The basic idea of standardized tests is to compare groups of children or to compare individual performance to that of a group. Aside from whether that might have any value in and of itself, there is simply no way it can be called diagnosis. Standardized tests have virtually *no* diagnostic value, and to use their results as if they were diagnostic is to abuse them in the worst way. Decisions about individuals cannot be made on the basis of performance on a group measure. While diagnosis may involve standardized tests, it certainly need not, often does not. To ignore this basic understanding, a point cautioned in the manuals of many standardized tests themselves, is one of the easiest and most common ways to misuse them.

Let's look more closely at the basic idea, however, and try to strip away some of the façade of standardized tests as we view their complicated inner workings. There are seven reasons we might say that the basic idea, comparing individuals to groups or groups to groups on standardized test performance, is as insidious and dangerous as a wolf among the sheep.

1. There is nothing to suggest that the "average" performance of a group on a very particular task is necessarily a "standard" of performance for an individual which can be generalized to his or her performance overall. And yet that is precisely what we assume when we say "Johnny is

reading on a fourth-grade level" because he scored grade 4.0 on a standardized test of reading ability.

2. People are different in more ways than they are similar; in fact, every person is unique in every ability, reading ability most certainly. It is cruelly ironic that in a country built on "rugged individualism" we should judge success in school by conformity, that we should reward convergence and punish divergence with standardized tests.

3. Objective tests, of reading or any other skill, are graded so that only the answer to an item, not the reasoning behind the answer, will figure into the data for the final score. Yet, as the eminent child psychologist Jean Piaget noted long ago, the reason for a "wrong" answer may often be better than the reason for a "right" answer. "Wrong" answers on a standardized test are always plausible and often attractive to the creative reader. (That's why students are often told, "Your first guess is more likely to be right than your answer on second thought.) Clearly, the implication, and truth, is that thinking can get you into trouble on standardized tests!

4. Tests are set up in a subtle version of Joseph Heller's "Catch-22" so that a predetermined and rather large portion (actually 15.86 percent) of students will score "low," the same portion will score "high," assuming the group tested is like the group against which comparisons are being made. Now why the students score low or score high or whether on a different sort of test of the "same" ability or understanding they would score differently, is quite irrelevant, at least in standardized test terms. As a matter of fact, the likelihood is rather good that the test scores of people who score either very high or very low would change if the same test were given again. How they might score on a different measure altogether is practically anybody's guess. Whatever the case, extreme scores are the least stable and are the very ones for which the danger in accepting them at face value is the greatest. Yet it is exactly these scores, the ones of students whose performances are outstandingly good or bad, that are the basis on which most "diagnostic" decisions are made!

5. The more "representative" the sample of pupils against whom comparisons are being made, the less likely it is that comparison of a "typical" student's performance will be fair to that student. On the other side of this coin, for the so-called ethnic youngster, even if a number of Chicanos or blacks or Eskimos or whomever are included in the "representative" sample, the number will be so small as to be insignificant to the individual. On the question of representativeness, you're damned if you do and damned if you don't.

6. There seems to be a certain respect for numbers in the thinking of most people, a respect that is unwarranted. While numbers *are* precise, the application of numbers to results of imprecise measures makes those measures no less imprecise. A score of 3.8 on a reading test sounds very scientific, but it may not be so at all. The concept is a tough one, but there

is a very real qualitative difference between saying, for example, that a person is 103 months old and that that person reads on a grade level of 3.8. You can count the months since a person's birth, but you can in no comparable way "count" grade levels of achievement in reading.

7. We tend to assume that standardized test results must mean something. We publish reading scores in newspapers, comparing schools and school systems. We judge the quality of a program of free reading in a school on the basis of standardized reading test scores. We pass out scores to children and parents, make decisions to retain or promote individuals, all without realizing the basic assumptions we are making.

And what are these basic assumptions? They concern two ideas, each of which is as confusing as the other: reliability and validity. Whether one realizes it or not, every time a standardized test is used, someone very likely is assuming: (1) that the test is a reliable measure, and that this means something about its quality as a measurement tool; and (2) that the test is a valid measure, and that evidence for validity is available somewhere for anyone who would want to look at it. Both of these assumptions are false enough to give anyone who realizes it pause to wonder about the whole idea of standardized tests.

For a test to be reliable merely says that it agrees with itself, that for example, any half of the test items would agree with the other half. It's called "internal consistency," in fancy words. Yet no matter how consistent it might be, any test can at the same time be completely useless as a measurement tool.

For example, we could administer a reading test written in Latin to a group of third graders. The test would probably be very "reliable," since the students would score about as well (or poorly, it doesn't make any difference so long as it is consistent) on one item as on the next. You might say this is nonsense since no one would do such a thing anyway. Right you are. But let's administer the same reading test, written in English this time, to a group of third-grade Spanish-speaking children. Or to a group of inner city black youngsters. In the same vein as our Latin example, the results would be highly reliable, and yet this fact would say nothing about the quality of the test or its results for these children.

In its common sense, "reliable" means "dependable," and connotes a good quality—usually. Just as even the habitual criminal is reliable, in the technical sense the word means only "internally consistent," and to label a test as such is to say very little about its value. Of course, we would want a test to be reliable, but only in *hopes* that it might be valid. Knowing a test is reliable gives us no *assurance* at all of its validity.

And now to the *sine qua non*: VALIDITY. Does the test measure what it says it measures? Does the reading test measure reading ability, does it measure achievement in reading? Test makers try to say yes by pointing to either one or both of these facts about their test:

1. Experts think it does, or it looks like it does, if you accept that these skills, the ones we think our test items measure, are what define ability and achievement in reading.
2. The test measures as well as other reading tests since we know that scores on the two tests tend to be very similar.

In fact, that's very little reason to think a test is valid. The first claim depends on acceptance of what amounts to a very narrow and probably unrealistic definition of reading. The second claim is circular: Test 1 is like Test 2 which is (when you look at it) like Test 3 which is (when you look at it) like Test 1. So all three tests are valid measures of reading?

We think not, actually. Reading comprehension is very complex. The criteria for its accomplishment are not to be captured in a number. In fact, reading comprehension defies quantification. To maintain otherwise is to trade teacher judgment in diagnosis for test reliability in measurement—a poor trade for those who make it.

Test performance is often very unlike real-life performance and only vaguely related to it. What students are asked to do on standardized tests of reading often doesn't even look like reading. It ignores the matter of interest, of reading strategy, of purpose for reading. Yet all these things are the critical factors that determine the success of the act of reading.

What tests do measure is performance on a test. The caution is clear: Make sure you know what performance on a reading test can and cannot be taken to mean before you use that performance to judge the ability of a reader.

Several Fundamentals

Can anything good be said about standardized tests of reading ability? Do they have any saving virtue to recommend them? We think so, though we hope we've made the point that they're no substitute for diagnosis. (The matter of reading diagnosis will be discussed in the next three chapters in terms of diagnosis of comprehension, vocabulary, and study skills.)

On the positive side of the question of standardized tests, we want to make these points:

1. That test results are reported in various ways, some more useful than others.
2. That standardized test results can be used as rough indices, useful for estimating the range of a group's achievement, and that from such results it is possible to make group instructional decisions.

3. That standardized tests can help in picking those children for whom specific diagnosis is to be recommended.

The Form of Test Results

Three common forms in which standardized reading test results are reported are: (1) grade equivalents, (2) percentiles, and (3) stanines. Of these, grade equivalents and percentiles are the most common, and stanines are the most reasonable way in which to express test results.

It is easy to think that a grade score, say grade 4.6, is equivalent to the performance on the test by pupils at the sixth month (February) of the fourth year of school. It is as if in the standardization process, students of all possible grade levels (scores) were tested. But not so, despite what "equivalent" may mean to most people. To test makers, "equivalent" means "estimated." It is likely that in a test standardization program a test is tried out at only one time of year with children of different grades. Then, taking the scores from each grade, it is possible to divide differences between grades into intervals and to thereby "interpolate" or at least roughly estimate the scores that would have been obtained had there been any children of such grade taking the test. For example, on a test intended for grades seven, eight, and nine it is possible to score such "grade equivalents" as 5.2 or 8.6 or 11.0, and yet no one at any of these exact grade levels would have taken the test. In fact, there is little if any real reason to think that if, for example, an eleventh grader or a fifth grader or an 8.6 grader has taken the test, he or she would have gotten the number of items correct which the grade equivalent score would lead one to believe. And so the grade equivalent is a guessed grade; it may or may not reflect anything very true about a person's real performance.

The percentile score is also estimated, but it has nothing to do with grade level. What it does express is the relative standing of a score in a group of 100 scores, pretending for the moment that 100 scores were obtained on the test. The fact that 100 raw score points is usually *never* the number of scores obtained simply means we're back to guessing. We take all the scores we do have and put them in a list from highest to lowest. We then take the score halfway down the list as the 50 percentile. Then we simply estimate the raw score which should be at a given percentile rank *or* we calculate the percentile of a given raw score on the basis of how many (what percentage of) scores fall above or below it. Then we say that someone scores at the 70 percentile or the 90 percentile or whatever. But a *warning* is in order. The difference between 50 and 70 in percentile terms is the same as the difference between 70 and 90. Yet the difference between a score at the 50 percentile and one at the 70 percentile is much smaller than the difference between a score at 70 and one at the 90 percentile. Because most obtained scores fall near the mean and few fall at the extremes, a small raw score difference can make a big percentile score difference among scores on the middle range while the opposite is true for scores at extremes. There is no doubt that percentile scores are tricky; like most test scores, they may not mean what they seem to mean.

Stanines are the easiest to understand, the safest to use, and yet may be the most difficult scores to accept. We say "difficult to accept" because test users often want more precision in a score than the stanine affords. But that's exactly the point. The manner in which results are expressed by stanines is about as precise as most standardized tests can measure to begin with, which is why we call them "safest."

Many standardized tests report results in stanines or, where this is not done, converting from some other "standard" score is a fairly simple matter. The most rudimentary text on tests and measurements should explain the procedure.

The basic assumption of any standard score, stanines included, is that whatever is being measured is "normally distributed." This in turn, assumes that most of the scores obtained on the test will be fairly close to the average score. Scores not close to the average are relatively few in number, and there are as many very low scores as very high scores.

Now back to the stanine score itself. "Stanine" is a coined word, from STAndard NINE-point scale. Stanines have values from 1 to 9. In the conversion to stanines, scores are divided into nine groups, each group a certain distance from the average. Actually, the average score is included in stanine 5, the middle group. And since it is the middle group and since most scores occur near the middle, a rather high percent of scores fall in stanine 5. By the same token, few scores fall in either stanine 1 or 9.

Table 4.1 expresses the story in a way that should make clear the meaning of stanines. Each number in the middle column is a stanine score. Per-

Percentage of Scores Represented	STANINE SCORE	Evaluation
4%	1	Poor
7%	2	
12%	3	Below Average
17%	4	
20%	5	Average
17%	6	
12%	7	Above Average
7%	8	
4%	9	Superior

centages of raw scores which are included in each stanine group are indicated in the first column. A guide to interpretation of performance indicated by a given stanine score is indicated in the third column of the table.

The Use of Test Results

You probably have the feeling that if we're right in our assessment of the situation, standardized tests are limited in their use. While this is true, they do have some uses, and in some ways are very efficient.

For example, we mentioned in chapter 1 that in a "normal" classroom the range of reading ability is quite wide. Certainly one of the most common problems of the classroom teacher is to identify the divergent reading needs and abilities of students in the class. No class is really "normal" though, and the formula we gave in chapter 1 can only demonstrate the diversity which is theoretically possible in a heterogeneous class. By using standardized test data, however, a teacher can get a much better estimate of the range of reading ability in a class. This is usually a matter of collecting standardized reading test data from students' folders and identifying the number of students that fall into each of the stanine classifications.

After studying such information about the group to be taught, the teacher can make selections of appropriate reading materials. The use of group test results in conjunction with readability formulas can provide guidelines for planning an instructional program or unit. Decisions can be tentatively made about who probably can or cannot read the textbook in the course. A lot of frustration might be avoided if a teacher were to know before being tempted to require the reading of a text that it was probably too difficult for many students to tackle alone. Naturally, standardized test and readability formula results are only part of the picture, in some cases a minor part. But our position is that if standardized test results are available anyway, teachers and others in schools may as well make the best use of them, taking every pain not to misuse them.

Picking Children for Diagnosis

We have tried to make the point that testing is what one does to groups, diagnosis is what one does to individuals. But to carefully diagnose the complex learning needs of all students is probably unnecessary, if not impossible. One of the strongest points in favor of group standardized tests is that they may help to pinpoint those students whose needs may be exceptional enough to warrant a detailed diagnostic workup. Students whose scores are in stanines 1, 2, or 3, or 9, 8, or 7, may be in particular need of special attention. (Recall, these stanines include roughly the lower and upper 20 percent of students.) The standardized test in this use is like a net whose openings are large enough to let through the students whose needs are more common while picking out others whose needs may be exceptional. The net will "catch" this latter group because of either suspected exceptional weakness *or* exceptional talent. Certainly, it won't always be accurate, for many reasons, but as a rough screening device, the group standardized test does have usefulness. With its results, teachers, guidance personnel, and other ancillary staff can cooperatively deal with instructional problems, treating individuals as individuals, once their needs have been identified by careful diagnosis.

CHAPTER 5   Measuring Attitudes

> Attitudes are a measurable outcome of learning.

Setting the Stage

Before you read over the summary of the chapter, we want you to begin with an activity. This will prove a point we will make later.

ACTIVITY 5.1

1. Identify several achievement tests that are used in your subject area.
2. Identify a scale that might be used to measure students' attitudes toward the subject you teach.

   [To do this, you might discuss the activity with fellow teachers and the guidance counselor or check publishers' catalogs and references such as Buros, *Mental Measurements Yearbook.*]

Overview

Attitudes of students toward school subjects are often misunderstood and usually ignored in assessment programs. However, there are scales available for measuring attitudes and there are techniques by which teachers can construct their own scales. Supplemented by informal but careful diagnosis, paper and pencil "tests" of attitudes could easily be a standard part of assessment of the objectives of instruction. Whether one would choose to measure attitudes, given the availability of techniques for doing so, probably comes down to a matter of priority.

The Estes Attitude Scales, one form for middle-school-age and up, another form for elementary school use, are a direct measure of attitudes toward English, math, reading, science, and social studies. Scale scores can best be interpreted in light of behavioral observations of students whose attitudes may be more extreme than those of their peers. Taken together, formal testing and informal assessment will likely yield the best information about attitudes.

The Importance of Attitude Measurement

Few teachers would quarrel with the notion that attitudes are critical determinants of learning. However, students' attitudes toward specific subjects or toward school in general are not usually included as a part of a school's regular testing program. Formal or teacher-made achievement tests are used almost exclusively to assess or plan teaching and learning. Why is this so? Why is attitude measurement so conspicuously absent from assessment programs? Need it be so?

While the selection is rather narrow, there are several good alternatives from which to choose in the measurement of attitudes. The reasons for absence of such measurement in most schools is anyone's guess, but two explanations seem most tenable to us. First, attitudes are not well understood by most people, other than to say they probably exist. The affective domain is not a major part of the professional study of teachers. Second, even among those who would wish to do so, few people really believe attitudes can be measured. While cognitive measures, the achievement and intelligence tests, are accepted with frightening indiscrimination, skepticism has been the common reaction to affective measures.

Despite their often misunderstood nature and the infrequent attention they receive, attitudes can and should be measured in planning for and evaluating students' educational experiences. To do so will require: (1) an understanding of attitude measures that are possible; (2) a familiarity with published scales that are available; and (3) some feeling for techniques of informal observation and assessment of attitudes.

Kinds of Attitude Measures

Basically, there are two ways of measuring attitudes, since attitude scales can be classified as either direct or indirect measures. Direct measures are distinguished by the fact it is clearly evident what the scale is measuring.

64

Such measures have the advantage of relatively high reliability, though critics will point out that answers to direct measures can be easily faked, that students may try to lie for fear of admitting dislike for a socially or academically desirable behavior. Research done on attitude measurement belies this criticism, however.

Indirect measures attempt in some way to disguise their true meaning. The supposed advantage to this is that students cannot easily "lie" to the scale. The main problem with indirect measures, though, is that one can never be sure that the attitude inferred from any behavior or judgment is justified. For example, when you see someone crying you may be tempted to conclude he is unhappy. You may, however, be wrong. If the person is happy, the attitude you infer (sadness) from the observed behavior (crying) is unjustified. In the same manner, many variables might be reflected in the scores of indirect scales, and the validity of purely inferential assessment is open to serious question.

Often, you may wish to measure pupils' attitudes toward something for which there is no available scale. For example, a department may want to know how pupils feel about a newly instituted elective program. A locally designed scale will have to be constructed for this. It is impossible for the commercial market to meet every conceivable need in educational diagnosis. Most tests given in schools will continue to be teacher-made, and so with attitude measures. The following two sections of this chapter concern the construction of attitude scales. Such information should also be helpful in selection of scales that are commercially or otherwise available for use. These will be given review in the next major section of the chapter.

Construction of Direct Measures

Direct measures are those which: (1) are rather obvious in intent and (2) require little if any inference in interpretation. Raw scores on such measures are directly interpretable; the higher the score, the better the attitude.

One of the most popular and perhaps the best direct method of measuring attitudes was designed by R. S. Likert (1932). Likert scales present the respondent with a series of statements related to a "psychological domain" (e.g., school, English class, curriculum design, or anything about which people might hold varying opinions). The task of the respondent is to indicate his or her agreement or disagreement with each statement. For example, in a scale to measure attitudes toward school, the following might appear:

5 will mean "I strongly agree"
4 will mean "I agree"
3 will mean "I cannot decide"
2 will mean "I disagree"
1 will mean "I strongly disagree"

	Strongly Agree	Agree	Cannot Decide	Disagree	Strongly Disagree
1. School is worthwhile.	5	4	3	2	1
2. Most courses in school are useless.	5	4	3	2	1

There are two points to be made concerning these items. First, notice that item 1 is positive, item 2 is negative. This means that the scored values of responses to the items are opposite in magnitude. For example, *strongly agree* to item 1 would be scored 5, whereas *strongly agree* to item 2 would be scored 1. (The numbers in the response boxes merely refer to response choices.) The general rule is this: from *strongly agree* to *strongly disagree*, score positive items 5, 4, 3, 2, 1; score negative items 1, 2, 3, 4, 5.

The second point about scoring is that an individual's score on a scale is the sum of response values across all items. For every item, an individual's response is scored 5, 4, 3, 2, or 1. These values are then summed across all items on the scale. The total represents a quantification of the person's attitude. For example, if a scale had 15 items, the possible scores for any individual would range from 15 to 75, or 15×1 to 15×5. Do you see why?

The writing of items for any attitude scale is the most critical step. Criteria for items have been published by Edwards (1957) in an excellent little book called *Techniques of Attitude Scale Construction*. The following suggestions for writing items are adapted from Edwards' list. Examples are provided to illustrate the criteria. Each item refers to and should call to mind the school subject "Science."

1. Avoid statements referring to the past rather than the present.
   Poor: Science was an exciting subject in elementary school.
   Better: Science is an exciting subject.

2. Avoid factual statements.
   Poor: Science is a required subject in the eleventh grade.
   Better: Science should be a required subject in the eleventh grade.

3. Avoid statements capable of multiple interpretation.
   Poor: The job of the science teacher is to transmit information. (Is *to transmit information* good or bad?)
   Better: The study of science offers the opportunity for search and discovery.

4. Avoid statements irrelevant to the subject.
   Poor: School is worthwhile.
   Better: The study of science is worthwhile.

5. Avoid statements likely to be endorsed by almost anyone or no one.
   Poor: All of man's progress has stemmed from his scientific endeavor.
   Better: The most important aspects of man's progress stem from scientific endeavor.

6. Use simple, clear, direct language in the form of concise statements.
   Poor: The study of science, while beneficial to the welfare of mankind, is nevertheless a double-edged sword, since it has the potential for accruing to man either his guaranteed immortality or his inevitable destruction.
   Better: Scientific endeavor provides a better way of life.

7. Each statement should have only one complete thought. (See examples for 6.)

8. Avoid terms such as *all, always, none, never, only, just,* and *merely.*
   Poor: All students should try to major in science in college.
   Better: Majoring in science in college would be worthwhile.

9. Avoid use of words perhaps incomprehensible to students.
   Poor: Indefatigability is high during the study of science.
   Better: Studying science is less tiring than studying other subjects.

10. Avoid use of double negatives.
    Poor: It is not true that not enough science is offered in high school.
    Better: More science should be offered in high school.

The use of these criteria is essential. By adhering to them, the content validity of the attitude scale is achieved. To the degree that items conform to the criteria, the scale is likely to provide a true measure of attitudes. For example, you might examine the attitude scale included in Peggy Greenfield's unit on the American Legal System found in Chapter 16.

Published Scales

Until recently, there were very few scales available for measuring attitudes toward school subjects. Those that were available were typically constructed for use in research or evaluation projects where the validity of the scale was not a primary concern. In 1967, Shaw and Wright, in their book, *Scales for the Measurement of Attitudes,* pointed out that most scales of attitude toward school courses were to measure attitudes of college students. They chose to exclude many existing scales from their compilation because of generally poor quality. In their terms, the "functional characteristics" of many scales were unsatisfactory.

In the ten years since the Shaw and Wright book appeared, the picture has changed somewhat. Alexander and Filler (1976) list eighteen attitude assessment instruments in their booklet, *Attitudes and Reading*. Only four of these bear pre-1967 dates. Most have appeared since 1970. Note that these are only scales to measure attitudes toward reading, which says nothing of scales that may have appeared as measures of attitudes toward other school subjects.

It was in response to the conditions deplored by Shaw and Wright that Johnstone (1973) sought to validate the Estes Attitude Scales. The success of her study led to the subsequent publication of the scales which are now available from Pro-Ed publications (Estes, Estes, Richards, and Roettger, 1981) in both a secondary and an elementary form. Dulin and Chester (1974) have provided good evidence of the validity of the scales and the scales have had favorable reception in reviews and reports (Summers, 1977; Payne, 1977; Tuinman and Kendall, 1980). Replications of the studies of the scales continue to bear out their consistency in measurement (Richards and Clark, 1983).

The main value of the scales is that they allow teachers to: (1) pinpoint students' present positive or negative attitudes expressed in interpretable terms; (2) make curricular and instructional modifications in response to those attitudes; and (3) observe changes in attitudes over time, when the scales are administered on a pre/post basis.

Informal Observation and Assessment

Formal, paper-and-pencil tests of attitudes are but a part of measurement in the affective domain. Certainly they allow quantification of attitude, but careful and sensitive observation is the best method of "qualifying" pupils' attitudes. Numbers on tests are impersonal. They say nothing of why a person's attitude is what it is, let alone how the attitude is expressed in behavior. Informal assessment, on the other hand, gains in personalization what it gives up in precision. The implicit suggestion for all measurement is clear, especially for affective measurement: for screening and testing of groups, use formal scales; for diagnosis and counseling of individuals, add informal observation.

An attitude is both a feeling and a disposition toward a class of tangible or intangible objects to which the attitude is related. Behaviorally, this often translates to verbal statements and approach-avoidance actions, especially where alternative behaviors are available. For example, a good attitude toward reading will lead a person to read instead of watch television when the goal is entertainment. Obviously, there are exceptions where good television wins out over mediocre reading. But the general choice of reading over television can be attributed to a person's relative feeling for reading and television as entertainment. Therefore, observation of behavior should be indicative of attitude.

When a student has been identified by a screening test as having a poor attitude, or where the teacher thinks that attitude may be a problem, there are certain questions that can be asked. Answers to these, derived from informal observation, will bear qualitative implications for the student's attitudes. Thus, answers to carefully framed diagnostic questions can suggest modifications in a child's school experience.

1. What does the student's cumulative record indicate about past experience with similar courses?

It is as true that experiences determine attitudes as that attitudes determine behaviors. If a child seems to have an unfavorable attitude toward school or a particular subject, you might ask whether previous experiences with school or certain courses have been negative. It is possible that even the student does not realize the source of his or her feelings or what to do about it. A frank and open discussion about the causes of a poor attitude can be helpful.

2. Does the student express anxiety and fear about a subject?

People will often verbalize their attitudes when given an opportunity. Where a student has developed an unrealistic fear of a subject, he or she may say so in different ways. Graduate students, for example, often are afraid of measurement and statistics courses, or so they say. But more often than not, what they are really afraid of is having to memorize things that they do not understand. What they need is to be counseled into a section of the course that is likely to be taught on an intuitive level rather than an algorithmic level. For high school students, the story is similar.

3. Is the work the student does in a course careful or careless?

To continue the example of the graduate student and statistics, tests and measurements professors often complain that their students "can't add a column of figures, let alone multiply a negative and a positive and get a negative product!" But is it really that the students can't perform simple operations or is it that their predisposition toward mathematics, stemming from whatever source, leads to carelessness? When an attitude of fear mitigates against learning, the student needs counseling about the fear more than teaching directed to a weakness that doesn't really exist. The story is the same, repeated endlessly for countless "failures" in school. Diagnosis of attitude can have far-reaching effects on a student's academic life if followed by attempts at attitude modification. (This topic will be treated in Chapter 13.)

4. By class participation, or lack of it, what is the student saying about his or her attitude toward the course?

Certainly not everyone who is quiet in class has a poor attitude and not everyone who participates in discussions has a good attitude. But by the way they do or do not participate in class activity and discussion, students may reveal their feelings toward a course. If the teacher is sensitive to this, he or she can often know when steps to remediate a poor attitude are in order. The antagonistic participant and the passive aggressive withdrawal are perhaps demonstrating similar attitudinal problems that demand attention.

5. What are the student's expressed personal and/or professional goals and how are these related to the course?

Students with good attitudes toward a course often aspire to occupations and endeavors that relate to the subject. Conversely, a student who sees no relationship between his or her goals and the requirements and content of a course will likely have a poor attitude toward the course. An informal survey of student interest and aspiration, given early in a course, can serve as part of an informal attitude assessment. Careful analysis of results may reveal the need for exploration of the relevance and relationship of students' interests and course content.

This brief list of informal questions is representative of the kinds of behaviors and statements that often indicate attitudes. Answers to such questions can be helpful in making decisions about causes and remedies of poor attitudes. There are, however, few if any simple solutions to attitudinal problems. Attitudes form over years and change slowly. To complicate matters further, the question of attitudes and behaviors is a question of chickens and eggs. While it may be logical to say that attitudes determine behaviors, it is as easy to say that behaviors can modify attitudes. This may, in fact, sometimes work to a teacher's advantage. For example, a social studies teacher might have a group of students who are very negative toward reading the text, discussing it in class, listening to the teacher, and taking tests every Friday. So, the teacher tries a completely different approach and sets up an activity-centered syllabus that includes many options for modes of learning the same thing. If not all, certainly many students give it a try and begin to behave as if they do like social studies—in fact, they come to do so because they are doing things in their study that they like and this affects their whole outlook on the subject. (Remember *Foxfire?*)

CHAPTER 6

Analyzing Reading Comprehension

Reading comprehension is the best window through which to observe reading ability.

Overview

From an informal analysis of a student's reading comprehension, we can generate hypotheses about that student's reading ability. As we do this, we can consider how well a student reads on three levels: (1) literal, (2) inferential, and (3) applicative.

In designing a program for informally diagnosing reading comprehension, a teacher should consider several factors. First, the abilities that one wants to assess must be identified and the type of selection process must be chosen. Second, the questions which are to be asked on the comprehension check should be designed in relation to the purposes for administering the test. Third, the administration of an informal reading inventory in a content classroom can serve several purposes. Fourth, interpreting the results of an informal analysis requires more than simply scoring a test objectively; it requires insights and perceptions which are developed through practice.

What's It All About?

Reading is a controversial matter surrounded by much heat and little light. Our earlier guess was, however, that as you defined reading you included a dimension related to comprehension. To try to do otherwise would be like trying to define the game of football without mention of the attempt to advance the ball. Whatever else it is or is not, football is a game of moving the ball. It is indefinable without that idea. Reading is also essentially indefinable without the element of comprehension. Comprehension is the object and the essence of reading; it is what reading is all about.

Theoretically, it is possible that a football game could be played in which neither team was able to move the ball. Such a game, however, could only be called football because both teams were attempting to advance the ball, and that is the object of the game. So it is with reading. It is possible to say, "I have read this, but I can't comprehend it." But the person who says this can be said to have read only because he or she was attempting to comprehend. The fact that the person did not comprehend suggests that his or her attempt to read was unsuccessful. The success of the attempt to comprehend determines the quality of the reading act. Whatever else it is or is not about, reading is about comprehension.

Levels of Comprehension

Comprehension is the object and the product of reading. As such, comprehension is the best window we have for observing reading ability. That window may be frosted, and we may see through it darkly, but it is the best we have at the moment.

Through the diagnosis of reading comprehension, one can generate inferences about the quality of a student's reading ability. On the basis of these inferences, hypotheses can be formed about the expectations one might reasonably establish for a student's reading. Inferences may also be drawn for instructional activities appropriate for the student. Comprehension, then, is the key to effective reading diagnosis.

Perhaps the easiest way to understand comprehension is to realize that a reader can (1) read the lines, (2) read between the lines, and (3) read beyond the lines. Reading the lines is equivalent to *literal comprehension,* that is, comprehending what the author says. To read between the lines is to interpret what the author means and is *inferential comprehension.* The third level is reading beyond the lines by applying what is read and is called *applicative comprehension.* Analytical and syntopical reading require that a student function on both the second and third levels of comprehension. Thus, an analysis of a student's ability to comprehend on each of these three levels is an important aspect of diagnosis.

Literal comprehension is what most students obtain when they read material that is within their instructional reading level. It is what can be verified by referring directly to what an author has stated; there is no guesswork involved. Consider, for example, the following sentence, typical of an eighth-grade, history textbook:

When Abraham Lincoln, the sixteenth President of the United States, took office, he faced the most difficult challenge in our history—to preserve the Union in the face of determined secessionists.

Assuming that the statements in this sentence are true, a student's literal comprehension will be determined by the ability to understand what the author said. If a student reads this as "Lincoln's challenge was to preserve the Union," he or she has comprehended literally what the author said. Literal comprehension is sometimes called factual recall because it refers to the facts that the reader remembers.

Inferential comprehension is based on one's interpretation of the facts that are presented. In a very real sense, inferences are the result of an "educated guess" because they cannot be proved by what is specifically stated. For example, in the passage about Lincoln, the author does not state why Lincoln's challenge was the most difficult in our nation's history. A student must infer from the evidence and make an informed guess about what the author meant. Thus, inferential comprehension is the ability to take what the author says and logically derive what is meant. Main ideas of passages are often left to inferential comprehension because they are not stated outright; students often need to be able to read on the inferential level if they are to identify the important concepts in a passage.

The applicative level is important because it is primarily through application that reading becomes meaningful and practical. The ultimate purpose of reading is to be able to apply what is learned through reading. Many students cannot transfer what they read to their own lives and situations, and reading for them is often perceived as a pointless and useless task. Reading a driver's manual and similar material may have obvious application to them, but a science textbook or a passage from *Walden* . . . ? Mature, critical readers actively seek application as they read, so their ability to comprehend and to analyze what they read far surpasses that of the reader who rarely transcends the literal level. The key to effective analytical reading is asking questions, and the student who constantly seeks application in his or her reading is the one who most easily learns to read critically. In addition, when a student comprehends on the applicative level, he or she is far more likely to remember the material because it has greater meaning for the student than for one who cannot apply what he or she reads.

Informal Diagnosis

When reading specialists diagnose reading comprehension, they rely on their knowledge and skills of observation more than anything else. The strategy they most commonly use is an informal reading inventory. It consists of pro-

73

viding a student with several reading selections, observing the student as he or she reads, and checking the student's comprehension when the reading is finished. Since the selections are of increasing difficulty, the diagnostician has an opportunity to determine what the student can do when reading easy material, challenging material, and difficult material. Because the testing situation is informal, the examiner can pursue a student's responses to determine exactly what has been learned and, in some cases, can even probe to ascertain how or why the student has learned.

The basic principles underlying the informal reading inventory (IRI) can be applied by classroom teachers in constructing and administering a content area informal reading inventory.

A systematically designed program to assess students' comprehension of content materials can be as simple or as elaborate as one wants. It should be designed to accommodate the needs of the teacher, and it can be as basic as giving a single passage to an entire class or as extensive as administering a series of passages to individual students. It might be best to consider something in between the two extremes. Whatever the case, careful attention should be given to preparing the testing material and to interpreting the results if the diagnosis is to be accurate and meaningful.

Constructing a Testing Device

Whatever one hopes to determine from an informal diagnosis of reading comprehension, the value of the findings often depends upon how well the testing device has been constructed. At best, a testing situation can only provide *clues* about what a student knows or does. The accuracy of a reading diagnosis is determined, in part, by the degree to which the test reflects a realistic reading situation. In constructing a content informal reading test, a teacher must consider (1) what abilities he or she seeks to diagnose, (2) the selection of the passages that will measure those abilities, and (3) the design of the questions to be such that they do measure the identified abilities.

A content IRI must be constructed in relation to well-defined objectives. Identifying exactly what you want to discern is the first step in constructing such a device. For example, do you want your content IRI to:

1. assess abilities with material only from your specific content field?
2. assess abilities across a range of difficulty (i.e., multi-level materials)?
3. assess abilities with varied types of material (i.e., narrative, descriptive, expository, word problems, etc.)?
4. assess ability to identify main ideas?
5. assess ability to "read between the lines"?
6. assess ability to use context clues to identify new words?
7. assess ability to apply what is in the selections?

74

These and other questions must be answered before a test or inventory can be constructed if you are to be reasonably confident that the results you obtain are accurate.

Consider the objectives for a content IRI in your classroom. What objectives would you identify on which to base the construction of your inventory or test? Are there areas that need to be considered that we have not suggested in our list of questions? What are they? A word of caution: because you identify your objectives does not guarantee that the inventory, when constructed, will provide accurate results. You must constantly monitor yourself during the construction process to determine how accurately the test reflects your objectives. If you lose sight of your objectives, it is likely that your inventory will diminish in its ability to yield accurate and meaningful information.

Having established the objectives for your inventory, carefully choose the passages you will include. Above all, the selections must be representative of the material students will be asked to read in your classroom. In selecting the passages, consider (1) the varied levels of difficulty for your course, (2) the predominant types of passages students will read, and (3) the length of the passage needed to obtain accurate results.

It is hoped a content teacher will be able to provide multi-level materials in his or her classroom. The diversity of reading ability in a content class has been discussed in chapter 1, and the need for multi-level materials is evident if one is to avoid frustrating reading assignments. If multi-level assignments are to be used in instruction, a content IRI should be constructed from material at each of the available levels. This provides the teacher with an opportunity to analyze students' abilities at several levels of difficulty and makes it easier to determine which students would learn best from assignments in which materials. In addition, when a student's ability is sampled across several levels of difficulty, the task of planning instructional activities becomes easier because reasonable expectations are more likely to be established and the teacher's prognosis can be made with increased confidence.

If, on the other hand, circumstances require that a single textbook be used predominantly, the passages chosen for the IRI should be selected to reflect the variability of reading levels within that text. While one can ascertain an overall readability level for a textbook, rarely is that level consistently maintained throughout the book. Most textbooks include a wide range of readability levels, and the assigned readability level is only an average within that range. Thus, it would be prudent to include several selections from a single adopted textbook to assess students' abilities with material on the varied levels within that text.

Closely related to the diversity of reading levels are the varied types of passages students typically encounter in content area reading assignments. With the exception of that required in their English class, students read material which is almost exclusively nonfiction. The experience that many students have had with nonfiction material is limited and their problems in reading content material are often related to this lack of experience. Assessing ability to learn from descriptive and expository selections is an important purpose of a content IRI. In selecting passages for a content IRI, then, one should include those types of material that dominate a specific field. For example, at a minimum, a math IRI should include expository passages and word problems; an English IRI, narrative passages and perhaps even a poem; a history or science IRI, descriptive and expository passages. The selections in a content IRI must reflect the type of material that students will typically be asked to read.

A third factor to consider in the selection of passages for a content IRI is their length. On the surface this may seem trivial, but one of the major problems with many reading tests is that they create atypical reading situations by using selections far shorter than what is normally read. This results in a distorted image of a reader's ability. We believe that a selection of 200 to 250 words is minimal. The number of words, however, is not of prime importance. The objective of the content IRI is to determine how well a student will read a typical selection. We suggest a passage of this length because that will probably be necessary to assure that the selection is inclusive and has continuity.

The passage chosen should have a logical beginning and conclusion, the body of the passage clearly reflecting the development of a topic. Accurate comprehension of passages excerpted from the middle of a larger body of material is often dependent upon what has preceded that excerpt and what follows it. Thus, the length of a passage in a content IRI must be determined by the degree to which it is continuous and inclusive.

Formulating Comprehension Questions

Good diagnosis depends upon the quality of the questions designed to assess comprehension; in the absence of good comprehension questions, the diagnosis of reading comprehension is almost surely inaccurate. Good questions can be formulated if three aspects of their design are considered. The neglect of any one of these is likely to result in an invalid assessment and a meaningless diagnosis.

IRI questions must measure the areas identified by your objectives. Typically, several aspects of comprehension are checked: (1) comprehension of main ideas, (2) factual recall, (3) inferential comprehension, (4) ability to apply and relate what is learned, and (5) ability to use context clues to understand unfamiliar vocabulary. You need not check all of these areas, but it is essential to know what areas of comprehension are being assessed. To check predominantly factual recall and then conclude that a student can or cannot comprehend the material can be both inaccurate and misleading. To conclude that the student can or cannot comprehend the material on a literal level may be accurate, but no information would have been gathered about other aspects of comprehension.

Exactly which aspects of comprehension to assess is each teacher's decision. We suggest that a teacher should check comprehension of main ideas, facts, and inferences. When these aspects of comprehension are assessed, the responses will provide information that can be used for an overall analysis of a student's comprehension. Each of the major aspects can be analyzed separately, and the interaction effect among them can be assessed. That is, if a student has difficulty with inferences, his problem may be an inability to recall the facts which are needed to make the proper inferences. An attempt to determine this should be made.

Questions that are not "passage dependent" may not be measuring what a student comprehends from that passage. This is not to suggest that one should avoid questions that assess a student's ability to relate what is learned from a passage to situations outside the selection. When you do so, however, be sure that the question incorporates *both* what is in the selection and what may be outside the passage's boundaries. For example, consider again the statement about Lincoln:

> When Abraham Lincoln, the sixteenth President of the United States, took office, he faced the most difficult challenge in our history—to preserve the Union in the face of determined secessionists.

An inappropriate question based on this statement might be: "Why might the challenge that Lincoln faced be more difficult than Washington's problems with his cabinet?" A student could answer this question from knowledge of Washington's problems and a general awareness of secession; he or she need not know the specifics of Lincoln's challenge. A slightly more "passage dependent" question might be: "Compare the magnitude of Lincoln's challenge to the problems Washington faced with his cabinet." But this "question," too, is probably inappropriate. Here the student must be aware of the details of the early problems of both presidents. If he or she cannot answer such a question, one must then ascertain whether this is because of (1) not knowing what Lincoln's challenge was, (2) not knowing how great the challenge was, or (3) not knowing about Washington's problem. Then and only then could an accurate diagnosis be made. If the diagnosis of comprehension is to be accurate, it must be directly related to the selection being read.

Another consideration in the formation of comprehension questions is that questions should not provide information about the answer. Frequently, too many clues about the right answer are included in the question itself. For example, consider the question "What problems did Lincoln face with the secessionists?" Immediately, the student is cued to secessionists. If he or she knows who the secessionists were, a reasonable answer can be provided

77

without reading the passage. A better question might be "What was the essence of Lincoln's challenge?" The answer can now provide a better clue to what the student learned from the reading.

In forming comprehension questions, it is important to bear in mind what you expect the students to learn from their reading. The questions should be similar to those you might ask on a test such as a weekly quiz or grading period examination, assuming now that those assessments accurately reflect your instructional goals and expectations. If the questions are easier or more difficult than what is typically asked, they may not help much in determining instructional strategies.

Finally, the questions you use in a content IRI should be designed to elicit short, essay-type answers. Sometimes, the answer may be only one word, such as a person's name, but you should avoid objective, multiple-choice questions. These questions tend to reveal too much information to the student and the answer may then be a guess based on the options made available. If there is to be a guess made, you want the student to guess on the basis of what he or she understands, not because you have provided a "right answer" and several distractors.

In summary, we might characterize good IRI questions as content related and open-ended. The classic open-ended question is "Retell what you have read," which may or may not be appropriate for a specific group administered content IRI. Certainly, the questions that are asked should require, by various degrees, retelling and evaluation of what has been read.

Administering a Content IRI

The way in which one administers a content IRI is an important aspect of informal reading diagnosis in a content classroom. This strategy may be used with an entire class or with individuals, but in either case, the emphasis must be on informality. By informal, we do not mean to imply overly relaxed, slouching students taking a test as they chat with their friends. Informal testing is to be contrasted with formal testing when the latter requires rigid, inflexible test administration. Flexibility is the byword of informal testing. A diagnostician is afforded a free hand in informal testing to pursue and probe students' responses in an effort to gain insights into their reading ability that are not immediately apparent from their responses. If a teacher takes advantage of the informality of a content IRI, the chances of obtaining valuable diagnostic information will be greatly enhanced.

When administering a content IRI, a teacher should consider several possible alternatives. The method that is eventually selected should, however, be in accord with the purposes and objectives established for using such a strategy in the first place. Among the available options, an individualized administration will provide the greatest opportunity for an in-depth analysis, but sheer numbers may make such an approach impractical for any but a small number of students. Another possibility is to administer group inventory to an entire class simultaneously. This procedure certainly has the advantage of efficiency. Another option is to administer the inventory in small groups, where some of the opportunity to pursue answers remains open. A teacher should consider all possibilities, as the best option may not be any one approach, given the various limitations of time, space, and need. Perhaps the most feasible and appropriate strategy lies in some combination of these alternatives.

The approach we recommend is to begin with a survey inventory administered to an entire class. A survey inventory may consist of one or several passages, depending on how much screening information is being sought. If you prefer to use a single passage, it should be as typical as possible of the material you will use most often in your course. If several passages are employed, they should represent the range of available materials that will be used for instruction.

If you decide to use this group screening inventory approach, consider the following cautions. First, if you are interested in testing students' ability to recall what they have read, you should not allow them access to the passages as they answer the questions. If students can refer to a passage, you will be testing recognition, not recall, and those are two very different, though related, aspects of comprehension. Second, a major disadvantage of this screening approach is that students will have to write out their answers. This introduces a variable that may easily affect your results. If students write out their responses and their answers indicate that they had difficulty understanding what they read, one can never be sure whether the difficulty was in understanding the reading or in writing out the responses. For this second reason, if for no other, we suggest that you not limit your informal diagnosis of reading comprehension to a large group inventory.

The real value of this large group approach is to provide initial information which can be used to suggest additional diagnostic procedures. Since this is the primary value of this approach, you may prefer to use available standardized test data for screening purposes. (This is, we remind you, the most appropriate and valuable use of standardized reading tests.) Naturally, an informal screening inventory will yield results more directly related to your specific purposes than will a standardized test, and too, the inventory will be based more on material immediately pertinent to your course.

A second step in the approach we recommend involves the administration of several passages to small groups of students. These groups should be designed homogeneously on the basis of results obtained from the large group screening. Ideally, the size of these groups would be no more than four students, thus minimizing the interaction among the students as they respond to the comprehension questions.

When administering a small group inventory, ask the students to read each passage silently as they would an assignment in class. As they read, observe the students to identify any signs of strengths or weaknesses. For example, good readers may ask if they can write on the passage and may underline certain portions as they would when reading a homework assignment. A weak reader may indicate signs of difficulty or frustration by finger pointing, vocalizing, or being easily distracted. These observations during silent reading may be as important as the information obtained from the comprehension check.

When all the students have finished reading each passage, ask the comprehension questions orally. You will not be able to ask all students each question, but if you have a variety of questions, you should be able to determine to what degree each student was able to understand what was read. Having several students together can also be advantageous if you ask others to agree or disagree with a student's answer. You can then probe to find out why or how students arrived at their answers. If conducted properly, a small group inventory may provide you with as much diagnostic information as you will either need or want for most of your students.

After administering small group informal reading inventories, it is likely that you will want to obtain more information about a few of your students. This can be accomplished with individualized IRIs. When administering an IRI individually, you should pursue the same basic strategies used in the small group inventory. It should, however, differ in that you will have an opportunity to pursue and probe responses in greater depth. The student will assist in the diagnosis by explaining why he or she may be having difficulties. Also, in an individualized setting, you have the opportunity to provide instruction and to determine how well the student responds to your guidance and direction. Perhaps the student is totally disinterested in the subject and has no intention of trying to learn what is being read; if that is the case, you may be able to discover this problem and generate some interest in the material— at least enough to get the student to try to learn. On the other hand, you may want to have a chance to examine a good reader individually to determine exactly how far you can challenge him or her. Too, you may discover that a good reader can comprehend well on a literal level but has difficulty abstracting thoughts beyond the factual to more inferential or applicative levels of comprehension. One can discover much from an individualized testing that cannot surface in even a small group setting, and the limitations of such a diagnosis are determined only by the amount of perceptiveness and imagination that a teacher can provide.

Interpreting a Content IRI

A good reading specialist interprets an informal reading inventory with the intensity of a bionic eye. Analyzing the facts and the implications in the Sherlock Holmes tradition, the diagnostician has but one purpose in mind—prognosis and recommendations; without these applications, diagnosis is of little import. Primarily, the intention is twofold: (1) to identify a student's instructional reading level (the level at which the student will benefit most from instruction); and (2) to determine the specific strengths and weaknesses of a student's reading ability.

When interpreting the results of a content IRI, one can begin by examining the percentage scores obtained by each student on the selections. These scores can *indicate* proficiency with similar material and can provide a rough, initial guideline for diagnosis. The following percentages are offered as estimates of several degrees of reading competence:

If a comprehension score is	*that material is likely to be on the student's*
90–100,	independent reading level.
70–90,	instructional reading level.
below 50,	frustration reading level.

If the score falls in the gray area between 50 and 70, it suggests that a student may find the material too difficult or that he or she may learn from it effectively when the reading is supplemented with appropriate instruction. When a score falls in this range, however, further analysis is required to suggest an appropriate competence level.

A word of caution is essential at this point. These scores can be misleading at times. Hence, we advise that the percentage scores be used only as initial indices or as evidence to corroborate findings based on more thorough analyses and understandings of a student's specific responses. For example, if a student skips, misreads, or misunderstands a major idea as the selection is read, it is conceivable that the student's total percentage score can be affected as much as forty points, depending upon how many comprehension questions are based on or are related to that idea. Therefore, accurate diagnosis can only be generated from an in-depth analysis of responses; it rarely emanates from a cursory examination of total percentage scores.

The in-depth analysis to which we refer is usually a result of an item-by-item examination of the responses to questions from each selection and from among various selections of varying degrees of difficulty. You should seek to identify trends in various areas of comprehension such as factual, interpretive, and applied. By determining specific strengths and weaknesses, you can relate the specifics to the whole picture and more readily understand what a student's real capabilities are.

ACTIVITY 2.2

In this activity we have provided a passage typical of a ninth-grade history textbook. It has a tenth-grade readability level (Fry graph). Following the selection are ten questions. To help you apply the principle of interpreting

IRI findings, we suggest that you read this selection and answer the questions after it. This should help familiarize you with the selection and enhance your understanding of our discussion of the several examples which will follow.

Directions: Read this silently to find out why the Shenandoah Valley was valuable to both the North and the South in the Civil War.

Phil Sheridan in the Shenandoah Valley

During the Civil War, it was known simply as the Valley: an open corridor slanting off to the southwest of Virginia from the gap at Harper's Ferry. It was a broad land, lying between blue mountains with the bright mirror of a looped river going among golden fields and dark woodlands, and with pleasant towns linked along a broad undulating turnpike and rich farms rolling away to the rising hills.

Queerly enough, although it had been a vital factor in the war, in a way that war had hardly touched it. Stonewall Jackson had made it a theater of high strategy in 1862, and there had been hard fighting along the historic turnpike and near quaint villages like Front Royal and Port Republic, and most of the fence rails on farms near the main highway had long since vanished to build the campfires of soldiers in blue and gray. Yet, even in the summer of 1864, the land bore few scars. East of the Blue Ridge and the Bull Run Mountains the country along the Orange and Alexandria Railroad had been marched over and fought over and ravaged mercilessly, and it was a desolate waste picked clean of everything an army might want or a farmer could use. But the Valley had escaped most of this, and when Phil Sheridan got there it was much as it had always been—rich, sunny, peaceful, a land of good farms and big barns, yellow grain growing beside green pastures, lazy herds of sheep and cattle feeding on the slopes.

An accident of geography made the Valley worth more to the South than to the North, strategically. Running from southwest to northeast, the Valley was the Confederacy's great covered way leading up to the Yankee fortress, with the high parapet of the Blue Ridge offering concealment and protection. A Confederate army coming down the Valley was marching directly toward the Northern citadel, but a Yankee army moving up the Valley was going nowhere in particular because it was constantly getting farther away from Richmond and Richmond's defenders. Nor did a Confederate force operating in the Valley have serious problems of supply. The Valley itself was the base, and it could be drawn upon for abundant food and forage from Staunton all the way to Winchester and beyond.

When the 1864 campaign began, Grant tried to solve the problem of the Valley, and the solution then would have been fairly simple. All that he needed was to establish a Federal army in the upper Valley—at Staunton, say, or Waynesboro, anywhere well upstream. That would close the gate, and the Confederate's granary and covered way would be useless. But nothing had worked out as he planned. First Sigel went up the Valley, to be routed at New Market. Then Hunter took the same road only to lose everything by wild misguided flight off into West Virginia. So now the problem was tougher, and the solution that would have worked in the spring was no good at all in midsummer.

Grant studied the matter, fixing his eyes on the fields and barns and roads of the Valley, and he had a deadly unemotional gaze which saw flame and a smoking sword for devout folk whose way led beside green pastures and still waters. The war could not be won until the Confederacy had been deprived of the use of this garden spot between the mountains. If the garden were made desert, so that neither the Southern Confederacy nor even the fowls of the air could use it, the problem would be well on the way toward being solved.

Grant put it in orders. In a message to Halleck, sent before Sheridan was named to the command, Grant was specific about what he wanted: an army of hungry soldiers to follow retreating Rebels up the Valley and "eat out Virginia clear and clean as far as they go, so that crows flying over it for the balance of the season will have to carry their provender with them." He spelled this out in instructions for the Union commander: "He should make all the Valley south of the Baltimore and Ohio railroad a desert as high up as possible. I do not mean that houses should be burned, but all provisions and stock should be removed, and the people notified to get out."

The war had grown old, and it was following its own logic, the insane logic of war. The only aim now was to hurt the enemy, in any way possible and with any weapon: to destroy not only his will to resist but his ability to make that will effective.

Comprehension Check

Do not refer to the selection while answering these questions. Write out your answers:

1. In the summer of 1864, Grant gave Halleck some specific orders about the valley. What was the essence of those orders?
2. Why didn't Grant just forget about the valley?
3. As used in the passage, what does *granary* mean?
4. Why was the valley strategically more valuable to the South than to the North?
5. After Halleck received Grant's orders about the valley, who was put in charge of the troops that were to carry out those orders?
6. Why did Grant specify "an army of hungry soldiers"?
7. How had Grant tried to solve the problem of the valley in the spring of 1864?
8. Why hadn't that plan worked?
9. What was the name of this valley that attracted so much attention in 1864?
10. What did the author mean when he referred to "the insane logic of war"?

The format of an answer sheet for this comprehension check would be just like the one you just completed if it were given in a written testing situation. If, however, it were designed for an oral testing situation, the format would resemble the one below. Note that the type of question is indicated in the margin by code for quick reference by the tester; namely,

MI represents a main idea question,
F represents a factual, hence literal, question,
I represents an inferential question, and
V represents a vocabulary question.

The answers which are provided in parentheses after each question are placed there for the tester's reference, but they are intended only as suggested responses, especially in the case of inferential and main idea questions.

In an oral testing situation, the tester must record the student's responses verbatim. (A tape recorder can be useful here.) Thus, when you prepare a comprehension page for an oral testing situation, you must leave ample room to record what the student says. If you administer such a test in a small group situation, you should indicate by some code which students answer which questions. Perhaps more than one student responds to a question, and you will need to record that information for reference when you analyze the data.

CONTENT INFORMAL READING INVENTORY: U. S. HISTORY

Comprehension Check

(Sheridan in the Shenandoah Valley, Fry Graph = 10th Grade)

(F)   1. In the summer of 1864, Grant gave Halleck some specific orders about the valley. What were those orders? *(to take complete control and to make it desolate)*

(MI)   2. Why didn't Grant just forget about the valley? *(it provided supplies and a concealed avenue for attacks on the North; for other offensive maneuvers to be effective, the valley had to be destroyed)*

(V)   3. As used in this passage, what does *granary* mean? *(an area producing enough food to sustain an army)*

(F)   4. Why was the valley strategically more valuable to the South than to the North? *(it went toward Washington and away from Richmond)*

(I)   5. After Halleck received Grant's orders about the valley, who was put in command of the troops that were to carry out those orders? *(Sheridan)*

(I)   6. Why did Grant specify "an army of hungry soldiers"? *(high incentive to accomplish the purpose of destruction)*

(F)   7. How had Grant tried to solve the problem of the valley in the spring of 1864? *(establishing a Federal army in the upper valley to cut off supplies to the enemy and eliminate the concealed passageway)*

(F)   8. Why hadn't this plan worked? *(Sigel routed at New Market and Hunter forced to flee into West Virginia.)*

(F)   9. What was the name of this valley that attracted so much attention in 1864? *(Shenandoah Valley, in Virginia)*

(V,I) 10. What did the author mean when he referred to "the insane logic of war"? *(the logic of war meant that Grant had to destroy and hurt the enemy any way possible but it was insane because it caused so much hurt)*

As an introduction to informal comprehension analysis, we suggest that you compare your answers with those suggested following each question. Score each answer accordingly, allowing a maximum of ten points for each answer. (Partial credit may be given.)

When you have finished, answer this question:

How does your score compare with your overall feeling about how well you think you understood the selection?

Now, consider your responses and your score in relation to the criteria established for each question and what each question was intended to determine.

The most important question asked was item 2—the main idea question. *Students* who could answer that question would probably be able to adequately read material that this selection represents—that is, the text from which it was excerpted. This item cannot, however, be considered exclusively, and if you noticed, closely associated with item 2 is the factual first question which sets up the succeeding main idea question. These two questions, when taken together, will reveal a great deal about a student's overall comprehension of the selection. We placed these two questions in this position to provide us with an immediate indicator of a student's general awareness of what he or she had read. If the student could not answer these questions, we can anticipate problems with later questions, as they are designed to extend diagnostic insights.

The three remaining factual questions are all intended to provide varying degrees of information about a student's recall. Item 4, for example, deals with a major fact about the importance of the valley, and a student's response to this question will provide further insight into the depth of his or her understanding. If a student misses items 1 and 2, we would also expect the student to miss 4; if, on the other hand, he or she misses 1 and 2 but answers 4 correctly, we have additional data to try to figure out exactly what was learned from the passage. Thus, the interrelationships of a student's responses become a very important aspect of informal diagnosis.

85

Items 7 and 8 are less important details in terms of an overall understanding of the passage, but they can provide valuable information about the kinds of thing a student learns as he or she reads. Item 9 is a minor, almost inconsequential, detail, but one which a student who thrives on isolated bits of information might get right, although he or she may have missed all of the other questions. The relevance of these three factual questions in terms of an analysis will become clearer as we undertake to examine several examples of students' responses.

The two vocabulary questions, items 3 and 10, are not arbitrarily chosen to test a student's ability to deal with unknown words in context. Instead, a student who can properly answer these items is likely to possess a depth of understanding well beyond the literal level and is probably indicating a comprehension at the upper ranges of the inferential level. Both items deal with connotations that require thought and nuances in conceptual awareness which may be beyond all but the very perceptive student. Good students will be apt to identify themselves by their ability to answer these questions.

The more typical inferential questions, items 5 and 6, really provide information about interpretive thinking more like that expected of average students. Item 5 is a very low level inferential question, while item 6 requires more of an intermediate level of inferential thought. Students' responses to these questions will reveal information that will allow an in-depth analysis that could not occur without them. In essence, with the inclusion of the two vocabulary questions as indicators of upper level inferential awareness, items 5 and 6 provide insights into a different dimension of inferential comprehension.

Responses to these ten questions can yield valuable information about students' reading comprehension. The total score, however, may not reveal very much as the succeeding examples will illustrate. The best chance of obtaining maximally useful information depends upon the selection of appropriate passages, the creation of incisive questions that will produce meaningful information, and an analysis which examines each item in relation to what information is being sought. With these ideas, criteria, and guidelines in mind, now examine several specific examples of students' responses and see how well you can interpret the results.

Name of Student—Liz[1]

Write out your answers to these questions:

1. In the summer of 1864, Grant gave Halleck some specific orders about the valley. What was the essence of those orders?

[1]All names in the examples that follow are fictitious, but the answers are from real students at Marana High School, Marana, Arizona.

To burn the valley so no one would want to use it. Then they'd move in so they could get to the Confederates.

2. Why didn't Grant just forget about the valley?

Because he needed to gain control over the South.

3. As used in this passage, what does *granary* mean?

4. Why was the valley strategically more valuable to the South than to the North?

South

5. After Halleck received Grant's orders about the valley, who was put in charge of the troops that were to carry out those orders?

6. Why did Grant specify "an army of hungry soldiers"?

Because a hungry soldier would have need for more than one who was not. And a hungry soldier would think of things other men might not.

7. How had Grant tried to solve the problem of the valley in the spring of 1864?

He tried to set up a fort upstream to close off the valley.

8. Why hadn't that plan worked?

The person in charge of the troops that was to take over the valley ran away.

9. What was the name of this valley that attracted so much attention in 1864?

Shenandoha

10. What did the author mean when he referred to "the insane logic of war"?

He meant that how could there be anything logical about something as illogical as war.

Analysis of Case 1

As we describe our analysis of Liz's responses, try your hand at each step before considering our interpretation. Your first attempt at informal comprehension analysis may be a bit wobbly, but give it a try.

Step 1. Begin by examining questions 1 and 2 on Liz's answer sheet. Read her answers, score them, and determine what they indicate about her comprehension. You may then wish to compare your analysis to ours, which follows in italics:

Liz's answers to both questions 1 and 2 are satisfactory. The response "needed it to gain control over the South" is somewhat vague but it indicates at least a general understanding, especially when considered in relation to her answer to item 1. (We would give full credit of 20 points for these answers.)

Step 2. Now examine question 4 since it is a major fact related to the ideas checked in questions 1 and 2. Again, make notes of your analysis before considering ours.

Here Liz has not done well, but she indicates something important about her comprehension. She has responded on a very literal level—"South"—as if the question were "To which side was the valley more strategically valuable?" Her answer indicates that she may have problems with "why" questions, and probably with inferential questions as well. That, then, is something to look for as you proceed. (We would give no credit for Liz's response to this question.)

Step 3. To continue examining her literal comprehension, move to items 7 and 8, then note item 9. (Remember, try your own hand at it before looking to our interpretation.)

Here Liz reinforces what she has shown us in her answers to items 1, 2, and 4. She seems to have a general idea of what happened. First, in item 7, she remembered the idea of establishing an army in the upper valley to close it off. Note that she said "fort," a term she associates with "establishing an army." While this may well reveal a misconception, it nonetheless does indicate a fairly good understanding of an important detail in the selection. (We would give full credit to Liz for this answer.) *In item 8, Liz shows again a general understanding of the idea, but not much more. "The person in charge . . . ran away" does not accurately describe what happened.* (Here, we would probably want to give half credit for her answer.) *Liz answered item 9 correctly; perhaps the name of the valley stands out because of the title, perhaps because of the river or a song she recalls. In any case, item 9 reveals little to us for analysis purposes, except that she remembers specific details.* (We would give full credit for the answer.)

Step 4. Now examine Liz's answers to the inferential questions, specifically questions 5 and 6. As you work out your analysis, remember the hypothesis we projected in step 2. There we saw reason to think she might find inferences difficult.

Liz's responses to these items are interesting. She doesn't remember Sheridan; why, we don't know. Apparently, the title of the selection did not impress her or perhaps she is confused by something in the question. Item 6 gives us an indication of what Liz can do, so we now have some indication of her true ability. She does not directly state the inferred answer, but she certainly hints at it—enough so that we know that she can read "between the lines" to some extent. (Thinking back, could it be that the answer to item

5 *was too obscure to allow Liz to pick up the answer?*) (Full credit for item 6, if we read between her lines!)

Step 5. Next, you need to see how well Liz did with questions 3 and 10. Before you do, though, on the basis of what we know up to this point about her performance, how do you think she will have done? Take a guess, then check it out as you analyze her answers.

Was your anticipation verified? Here's what we guessed we'd see. We judged, for two reasons, that she would completely miss item 3. First, she tends to deal with general ideas, not specifics, and "granary" is very specific. Second, she has never mentioned the concept of supplies—food, grain, and the like—and it seemed unlikely that she would answer item 3 correctly. Checking her paper verifies our guess, though we must suspend our judgment on the reasons for which she left the answer blank.

Item 10 deals with a general idea, so we guessed Liz might be able to provide a reasonable answer. That was our hypothesis, and WOW! what a guess! What more synthesized and appropriate answer from a fourteen-year-old? The final paragraph of the reading selection is subtle and powerful, and it has obviously struck Liz. (Ten points for Liz, more if we had it.)

Step 6. Now sum the objective score. On the basis of the item analysis, determine whether Liz can read this material independently, instructionally, or cannot read it with success.

In objective scoring, Liz gets a 65. But what does that tell us? What could any objective score really mean? A diagnosis of Liz's comprehension forces us to examine the general quality of her answers to our questions. That's quite a different matter from adding numbers, which can often be dangerously misleading. A score of 65 is marginal, but is Liz's reading so? She seems to grasp major concepts and general ideas, she draws logical inferences. Her weaknesses lie in recall of specific details ("granary," "Sheridan," and the like). But the material on this IRI is well within her instructional level, *objective sums notwithstanding*.

Before moving on to a second case, we feel compelled to iterate the value of examining a student's responses collectively. When considered all together, rather than in isolated segments, the responses usually represent the most accurate picture of the student's comprehension one can obtain. If we had asked Liz what this passage was about, her response might have been, "It's about Grant's burning the valley so no one could want to use it; then he'd move in to get to the Confederates. He needed it to gain control over the South. He told some hungry soldiers to do it because a hungry soldier would have need for more than one who was not and he would think of things to do which other men might not. Grant tried to do this by setting up a fort upstream to close off the valley but the person in charge of the troops that were to overtake the Shenandoah Valley ran away. None of it was logical, but how could there be anything logical about something as illogical as war?"

Look closely. We compiled this overall answer by simply tying Liz's specific answers together. Taken as a unified response, her answers certainly indicate a rather good understanding of the passage—and that's what we were trying to find out. The emphasis of this type of analysis must, then, be on what the student comprehends, not on any cumulative, objective score. The score itself is really of little value except when it might support a general conclusion suggested by a unified analysis.

Try the next example on your own and then compare your analysis with ours.

Follow the basic steps outlined for Liz's case:

1. Check the main idea and related factual question (items 1, 2). These should provide a major clue for you.
2. Examine the factual question, item 4, as it is closely associated with items 1 and 2.
3. Analyze the other three detail questions for factual recall (items 7, 8, and 9).
4. Examine the responses to the lower level inferential items (numbers 5, 6).
5. Analyze the responses to the upper level inferential items (numbers 3, 10).
6. Evaluate the responses in total and synthesize your conclusions about the student's comprehension.

Name of Student—Ron

Write out your answers to these questions:

1. In the summer of 1864, Grant gave Halleck some specific orders about the valley. What was the essence of those orders?

   To turn the garden into a desert

2. Why didn't Grant just forget about the valley?

   Because it was a natrul road to the Yankee citadel

3. As used in this passage, what does *granary* mean?

4. Why was the valley strategically more valuable to the South than to the North?

   Because it ran southwest to north east.

5. After Halleck received Grant's orders about the valley, who was put in charge of the troops that were to carry out those orders?

6. Why did Grant specify "an army of hungry soldiers"?

   so soldiers would eat most everything.

7. How had Grant tried to solve the problem of the valley in the spring of 1864?

   tryed to set up a camp at the end of the valley

8. Why hadn't that plan worked?

*his men had been attacked
and run off*

9. What was the name of this valley that attracted so much attention in 1864?

just, valley

10. What did the author mean when he referred to "the insane logic of war"?

*when you take sides in a war
you try to help your side win
even thogh you have to do some of
the most logical things in a war,
any other time they would consider
it insane.*

Analysis of Case 2

Let's begin this analysis by examining our conclusions. You compare your conclusions to ours. Then we'll look at the specifics that led to the conclusions.

Ron is probably on a high instructional level with this material; perhaps he is independent with it. He has understood the main ideas of the passage in terms that are directly related to the passage. His ability to handle the inferential questions is basically sound even though he did not seem to pick up the concept of the valley being a source of food and supplies to the Confederate armies. His weakness lies in the area of specific details, but not in the same way Liz had trouble. Ron recalled some details that were important to his understanding the main ideas of the passage and they are reflected in his answers. Liz could not do that as well as Ron; her understandings were more general. If the instructional purpose of this passage is to have the students understand concepts rather than recall isolated pieces of information, then Ron has demonstrated his ability to do that.

If you are to learn much from comparing our overall diagnosis of Ron's responses, we need to go through the analysis step by step. Even if you came to the same conclusions we did, you may have arrived at them for different reasons. If you disagreed with our conclusions, then the following analysis may help you to see where we differ in our thinking.

The first thing we noticed was that Ron understood the main idea of the orders and why they were given; this can be determined by his responses to items 1 and 2. His answer to question 4 may appear superficial and insufficient unless it is examined in relation to the first two questions. We decided, therefore, to examine the interrelatedness of the answers Ron gave to items 1, 2, and 4. "Because it ran southwest to northeast" doesn't really reveal too much by itself, but when combined with "a natural road to the Yankee's citadel" the basic concept of the details and the main idea are clearly evident in his reasoning. Why didn't he repeat the idea of a possible invasion route in his response to item 4? Perhaps he saw little need to repeat himself from item 2. That is only a guess, but his answer satisfied us. Granted, there is a certain depth missing in his answers to questions 1, 2, and 4. He failed to mention the concept of supplies and the idea that Grant had to keep pressure on Lee at all points. All things considered, we felt that Ron's answers to these three questions, considered together, would warrant about two-thirds credit, or 20 points.

In the detail questions—items 7, 8, and 9—Ron does demonstrate a general understanding of what happened although he has not retained specific names of people and places. Consider the nature of these questions, though. Can we expect readers to recall such detail? Would we want them to? We think not. In fact, though Ron's attention and memory for detail is imperfect, it is quite sufficient for his purpose of general understanding and comprehension. Much better that than the other way around, we'd say! (So, we would give full credit for 7 and 8, none for 9.)

Among Ron's four remaining responses, we can see a confirmation of everything that the analysis has indicated so far. He missed the specific, low-level inferential item, but he did perceive why hungry soldiers might be more effective in carrying out the orders. The "granary" question we'd expect him to miss because, like Liz, he has not mentioned the concept of supplies and he does not seem to rely on specifics for his understanding. His detailed explanation in response to item 10 reinforces everything we have been led to expect by his previous answers. When scoring these items, we'd give no credit for items 3 and 5 and full credit for items 6 and 10.

To summarize Ron's case, his objective score is 60, but his comprehension is clearly greater than 60 percent. This analysis reiterates the inherent fallacy of objective scoring and the need for comparative, in-depth analysis of student's responses. Whether Ron can learn from this passage with independent level comprehension is dubious, only because he missed the idea of the valley as a supply source, and not for any specific details he may have failed to remember. To our way of thinking, Ron has demonstrated a very sound, mature approach to a reading task; hence, any instructional assistance he may need would be minimal.

It is hoped that Liz and Ron's cases both demonstrate the variability that can exist in students' answers and the fallacy of relying on strictly objective scoring. In an analysis of a student's comprehension, little is definitive; one must constantly seek clues to what each student has perceived and to each reader's success with the act of reading. The variability that exists among students is, to us, the exciting part of diagnosis and of teaching.

Now for another case. This one you may find a bit different from the others, but see how you would analyze Karen's comprehension, then compare your analysis with ours.

Name of Student—Karen

Write out your answers to these questions:

1. In the summer of 1864, Grant gave Halleck some specific orders about the valley. What was the essence of those orders?

   To take over the valley

2. Why didn't Grant just forget about the valley?

   It was good land.

3. As used in this passage, what does *granary* mean?

   his army

4. Why was the valley strategically more valuable to the South than to the North?

5. After Halleck received Grant's orders about the valley, who was put in charge of the troops that were to carry out those orders?

a hungry army

6. Why did Grant specify "an army of hungry soldiers"?

To eat out Virginia clear and clean as far as they go.

7. How had Grant tried to solve the problem of the valley in the spring of 1864?

8. Why hadn't that plan worked?

9. What was the name of this valley that attracted so much attention in 1864?

10. What did the author mean when he referred to "the insane logic of war"?

The weird way the war thought and worked.

Analysis of Case 3

The first reaction one probably has when analyzing Karen's responses is that she is clearly frustrated by this selection. After all, her objective score is approximately 25! In every instance the answers she gave indicate minimal understanding, and she failed to respond to 4 items. But if we are to accept such conclusions, we must first reject several alternative possibilities. For example, is the problem here that she cannot express her ideas well enough in writing to handle the response part of the task? That is, can she do the reading but finds herself unable to compose written responses to questions on it? Obviously, this would require first-hand knowledge of Karen and her language abilities. We mention this, however, because it is a plausible explanation that cannot be dismissed lightly. On the basis of her teacher's observations, however, we can eliminate this possibility because the fact is that Karen can write reasonably well when given a task with which she is comfortable. A second alternative which must be explored is that Karen simply doesn't want to be bothered with this task. Interestingly, there is evidence that can be used to make a reasonable guess as to the probability of this alternative. Notice her answer to item 5, "a hungry army." This response seems to come from the wording of question 6! That Karen would go to the trouble to even attempt to manipulate the available information to fit another question is evidence that she has not taken the task lightly. In addition, her teacher knows that she is not the type of student who would simply throw down a few answers just to make it appear as if she had at least tried. She is a very conscientious student. Thus, the second alternative can be discounted along with the first.

There is one remaining point to be made about analyzing reading comprehension from this example. The fact that a student *does not* perform should not be taken as evidence that the student *cannot* perform. The IRI, as you may have guessed, is designed to give information about what students can comprehend. When a reader *fails* to comprehend, we may wonder why, but the answer to the primary question posed by the IRI must await further exploration.

Now, how are you doing? We want to present you with one final example of a student's responses to this comprehension check for two reasons. First, we think you can probably use a little more practice. Second, there are a few more things about informal comprehension analysis that we'd like to point out to you and they can be discussed in relation to the next example. Try your hand with Mary's case and then compare your analysis with ours.

Name of Student—Mary

Write out your answers to these questions:

1. In the summer of 1864, Grant gave Halleck some specific orders about the valley. What was the essence of those orders?

   To take over the valley

2. Why didn't Grant just forget about the valley?

   Because the land, was rich, sunny.

3. As used in this passage, what does *granary* mean?

4. Why was the valley strategically more valuable to the South than to the North?

   North because the valley was a passage way to the Yankees fort.

5. After Halleck received Grant's orders about the valley, who was put in charge of the troops that were to carry out those orders?

   Jackson

6. Why did Grant specify "an army of hungry soldiers"?

7. How had Grant tried to solve the problem of the valley in the spring of 1864?

8. Why hadn't that plan worked?

Because one troop was going to the New Market. The other lost almost everything.

9. What was the name of this valley that attracted so much attention in 1864?

Shendoah

10. What did the author mean when he referred to "the insane logic of war"?

Analysis of Case 4

An analysis of Mary's answers stimulates more questions than it provides answers about her comprehension. A cursory analysis strongly suggests frustration, but a further examination causes one to wonder. That is, we think she is probably frustrated, but we can't be sure. Her answers to questions 1, 2, and 4, the main ideas and associated supporting detail, suggest a paradox of sorts. She remembers certain details related to the main idea but her response to the main idea question indicates confusion. Apparently, she thinks Grant wanted the land because it was good land. Her answers to items 1 and 4 tell us more about her comprehension. "To take over the valley" is an acceptable response and so is most of her answer to item 4, but why did she begin her response to number 4 with the word "North"? Does she think that the Yankees and the North are terms for different sides in the war? She has understood why the valley was strategically more valuable, but has she confused the two sides? Whatever the case, note that she may have provided us with a clue to her comprehension by getting several details correct, even if in a somewhat confused sort of way.

As we examine the three other detail questions, 7, 8, and 9, we are even more puzzled. "New Market" and "Shendoah" stand out, but the sense of her response to item 8 seems confused. The thing that creates confusion is the inclusion of "the" before New Market. What is her concept of this place, New Market? Is it a place to buy food? Or is this just a linguistic slip? We don't know, but we sure would like to know. Also, how does she remember the gist of the spring offensive if she doesn't remember what it entailed? Again, her answers suggest more questions than they provide solutions, and the more we see, the further we seem to be from being able to analyze what she has comprehended.

What, then, does she reveal in her responses to the higher level questions? Aha! Finally, we can say something with some confidence. Mary has missed all four questions—3, 5, 6, and 10. That we know, but that's really *all* we know! Can Mary handle inferential questions? How can we judge? She cannot read "between the lines" with this selection, or doesn't seem able to do so, but *why* can't she? We haven't many clues, but perhaps she is simply not interested in war stories. Our only recourse is to give Mary another passage at a different level of difficulty in an attempt to find something she *can* comprehend. Only then will we be able to judge the quality of her comprehension.

Where to from Here?

Now that you've had the introduction and some practice, if your wobblies are beginning to go away, then we have accomplished as much as we hoped. After all, analyzing reading comprehension is rather complicated and one becomes good at it only through practice. Where to from here? We suggest that you create some passages for your own content area, collect some data, and analyze them. Then compare your diagnosis with a colleague and slowly, but most assuredly, you'll begin to feel confidence in this testing method.

CHAPTER 7   Vocabulary Diagnosis

> Vocabulary and conceptual development are essentially related.

Overview

Vocabulary diagnosis is diagnosis of the meanings which students hold for words related to the concepts they are developing out of their experiences. The overriding purpose of vocabulary diagnosis is to determine simultaneously students' conceptual development and their vocabulary facility. Different instructional approaches will be implied by such diagnosis, depending on whether misunderstandings arise out of a failure to conceptualize or a failure to acquire the vocabulary necessary to express adequate conceptual awareness. Our position is that "vocabulary" problems may often be the manifestation of a more serious problem, a lack of proper conceptualization. Furthermore, it is impossible to separate conceptualization and experience from the vocabulary that ties the two together in the mind of the learner or the language the learner speaks.

Several techniques of vocabulary diagnosis are possible, each a different twist on the prevailing idea of conceptual analysis as we define it. Word association activities for groups, a modified synonym-production task, an adaptation of cloze—all are aimed at finding out what sort of balance exists in the student between what is understood and what words the student can use to express that understanding. We are not particularly concerned with word analysis skills that traditionally fly under the banner of vocabulary—phonics, structural analysis, context, use of the dictionary. We are, rather, concerned

101

with word meaning and its relation to conceptual development, which we view as the proper concern of the content (reading) teacher and, frankly, the more appropriate concern of any teacher involved with reading as an activity directed at comprehension.

Concepts, Experiences, and Vocabulary

In their thorough review of the role of vocabulary knowledge in reading comprehension, Anderson and Freebody (1979) concluded that word knowledge is essential to reading comprehension and that "people who do not know the meanings of very many words are most probably poor readers" (p. 42). Perhaps we state the obvious, but vocabulary is the single factor most consistently associated with comprehension. To comprehend, one must recognize the words through which meaning is conveyed.

When we discuss vocabulary instruction in Chapter 12, *Developing Meaningful Vocabularies,* we stress the relationship between one's vocabulary and one's conceptual awareness. In this chapter our major point is that vocabulary diagnosis cannot focus solely on whether students know words; if students have difficulty understanding what they read, it may be more than words that they don't know. They may not have a firm grasp on the ideas that the words represent. In such instances, it is likely that students' experiences (learning) have been insufficient for the development of the concepts that the words represent. We all know that experiences provide the basis for conceptual understandings that are subsequently expressed by words. In vocabulary diagnosis, conceptual assessment is often more important than a word-knowledge test.

That master of the English language, Sir Winston Churchill, in an excerpt from his autobiography, *My Early Life,*[1] conveys in a negative way the essence of our disposition toward vocabulary:

> I was taken into a Form Room and told to sit at a desk. All the other boys were out of doors, and I was alone with the Form Master. He produced a thin greeny-brown, covered book filled with words in different types of print.
>
> 'You have never done any Latin before, have you?' he said.
>
> 'No, sir.'
>
> 'This is a Latin grammar.' He opened it at a well-thumbed page. 'You must learn this,' he said, pointing to a number of words in a frame of lines. 'I will come back in half an hour and see what you know.'
>
> Behold me then on a gloomy evening, with an aching heart, seated in front of the First Declension.

---

[1]Reprinted by permission of Charles Scribner's Sons from *My Early Life: A Roving Commission* by Winston Churchill, © Copyright 1930, Charles Scribner's Sons. Also reprinted by permission of the Hamlyn Publishing Group Limited.

102

Mensa	a table
Mensa	o table
Mensam	a table
Mensae	of a table
Mensae	to or for a table
Mensa	by, with or from a table

What on earth did it mean? Where was the sense in it? It seemed absolute rigmarole to me. However, there was one thing I could always do: I could learn by heart. And I thereupon proceeded, as far as my private sorrows would allow, to memorize the acrostic-looking task which had been set me.

In due course the Master returned.

'Have you learnt it?' he asked.

'I think I can say it,' I replied; and I gabbled it off.

He seemed so satisfied with this that I was emboldened to ask a question.

'What does it mean, sir?"

'It means what it says. Mensa, a table. Mensa is a noun of the First Declension. There are five declensions. You have learnt the first singular of the First Declension.'

'But,' I repeated, 'what does it mean?'

'Mensa means a table,' he answered.

'Then why does mensa also mean o table,' I enquired, 'and what does o table mean?'

'Mensa, o table, is the vocative case,' he replied.

'But why o table?' I persisted in genuine curiosity.

'O table,—you would use that in addressing a table, in invoking a table.' And then seeing he was not carrying me with him, 'You would use it in speaking to a table.'

'But I never do,' I blurted out in honest amazement.

'If you are impertinent, you will be punished, and punished, let me tell you, very severely,' was his conclusive rejoinder.

Such was my first introduction to the classics from which, I have been told, many of our cleverest men have derived so much solace and profit. . . .

As young Winston was so emboldened to suggest, a knowledge of vocabulary without an understanding of its meaning (the concepts and experiences it expresses) is useless.

Einstein said that concepts develop in two ways, both of which are necessary to understanding. The first is by logical analysis, the procedure by which we see how concepts and judgments depend on each other. The second is by connection of our logic to experience.[2] In both cases, vocabulary is used.

[2]Albert Einstein, from "The Problem of Space, Ether, and the Field in Physics" in *The World As I See It.*

But only when that vocabulary becomes the bond between conceptualization and experiences will either the conceptualization, the experience, or the vocabulary have any meaning.

This implies a firm conclusion regarding vocabulary diagnosis: *to assess students' understanding and use of vocabulary is tantamount to assessing the sophistication of their conceptualizations.* This conclusion is justified because one's understanding of concepts is reflected in and demonstrated by the vocabulary one uses to express those concepts.

Lest we make our case too strongly, however, it is true, of course, that at times a student may fail to understand something because of unfamiliarity with the vocabulary in which it is expressed. One's understanding depends on the appropriateness of the vocabulary with which an idea is expressed. That is, if a reader is to comprehend, the vocabulary of what is being read must be appropriately suited to the level, or stage, of conceptual development. If someone fails to understand what he or she reads, given at least minimal quality and style in what the person is reading, one of three things may be the case: (1) The concepts expressed may be so far removed from the reader's experience that little meaning is possible for what is said, even though individual words may seem familiar; (2) The vocabulary with which the ideas are expressed may presume a familiarity not yet acquired by the reader, even though the concepts might be understood if put in less sophisticated wording; or (3) Neither the concepts nor the vocabulary have places in the reader's cognitive store and thus it is all "rigmarole," to borrow Sir Winston's term.

To illustrate this point, we ask you to join us in a little exercise. Begin by reading this paragraph.

> It is particularly true in reading that the larger the context, the greater is the redundancy. And the more redundancy there is, the less visual information the skilled reader requires. In passages of continuous text, provided that the content is not too difficult, every other letter can be eliminated from most words, or about one word in five omitted altogether, without making the passage too difficult for a reader to comprehend—provided that he has learned the rules related to letter and word occurrence and co-occurrence.[3]

How well were you able to understand what the author is discussing? If you had difficulty, perhaps you feel that you lack the conceptual background to understand the meaning of the passage. Before deciding definitely, however, read this paragraph.

> In many reading selections, ideas are repeated several times, especially when the selection is of moderate length or longer. As

[3]From *Understanding Reading*, by Frank Smith, New York: Holt, Rinehart, Winston, 1971, p. 23.

the ideas are repeated, a reader has more chances to pick up the ideas and thus his chances of understanding the selection are increased. A reader can rely on this repetition instead of having to identify every letter or word in the selection. To prove this point, in many passages it is possible to eliminate every other letter from most words or eliminate every fifth word and yet not significantly impair a reader's comprehension. That is to say, the good reader is familiar with the rules of letter sequences within words and the rules of word sequences within sentences, and he can anticipate the letters and words which should come next. His comprehension is not dependent upon letter perfect or word perfect reading.

Now, compare your understanding of this paragraph to the previous one. If there were differences, can you determine what caused them?

When we have done this with teachers in person, we have seen one of three things happen: (1) they find both paragraphs difficult to understand; (2) they find that both paragraphs are clear; or (3) they find the second paragraph to be clearer than the first. We suspect that you found one of these to be true in your own case. What, though, are the implications of what occurred?

Typically, the teachers with whom we have conducted this exercise find that they understand the second paragraph far more easily than the first. Interestingly enough, the teachers who find the first paragraph considerably more difficult conclude that it is due to the complexity of the ideas. The intriguing thing here is that the ideas, i.e., the concepts, in both of the paragraphs are identical. In other words, the complexity of the first paragraph is inherent in the words chosen to present the concepts rather than in the concepts themselves, and any differences between the two paragraphs are merely rhetorical. Thus, if you found difficulty with the first paragraph but not with the second, then the factor that interfered with your understanding was the vocabulary in which the ideas were expressed rather than with a failure to understand the concepts or ideas.

When we diagnose students' vocabulary knowledge, we must also determine whether they understand the concepts associated with words. The purpose of vocabulary diagnosis is to determine what has to be taught so that students can learn. Recall, the first principle of instruction is that what to teach must be determined by what can be learned. If students understand concepts, the task is to help them learn new labels for their ideas, to bring their vocabulary up to par with their understanding of the concepts. If, on the other hand, students have superficial, inaccurate, or no understanding of a concept, they have little use for the vocabulary by which such understanding might be expressed. For these students, instruction must begin with a focus on concepts. While this latter case may be more difficult pedagogically, it is the more typical case. Vocabulary instruction comes down to providing experiences through which concepts and understandings may develop.

Let's return then to a consideration of the two paragraphs in our exercise, keeping in mind that the purpose of vocabulary diagnosis is to determine what students know of both vocabulary and the concepts it represents. If you found the first paragraph more difficult than the second, your difficulty with that material was with the vocabulary, not the concepts. Our instruction would then be designed to build on the concepts you knew by helping you associate new words with old concepts. If, however, you found both paragraphs difficult to understand, the implication is that you had problems with both the concepts and the vocabulary. In that case, instruction would probably need to provide opportunity for conceptual development. If you were among the lucky few who had no trouble with either paragraph, you probably understood both the vocabulary and the concepts, and for you instruction in either would be unnecessary.

Tolerance-Tolerate: A Case in Point

Students' conceptual awarenesses may not be what we assume them to be. For example, the following experience was shared with us by an English teacher who spent six weeks teaching a unit in which one of the key concepts was: "Social and emotional maturity is often exhibited through tolerance of others' ideas and beliefs." On the unit test, this teacher's students consistently indicated that tolerance meant "to tolerate." The teacher's dismay was understandable: her students hadn't understood the positive connotation of tolerance at all; how could they have understood the concept that characterized maturity as "exhibiting tolerance"?

Let's look closely at this common problem. The students had a preconceived idea of the concept associated with *tolerance*. Had the teacher realized that their idea was inappropriate in the context she was creating, she could have easily rectified the misconception at the beginning of the unit. Instead, problems arose for her students because she failed to analyze their conceptual perceptions. She made the unfortunate mistake of assuming that her meaning for a key word was similar to the meaning the students had for the word.

It is essential to begin vocabulary diagnosis by identifying (1) the most important concepts that are to be taught and (2) the terms that best convey those concepts.

By approaching vocabulary diagnosis from this perspective, instruction can be designed to meet both the students' conceptual needs and their vocabulary needs, in that order. To the credit of our English teacher friend, she did identify major conceptual objectives and the key words which students needed to know if they were to understand and discuss those concepts. However, she didn't go the next step to determine what the students' perceptions of those terms and concepts were. While it may sometimes appear that students understand terms and concepts, effective instruction is often

106

dependent upon taking specific steps to verify initial assumptions. The by-word of vocabulary diagnosis, then, must be conceptual analysis. Whatever method of vocabulary diagnosis might be chosen, one of its essential features must be an analysis of students' developmental stages of conceptualization.

Diagnostic Strategies

There are several approaches one might take to vocabulary diagnosis. The final decision in any situation will be influenced by two factors, namely effectiveness and efficiency. Which approach and activity will provide the most information in the least obtrusive manner? Which strategy is likely to secure the most valuable information from the largest number of students? Recall our thesis: *Instruction can only approach maximum effectiveness when it is designed to bridge the gap between what a student knows and what that student needs to know.* In vocabulary diagnosis, the object is to determine students' familiarity with the key terms and basic concepts that comprise the essence of the topic under consideration.

The decision regarding a specific approach or strategy involves several issues. First, what is to be assessed? Should students' familiarity with terms be evaluated or their awareness of concepts, or both? Next, what is the most appropriate context for the diagnosis? Would a formal pre-test be most revealing? Would an informal activity do as well? Or, in perhaps the best case, could vocabulary and conceptual awareness be tapped during various instructional activities?

Each instructional situation you encounter is unique; hence, your answers to these questions will inevitably vary. To help you make reasonable decisions, let us share with you some of the strategies that we have found effective and efficient under varied conditions. As we do, however, keep in mind that the purpose of diagnosis is to facilitate learning by determining what it is students need to bridge the gap between what they know and what they need to know. The object is not to discover what they do not know; instead the focus should be on what they do know and how it can be related to what they need to learn.

The Word Analysis Skills Approach

Typically, recommended vocabulary diagnosis strategies are more appropriate to a diagnosis of word analysis skills than to vocabulary *per se*. Word analysis skills include phonics; syllabication; use of prefixes, stems, and suffixes; and the ability to use context clues. Such skills are of little concern to us here. Instead, we will address the ways to determine what terms students know and what meanings they associate with those terms. Very few content teachers can or should be concerned with traditional word analysis skills, except as those skills might pertain directly to the meaning of the content which the teacher is trying to help students understand. We believe it would be as foolish to recommend that content teachers teach phonics as that they be teachers of reading. The sense in which content teachers are teachers of reading, we would maintain, is limited to the sense in which they attempt to stimulate and guide students toward understanding content, through reading or other means. This is to us the most realistic and practical spirit in which to approach vocabulary diagnosis in content area classrooms.

Conceptual Analysis

Of the several techniques or approaches we will suggest, this is the one that best represents the essence of vocabulary analysis. The idea is to find out (1) what meaning students have for specific concepts, and (2) in what terms they might express the concepts.

As part of the introduction to a unit of work in science, we recently asked several groups of students questions such as this:

> What does it mean to you when I say 'A knowledge of the way in which the earth changes helps make a better world'? Do you understand the statement? Tell me what it means to you.

(Notice that the statement is typical of concepts that might be developed in a social studies or science unit on ecology. Following our question, a dialogue roughly equivalent to the ensuing occurred. S is student, T is teacher.)

S_1: The world doesn't change.

S_2: Things are today pretty much like they were when Christ was here.

T: Nothing is different?

S_1: Well, except that we now have telephones and airplanes. But

T: those are inventions. They don't mean the *earth* is different. No, they don't. But what about other things, like pollution?

S_1: Men have always polluted. That's not different.

S_2: Except that now you get fined $30 if you do it!

T: But does the pollution affect the way the earth is, do you think?

S_1: No. Not really. Just the way it looks or smells.

These were elementary students, grades 3, 4, and 5, children of rather normal intelligence and achievement. We found that there were many things they did understand, of course. We tried the procedure on a wide variety of conceptual statements. Often, the students' wording was an improvement on

108

ours. We failed to guess how well they understood. Sometimes they had the idea, but required a little more explanation. But at other times, true misconceptions came out. Diagnostically, we were learning (1) what the students knew about the concepts, and (2) what vocabulary they used to express *their* meanings of the various concepts.

At the beginning of a unit, one of the best "pretests" possible is to ask of students "What is your understanding of the following concepts which we are going to study? In a few words, tell what each means to you." The answer students give to this sort of diagnostic question will tell much about what they understand and in what terms they understand it. The technique is invaluable, diagnostically, at any level of education, from primary school to graduate school. And, we might add, it is as effective a test as it is a pretest.

Word Association Tasks

A variation on the conceptual analysis technique is to engage the students in word association activities. These may be led by the teacher or played between teams of pupils under the teacher's supervision. The activities may call for student responses to stimulus words given by the teacher ("Tell me all the words which come to mind when I say_____.") or may be of the word-guess type. To get another team member to say a word in a given time, a person may say as many other associated words as he or she can think of, but not the word itself. Diagnostically, what pupils say will often represent the breadth and depth of their understanding.

The preparation of a word association task for vocabulary diagnostic purposes requires an identification of key terms related to concepts in a unit or reading selection. The diagnostic questions are, as you might guess: (1) what meanings do the students have for these words; and (2) what do they reveal about their level of understanding of the concepts to which the words are related? The advantage of the word association technique, used in whatever format, is that it tends to be "unobtrusive," in testing terms. That is, it is less easily perceived as a threat, as sometimes tests can be. We'll undoubtedly repeat, in a variety of ways, that the object of diagnosis is not to test but to structure an opportunity for students to demonstrate as naturally as possible what they do know and can do. That reveals what to teach and how to teach it.

Write It Down

Another variation of conceptual analysis is a "write down all that you know" strategy. This activity is similar to a stream of consciousness writing exercise. As you begin the study of a topic, ask students to put a piece of blank paper on their desks. Give them a key word related to the topic, but choose a word that you are sure will have some meaning for them. Then say, "If everything in the world that is known about (*insert your word here*) were written on that piece of paper, what would be there?" Students are then to write down everything they know about the topic. Avoidance of unfamiliar "association" terms is desirable because if students know nothing about "tillage," for example, they will sit for five minutes with nothing to write. Hence, in place of tillage, the teacher might offer the term "plowing" as a more familiar point of departure.

In this activity students must be told that spelling, punctuation, and other grammatical concerns are of no consequence. The issue is to record as many ideas as they can think of. Nor is unity or coherence of concern; students should brainstorm and free-associate as far as their experiences and awarenesses will carry them. Too, they will not be judged on whether they are right or wrong.

What emerges from this activity is a wide spectrum of information including the vocabulary that is comfortable and familiar to students. An additional advantage of this strategy is that the teacher has a record of what *each* student has written. Individual records help avoid the transgression of generalizing conclusions from the contributions of a few, as can easily happen with oral discussions.

Modified Cloze

The cloze technique can be modified in a variety of ways to increase its diagnostic and instructional value. One obvious modification is to analyze the "synonyms" that students use as replacements for deletions. If the selection is one of particularly relevant conceptual load, the replacements that readers make will reveal much about their understandings of the concepts being taught. At times, the cloze replacements may indicate a conceptual attainment of *higher* sophistication than that assumed by the author. Given an opportunity to discuss their replacement words in a whole class or small group setting, students will usually make very clear their familiarity with vocabulary and concepts. The question becomes not what word was chosen but why it was chosen. *Which* word was chosen is a test question; *why* it was chosen is a diagnostic question.

Another modification of cloze which is often desirable is this: Make deletions systematically, to include key conceptual terms. Then, rather than have students guess at the replacements, have them pick from a list of words those that belong in specific blanks. Include in the list the deleted words, common synonyms, and potentially "misconceived" synonyms, words likely to be chosen if the reader misunderstands the concepts behind the words.

People who know and love the cloze technique may object that our modifications make the test invalid and leave the percentage of exact replacement scores confused. This is a valid point but it is not our object here to test the appropriateness of material, in a readability sense of appropriate. What we are trying to get at is what the student knows. The key to diagnosis is a common sense understanding of what the student is doing, not an empirically derived percentage score that says nothing of why it is being done or what it means. The results could well mean avoiding the frustration of "Mensa . . . o table" when meaning takes first place among all vocabulary skills.

Contextual Synonyms

Another prudent approach to vocabulary diagnosis is to have students identify words that are unfamiliar and unexplained in the text. Emphasis should be placed on identification of important, key terms, but students should not be discouraged from noting other words of interest too. If the general approach to reading assignments in a classroom is to discuss what students understood from what they read, such a discussion could be followed by a sharing of the terms that students found difficult. The meanings could be discussed, the context in which a word appeared could be examined for clues to the meaning, and consideration could be given to the importance of the term relative to the major topics being studied.

Our experience has shown that students who are given a chance to identify problems and to explore questions become far more involved and interested in their studies than do students who rarely engage in such discussions. Further, words and their meanings are often fascinating to students, especially when ideas and issues become clarified as a result of group discussion.

A related activity is one we call contextual synonyms in which students try to identify alternative terms that an author could have used instead of specified "key" words. The teacher examines a reading selection and identifies certain words of interest or importance to the topic. As the students read, they list, on a separate paper, alternatives to the key terms that they think would suit the context about as well as the terms used by the author. They may either stop during their reading to consider alternatives or they may return to the words after reading the entire selection. In either case, if the "key" words are well chosen, the students will engage in word study, conceptual understandings, and in comprehension monitoring. In this regard, a conceptual synonym activity can work like embedded questions, engaging students in reasoning as they study. Students can then discuss their ideas in groups, as a class, or turn in their papers so that the teacher can detect each student's progress.

This activity would have given our English teacher friend (tolerance-tolerate) some valuable information. Her students would have suggested "tolerate" as a substitute for "tolerance." She would have been looking for "understanding" or "broad-mindedness," perhaps "sympathy"; she would have gotten (she found out too late) words like "put up with" or "endure," perhaps

111

"suffer." Information about the misconceptions students may hold, and reveal through their vocabulary misunderstandings, is invaluable diagnostic information.

Beyond Technical Terms

In the context of vocabulary diagnosis, it is natural to focus on technical terms that are particularly relevant to the topic under study. Terms such as metaphor, onomatopoeia, and blank verse apply to Shakespearean sonnets; carriage, alignment, and margins, to typing; harmonic, chromatic, and triad, to music; monarch, czar, and president to executive officers. Such a focus is appropriate; however, it is often necessary to examine non-technical terms because they are also potential obstacles to comprehension.

In a sixth-grade history class we recently heard the plight of a young student who had read a selection about castles, knights, and vassals and was mightily concerned about the serfs during times of armed conflict. He had read that the lords raised the drawbridge to provide protection to the castle and the "serfs took refuge behind the castle walls." He questioned his teacher, "Why didn't the lords allow the serfs into the castle?" Puzzled, the teacher responded, "Why do you think they didn't?" The youngster responded, "Well, the serfs stayed outside, out back of the walls. That way when the enemy came around one side of the castle, the serfs moved around behind the other side. Seems like the lords owed the serfs better than that." And so the puzzle becomes clear. To this student, at least, "behind the castle walls" meant outside the walls. What teacher could have ever predicted that interpretation?

Other "non-technical" terms can confound students' reasoning too. Consider this example taken from *Consumer Decision Making: Guides to Better Living,* a textbook in a tenth-grade consumer studies class.

All national banks are required to belong to the Federal Reserve System. State-chartered banks, known simply as state banks, may join the System if qualified and accepted by the Federal Reserve Board. Member banks must abide by the many provisions of the Federal Reserve Act, some of which are: (1) they must place legally required reserves either on deposit without interest at the federal reserve bank or as cash held in their own vaults; (2) they must honor checks drawn against them at par (i.e., no charge may be deducted for processing checks) when presented by a federal reserve bank for payment; (3) they must abide by loan and investment limitations stated by the Federal Reserve Board (p. 141).

Within this passage are certain technical terms such as "federal reserve board" that have been defined earlier in the text. What about "state-chartered," "reserves," "on deposit without interest," "drawn against," and "loan and investment limitations"? Nowhere in the text are these terms defined, nor are they even elaborated. Nothing further is mentioned about these terms. And do tenth graders know about reserves, interest, or investments? Should they be expected to know about these matters? We think not, at least not from everyday experiences.

At issue here are vocabulary terms that an author just assumes the reader will know—terms like "reserves" and "drawn against." Such terms are very clearly technical in that they all have special meanings in the context of business and banking. Although they are clearly technical to the field, the author seems to be so familiar with these terms that they are used as though they were as commonplace as terms like "bank," "school," and "bus." Our point here is that many words in texts pose difficulties for students yet are easily understood by adults because of experiential differences. As we work with teachers and their students, it seems that many more words pose problems for readers than solely the ones in italics. In fact, the words identified for emphasis rarely create comprehension problems because they are carefully defined in the text and are often pretaught before the lesson is assigned.

In vocabulary diagnosis, then, consideration must be given to the non-technical language used in the texts. Assuming it is of value for students to know something of the requirements of member banks in the federal reserve system, they must know more than their typical experiences will allow if they are to understand the sample selection we have shared. And what about the youngster who did not understand "behind the castle walls"?

Before you select the terms that should be included in any diagnostic activity, look carefully to determine if other subtle, surreptitious terms are lurking between those italicized words. In fact, we often recommend that the important "non-technical" terms be chosen for assessment in lieu of the technical vocabulary because the technical terms are often defined or clarified in the text.

Many of the strategies we suggest in this chapter require students to respond to words presented by the teacher. In word association tasks, for example, students try to recall any familiar information associated with the "cue" word. Often, students will not be able to provide responses to technical terms. Remember our suggestion to substitute "plowing" for "tilling"? We don't mean to imply that plowing and tilling are synonymous. We do believe, however, that if students know "plowing" they will provide us with important information about their awareness of concepts related to "tilling."

For similar reasons we do not recommend the use of formal pretests where students are provided a list of words and asked to define them. To test students' knowledge of key concept vocabulary before they have studied the concepts or the terms will usually be both ineffective and inefficient. To increase the potential of securing pertinent information about students' knowledge, choose the "cue" words from among terms likely to be familiar to the students. The result is likely to be fruitful diagnosis of vocabulary knowledge and conceptual awareness.

Instructional Diagnosis

We have previously suggested that one approach to vocabulary diagnosis is within the context of instruction. One need not create special activities for diagnostic purposes because diagnosis can be conducted during teaching situations. Throughout the third unit, *Diagnostic Instruction,* we offer techniques that can be manipulated in numerous ways to incorporate instruction with diagnosis and diagnosis with instruction.

We would be remiss if we left this topic without the reminder that the *raison d'etre* of diagnosis is to facilitate instruction. Too often diagnostic settings are contrived and do not correspond to the setting in which learning is to occur. The most reasonable context for diagnosis, then, is amidst students' learning. When sensitive, alert kidwatchers facilitate students' efforts to learn, diagnosis and instruction become indistinguishable, as they should be.

CHAPTER 8   Assessing Study Skills

> Analyzing students' study skills is an important aspect of diagnosis for a content teacher interested in improving students' ability to learn.

Overview

Good and poor students alike can often become more efficient learners if they are made aware of some basic, easy-to-learn strategies such as use of time, taking notes, and taking tests. The most logical place in the curriculum to diagnose and teach study skills is in the content classroom, for it is there that students find the greatest need and most appropriate application of such skills.

Several different methods of diagnosing study skills exist, both formal and informal. While there may be occasional need for the formal strategies, the informal assessments are usually more informative. Teachers who are interested in improving their students' ability to learn can devise their own program of study skills diagnosis based on the various techniques discussed in this chapter.

A Distinction

The ability to study efficiently is a distinctive characteristic of most good students. Conversely, many poor students are unproductive because they lack good study skills. A requisite for success in a content classroom may well be

115

the ability to distinguish between "studying" and "reading once-over-lightly." Good students make that distinction easily; poor students rarely do, but often they *can* do so if given the needed guidance and instruction to make them aware of the difference.

An improvement of students' productive learning in a content classroom is often directly related to a concomitant increase in their awareness of effective study skills. Of course, awareness is only the beginning, but without awareness, study skills development and application is haphazard at best. The ability to identify students' study skills and to discuss strengths and weaknesses with them may be among the most important diagnostic and instructional strategies for content teachers.

Delineating Types of Skills

Reading and study skills are often discussed as though they were one and the same; we want to maintain their separateness as they are two different aspects of learning which are, at times, related. To identify and correct weaknesses in study skills will enhance a student's ability to learn effectively; that is not, however, to be considered equivalent to improving reading ability. Skills are specific, overt, demonstrable capabilities that are required to perform a specific task. Smith (1982) has amply discussed the fact that reading proficiency does not develop through learning a series of isolated skills. The distinction between reading and study skills is of utmost importance. The primary difference is that as one becomes a more proficient, experienced reader, one will also become a better learner, but the reverse is not necessarily true. While an improvement in reading may cause an improvement in one's ability to learn, improved study skills will produce a better student, but not necessarily a better reader. If we have belabored this point, it is because we do not sanction instruction in study skills as a means to improving reading ability.

Study skills may be classified into four categories: (1) work-study habits, (2) locational skills, (3) organizational skills, and (4) specialized skills. Our discussion of the different skills within each category will necessarily be general since we have tried to focus our discussion on areas of concern to all content teachers. If you want to pursue the concept of study skills in greater depth in your own specialized content field, we refer you to Thomas and Robinson (1981) or Shepherd (1978).

Work-Study Habits

Many students have little or no concept of basic work-study habits which can help them be more efficient learners. They often study at haphazard times, whenever "the mood strikes them," and in places that actually detract from rather than facilitate learning. Good work-study habits can foster students' awareness that dependable learning is based on the intent to remember. Simple exposure to information does not guarantee learning, nor does the passive repetition of an experience. When students learn to organize their study time and to establish a familiar place for study, they can become more proficient learners.

Efficient study can result from students' self-analysis of their use of time. A daily schedule, however, is a personal thing and should vary with each individual. Once established, it can indicate to a student how much studying is being done and it can give a better indication of how well the student is doing in a class. If a student is frustrated by his or her inability to learn, a motivation factor might be the realization of how much time and effort is being wasted. Few students are bored by learning; instead, they are frustrated and "turned off" by nonlearning. If a student can be encouraged to establish a reasonable daily routine where chunks of time for study can be set aside, it is likely that he or she will become more involved in study and perhaps motivated to learn more.

Finding the best place to study is another aspect of good study habits that can result in marked improvement in learning. Some students have no place where they feel comfortable studying. Usually, the best place is a special place, perhaps in a corner of a bedroom set aside for studying, or in a library carrel. Each person must find his or her own place; it must, however, be a productive place! Often students study where they are too uncomfortable (or too comfortable) and they find difficulty keeping their minds on their work. It is possible that where a person studies may be more of a distractor than a facilitator of studying. *Where* may be as crucial as *how* one studies.

Locational and Reference Skills

Locational skills include knowing how to find information in various reference sources. Many students are as bewildered by a library as they would be if transported by spaceship or time machine to a remote place. They don't know what is there that can help them. *Readers Guide, Masterplots, Oxford Companions,* or even atlases, almanacs, and encyclopedias of various sorts are often totally unfamiliar and unusable to students. More often than not, students are intimidated by libraries and their rules. Likewise, many students do not know how to use the table of contents, index, chapter summaries, or glossaries in their texts. Deficiencies in these skills are not due to low intelligence or other ability-related deficiencies; most students lack the experience that would lead to facility with these skills. They need instruction and guidance. Often, and this may be especially true of junior and senior high school teachers, the assumption is made that students do know how to use various reference materials; such assumptions are unwarranted in the majority of

117

instances. Analyzing students' locational skill needs then is an important part of assessing their study skills. Deficiencies can often be rectified, and a whole new world opened for students.

Organizational Skills

One of the more common weaknesses among junior and senior high school students is the inability to organize the material they are supposed to be learning. Yet, efficient learning often depends upon how well a student can organize the information that he or she is trying to learn. Good students tend to be able to organize their thoughts and their learning far better than poor or average students and this ability gives them a distinct advantage. Of all the study skills that a teacher needs to diagnose and provide help with, this is probably the most crucial.

That students are often not allowed to underline or write in the margins of their textbooks is a fact of which we are all too well aware. Nevertheless, underlining is a skill that students should be taught and encouraged to use to highlight the most important things encountered in their reading. Students need to become selective in what they underline, so that they highlight the key words and the key ideas that can be tied together as a summary of what the author is trying to emphasize.

Outlining is probably one of the most complex skills in learning because it requires analysis and synthesis of a very fine sort. Outlining requires that a student recognize the main ideas treated in a passage as well as the supporting details, examples, and reasons that are related to those main ideas. Consider, however, that it is possible—even likely—that a student's inability to outline the material being studied is not an indication of failure to understand the system of outlining, but an indication of failure to understand the material being considered. The perceptive teacher will recognize that the problem may not be a lack of organizational skills but a mismatch between student and material. To remedy this, the teacher's next step would be to switch to supplementary materials more appropriate for the student in trouble or to provide help in breaking the code of the particular pattern of organization the author is using, whichever may be the problem.

Notetaking is another organizational skill at which few students are accomplished. As most often used, it takes one of two different forms, lecture notetaking and reading notetaking. Most students do neither well. In lecture notetaking, students are required to listen, analyze, interpret, and synthesize while writing. In some cases, the lecture they are hearing is not well organized, and this makes notetaking even more difficult. That they only have one chance to hear something creates additional problems because they are afraid they will miss something; when they do miss a point, they tend to give up and not get down whatever else is said. Reading notetaking is closely akin to underlining and outlining, as it too is a difficult skill with which students often need assistance. While taking notes during reading, a student must analyze, interpret, and synthesize. It basically involves identifying key points made by an author and converting these key ideas to the reader's own words. Such a skill often requires rather sophisticated reading and thinking abilities if the end product—the notes themselves—is to be valuable. This is a difficult, if not impossible, feat if the material is not appropriate for the student. Unfortunately, students usually find their notes to be a word-by-word duplication of the textbook, so they perceive notetaking as wasted effort. Since it is a rather complex skill even when done well, students should practice reading notetaking and receive guidance from their teachers.

Specialized Skills

Specialized study skills include those needed for very specific purposes such as taking tests. In many cases, students know enough information about the material in a class to warrant their receiving a high grade, but they are unable to convey their knowledge to the teacher when test time comes around. The ability to express what is known is a major determiner of a student's grade in a class. Unfortunately, some students become confused by reading too much into a matching exercise; others fail to realize that one false element in a true-false item can make the entire item false. In addition, students at times do not understand what is being asked on an essay test. All of these situations create testing confusion and the confusion often results in students' failure. Thus, there are many strategies in taking tests that students need to know.

Other specialized skills include following directions and using graphic aids. Following directions is a specialized skill which is developed with practice; yet many students do not follow directions well at all. Such students need to be made aware of this weakness, and they need help avoiding distractions that cause them to ignore or be confused by directions. Using maps, graphs, and other graphic aids are other skills that usually can be developed through experience and practice.

Such simple things as these specialized skills can increase students' confidence in themselves and can stimulate their learning. A teacher who exposes students to specialized skills in a classroom can perceive how well the students are able to handle them and can help those who are having difficulty.

Formal Assessments

A formal assessment of study skills may be obtained from a subtest of a standardized achievement test or from a standardized study skills inventory. As with other types of standardized testing devices, however, a teacher must exercise caution when interpreting the results of such devices. A formal assessment of study skills can be of value if it is used to indicate which students may have weaknesses in study skills. But to use these devices for purposes

119

other than rough indicators would be assuming that they are more accurate than they are.

Many standardized achievement tests, especially those designed for junior and senior high school students, include a subtest intended to assess study skills. Such subtests are usually designed around a multiple-choice format and examine only tangential skills such as library awareness, using a map or graph, using an index, and ability to alphabetize. That they often do not sample the more important skills such as outlining, notetaking, use of time, or test taking is a significant deficiency in these tests.

A standardized study skills inventory, such as the Preston-Botel *Study Habits Checklist* (1967) has several advantages over the subtest of a standardized achievement battery. First, most of these inventories cover major areas of importance such as use of time, notetaking, outlining, and taking examinations. Specific questions in these and other areas provide a greater degree of depth than an achievement battery subtest. A second advantage lies in students' responses. Rather than directly testing a specific skill, students are asked to analyze and describe their own study habits in reference to a very specific question. For example, students may be asked, "In taking examinations, do you read the directions and the questions with care?" (Preston and Botel, 1967). The response will be either "Almost always," "More than half the time," "About half the time," "Less than half the time," or "Almost never."

These inventories provide students with an opportunity to reflect carefully on their own study habits. This self-analysis is an important first step since areas of weakness may become immediately apparent. Such appraisals are of value to both students and teachers because they can serve as the springboard for fruitful diagnosis through private conferences.

If formal assessment devices of the standardized variety are to be used, we suggest the inventory over the achievement battery subtest. Each can be used as a screening device to indicate which students seem to have weaknesses in study skills that would impede academic success, but the inventory usually examines important areas rather than tangential ones. Each offers a teacher the chance to compare the students with established norms, but because of the nature of the questions posed, the inventory offers greater possibilities for intensive diagnosis based on an item analysis. The inherent dangers and limitations of any type of standardized device exist with both, but if a screening device of a survey nature is what is wanted, the advantages of the inventory are apparent.

Informal Assessments

An informal analysis of students' study skills may be the easiest aspect of diagnosis for a content teacher interested in helping students improve their learning abilities; it may also be the most important. Students who do not know how to learn are handicapped from the outset, and teachers cannot fairly assume that students, good and poor alike, automatically develop the necessary skills for effective study. Informal assessments are probably the most reliable and beneficial methods of evaluating students' study skills, and when appropriately utilized they can help perceptive teachers avert many problems before they arise.

One informal approach to study skills diagnosis is through daily observations of students as they perform the various tasks needed in the classroom. If lecture notetaking is important, a teacher can unobtrusively observe students as they attempt to take notes. Mental observations can be made of those who seem to be writing down the more important ideas which are expressed during the lecture. In fact, a written record may often be of value since a premium is not placed on remembering observations. Other skills that will enhance learning can also be observed in the course of daily routines such as test taking, outlining, and specialized skills such as knowing how to use a map or how to work a problem in math or science classes. A major advantage of this approach is that it requires performance and is based on realistic performance criteria.

A second means of informally assessing certain study skills is to create tests or exercises that are designed to assess specific skills. A tape might be made to check students' ability to take notes in a listening situation; a reading passage can be designed to assess underlining, reading notetaking, and outlining skills. A practice test can be devised that asks students to answer questions and then describe how they proceeded to take the test. To aid in study skills assessment, a checklist can be created to keep a record of strengths and weaknesses in those areas that seem to be most important in a given class.

Devising Your Own Program

The most efficient method of assessing study skills is probably a combination of all the strategies we have discussed in this chapter. With this in mind, let us suggest a series of steps, with some examples, which can guide you toward devising a study skills assessment program that will be most appropriate for your classroom.

First, analyze the courses you teach and the way you teach. What study skills are needed for success in these courses? Do students need to take careful reading notes because of your emphasis on the text and other outside readings? How important are lecture notes? Do students need to be able to outline material because the material itself is disjointed and needs to be tied together for clarity? Do they need to use maps and graphs, or research or locational skills? Is the terminology going to be very new and different so that they will need to refer often to a glossary? The identification of the specific study skills that are important in a course must be identified so that assessments can be related to the specific skills needed. As the year progresses, ask your students to help you revise the list; you may be surprised at some of their observations.

Second, once the list is compiled, construct a checklist. It may look something like Figure 8.1. We have based this checklist on specific skills identified as being important. The preparation of such a checklist will enable you to keep a record of individual students. Other formats can easily be devised that may be more suitable for you, but without such a checklist, you will be forced to rely a great deal on memory. If the idea of keeping track of each student seems too overwhelming, you might consider letting the students do their own record-keeping with individual checklists. If you do, periodically hand out the checklist and let them make revisions they think are appropriate. Perhaps a combination of your own observations kept on a separate sheet and the students' self-analysis will be appealing.

Third, prepare an inventory form to which students can respond with the emphasis placed on the skills you have identified as being important in your class. Published inventories such as those alluded to in the discussion of formal assessments can be used, but they frequently cover areas that are not of immediate interest to you and omit areas that might be vital in your class. If you do construct an inventory, it might look something like the one we have designed here.

Fourth, design some evaluation exercises that are based on the most crucial skills you have identified as being important in your course. Have the students do the exercises and then evaluate them for signs of strengths and weaknesses.

Fifth, observe your students in daily classroom activities. Such informal observations can be used to reconfirm any tentative conclusions you might have drawn as a result of "testing exercises" or from an inventory or self-analysis by means of a checklist. As you use the observations in diagnosis, you should look for trends and not assume too much from an isolated situation. Students' performances are not usually consistent since many external variables affect them at any given time.

Sixth, compare your findings with those of the students. Discuss with them the areas you consider important and design ways that will help them eliminate any existing problems.

In summary, then, these are the six steps:

1. Identify the study skills that students will need for success in your course.
2. Construct a diagnostic checklist to record your evaluations of students' proficiency with the specific skills of importance.
3. Prepare a self-analysis inventory based on the study skills you consider important.
4. Construct evaluative exercises to assess the most vital study skills.
5. Informally observe students' ability to use their study skills as they perform tasks during daily classroom activities.
6. Compare your findings with your students.

STUDY SKILLS CHECKLIST

_____
teacher

_____
course/period

_____
date

3 = can do well
2 = needs improvement
1 = very weak

SKILLS

NAME	KEY	Texts			Underlining						Notetaking — Reading					Notetaking — Lecture					Outlining						Uses Maps			Essay Test-Taking					
		table of contents	index	glossary	highlights important ideas	underlines key words	underlines supportive information				based on underlining	will make sense several weeks later	cross references with page numbers			brief, but clear	includes main ideas	includes supportive details			headings reflect main ideas	subheadings include supportive data	headings reflect parallel relationships			can use legends	can interpret historical data		reads directions and all questions before beginning	thinks before writing	organizes answer	proofreads		
Bell, J.	1																																		
	2																																		
	3																																		
Brown, S.	1																																		
	2																																		
	3																																		
Carver, T.	1																																		
	2																																		
	3																																		
Cotton, W.	1																																		
	2																																		
	3																																		
Horton, G.	1																																		
	2																																		
	3																																		
Ives, J.	1																																		
	2																																		
	3																																		
etc.																																			

FIGURE 8.1
Study skills checklist

STUDY SKILLS INVENTORY

_____
Student

_____
course/period

_____
date

Directions: Study skills will be important to your success in this course and this inventory is designed to find out what your strengths and weaknesses may be in these areas. Think carefully about each of the following statements and then *answer as honestly as you can.* This is NOT a test!!

Circle 1, 2, 3, or 4 next to each statement to indicate whether the statement would be true for you usually, sometimes, seldom, or never.

	USUALLY	SOMETIMES	SELDOM	NEVER
Use of Time				
1. I spend about forty-five minutes each day studying for each of my courses.	1	2	3	4
2. When I study, I can stick with it until I am finished.	1	2	3	4
3. I study where I will not be interrupted.	1	2	3	4
Using a Textbook				
4. I use the table of contents to help me understand how topics are related.	1	2	3	4
5. I use the index in my studying.	1	2	3	4
6. I use the glossary to find meanings of unfamiliar words.				
Underlining				
7. I underline all important ideas as I read.	1	2	3	4
8. I underline only key words and phrases, not whole sentences.	1	2	3	4
9. I underline details and examples.	1	2	3	4
10. I underline almost everything.	1	2	3	4
Notetaking				
11. When I study, I take notes from my reading.	1	2	3	4
12. When I take notes from my reading, they are clear enough to make sense several weeks later.	1	2	3	4

	USUALLY	SOMETIMES	SELDOM	NEVER
13. When I take notes from my reading, I put down the page numbers where I got the information.	1	2	3	4
14. When a teacher is lecturing in class, I take clear notes of what is said.	1	2	3	4
15. In my lecture notes, I make sure to write down the main ideas.	1	2	3	4
16. In my lecture notes, I include details and examples that help me clarify ideas.	1	2	3	4
Outlining				
17. I outline the major things I learn when I study.	1	2	3	4
18. In my outlines, I include main ideas in the primary headings.	1	2	3	4
19. In my outlines, I include details as subheadings that clarify the main ideas.	1	2	3	4
Using Maps				
20. I can use the keys and legends when reading maps.	1	2	3	4
21. I can interpret what the maps suggest about historical trends.	1	2	3	4
Taking Essay Tests				
22. When taking essay tests, I read the directions and all the questions before beginning to answer any of the questions.	1	2	3	4
23. When taking essay tests, I think about what I want to write before beginning.	1	2	3	4
24. When taking essay tests, I organize my answer so my ideas will be clear to the instructor.	1	2	3	4
25. I proofread my answers when I am finished and before I turn in my paper.	1	2	3	4
Taking Objective Tests				
26. When answering a multiple choice question, I try to eliminate first the obviously incorrect choices.	1	2	3	4
27. I trust my first guess when unsure of an answer.	1	2	3	4
28. I proofread to make sure no question is left unanswered, even if the answer is a wild guess.	1	2	3	4
29. I read through all of the choices given before marking an answer, even if the first or second one seems correct.	1	2	3	4
30. I look for clues in other questions that can help in answering questions of which I am unsure.	1	2	3	4

In addition to these six, two more might be added:

7. Help students improve their study skills by providing direct guidance and instruction.
8. Periodically discuss students' progress on an individual basis. Make suggestions that will help them improve further. Above all, provide encouragement!

Teaching Study Skills

Instruction in the various study skills we have described should be integrated into content reading lessons where the need arises. Students learn skills most effectively in a meaningful context. The inclusion of specific skills in this way, however, requires perceptive, diagnostic teaching. To fragment and isolate skills instruction will rarely accomplish the desired objective. Skills instruction which originates from an observed need will help students see value and purpose in the skill.

Consider study skills as a means to an end, rather than as a separate entity worthy of active pursuit for its own sake. Application is the byword and, more often than not, effective instruction will emerge from students' need to acquire, assimilate, or synthesize knowledge. As you proceed through the next unit, seek ways to incorporate meaningful skills instruction into your activities. Be on the lookout for occasions when your students might need your help and guidance in studying. However, be wary that as you begin to consider and appraise their needs that you plan to meet those needs in a meaningful context.

UNIT 3

Conceptual Objectives

1. What the reader knows is more important to comprehension than what the author says.

2. In their search for information, students may find opportunities to practice a variety of reading strategies.

3. The opportunity to reflect and react to what one has read solidifies learning.

4. Knowledge of vocabulary reflects a stage of understanding.

5. Attitudes toward school are changed by experiences in school.

A Synthesis

Diagnostic instruction is instruction designed to adapt the curriculum to meet the needs of the student. Unfortunately, students in secondary school classrooms are often passive and unenthusiastic. For most teachers, this inertia is perplexing, especially when the same students are often seen engaged in witty, dynamic, animated conversations outside classroom doors. It is as if going to class is a price they pay for precious moments of socializing with their friends.

In the final chapter of *Psycholinguistics and Reading* (1973), Frank Smith discusses "Twelve Easy Ways to Make Learning to Read Difficult and One Difficult Way to Make it Easy." His one difficult way is the substance of diagnostic reading instruction in a content classroom: "Respond to what the child is trying to do." In other words, *identify what the students are trying to learn and then provide them with activities that will help them succeed.* The object of diagnostic instruction is to facilitate learning.

Students learn by continually attempting to make sense of their world. Their inertia would suggest that they perceive much of what takes place in their classes as making little sense in their world. Thus, they make little or no effort to learn it. Learning is an active process; passivity is counterproductive to learning. When students perceive neither purpose nor sense in what they find in their classes, they make no effort—and without effort, they do not learn.

Putting these comments in other words, the following quote from Arthur Combs in *Helping Relationships* (1971) seems particularly apt:

> Learning is the discovery of meaning. The problem of learning . . . always involves two aspects: one is acquisition of new information or experience; the other has to do with the individual's personal discovery of the meaning of information for him. . . . The discovery of meaning, however, can only take place in people and cannot occur without the involvement of persons. (p. 91)

In *The Naked Children* (1971), Fader describes a student, Wentworth, who never participates in class activities and who might best be described as the model of classroom inertia. His teacher explained that Wentworth could not read and that was why he never took part in class activities. Further, she explained, his malady could not be rectified in spite of all efforts to do so. When Fader pursued this problem, he found that, in fact, Wentworth could read. As Fader describes it,

> Wentworth told me. "Sure I can read," he said. "I been able to read ever since I can remember. But I ain't never gonna let *them* know, on accoun' of iff'n I do I'm gonna have to read all that crap they got." (p. 17)

This vignette dramatizes the problem of inertia all too well.

Combating the Wentworth Syndrome

The diverse nature of students' backgrounds, interests, and needs is no more evident than in secondary content area classrooms. Similarly, the need for responsive, diagnostic instruction is nowhere more essential than in these classes. Through this type of instruction, a teacher can help students find sense and purpose in their study and can effectively combat the "Wentworth syndrome."

Diagnostic instruction is instruction organized by the teacher around the needs and interests of pupils with the goal of adapting the curriculum to allow pupils to find personal meaning in what they are doing. By accounting for the students' needs, teacher's goals, and curricular demands (discussed in chapter 2), and by creating a meaningful blend of these three instructional factors, a teacher can produce an activity-oriented classroom where students can learn in accordance with their own goals.

Students need to become involved, personally and collectively, in their learning. They need to discuss and debate the concepts being emphasized. They need to manipulate elements of the concepts and to make judgments about these concepts. They need to explore and examine issues in creative and meaningful ways, through open-ended questions where no "right" or "wrong" answers reign. They also need guidance in how to extract the personal content that will be meaningful and important to them.

Students in content classrooms need encouragement to ask questions—questions that will be self-stimulating, questions that will help them overcome inertia and guide them toward becoming active readers and learners. Students need the freedom to stick their necks out, to make intellectual progress. They need to ask questions, such as:

1. Why am I reading this? How can I best learn from it?
2. What do I want to know about this?
3. How can this information be valuable to me?

Such questions will help students pose more questions—probing questions of good quality that will help them make sense of their world.

What is more dynamic in an academic setting than to see and feel genuine learning taking place? When students become actively involved in learning, receive the proper amount of instructional guidance, and can have their creative drives nourished rather than stymied, they become as animated in the classrooms as they are in the halls. Such learning usually is characterized by the ability to answer three questions:

1. What am I doing? (This one's usually easy!)
2. Why am I doing it? (This one's essential!)

3. What am I going to be doing next? (This helps make sense in a larger perspective!)

Students must be able to answer these questions if they are to relate classroom activities to their world rather than to perceive them as arbitrary nonsense imposed by school. When students can answer these questions, diagnostic instruction is functioning at its best.

Activity and Selected Readings Key

Suggested Activities

	CONCEPTS				
	1	2	3	4	5
1. Carefully examine the examples of content reading lessons included in Chapter 16.	X	X	X	X	
2. Design and implement a content reading lesson.	X	X	X	X	
3. Try the structured overview process we describe on pp. 139–144, at first with a small group and then a whole class. Compare your dialogue with the one we offered as an example.	X				
4. Beginning with a brainstorming activity, try the PReP strategy described on pp. 144–149.	X				
5. Use the ReQuest procedure with a group of students, modifying it as you feel the need. (See pp. 149–150.)	X				
6. Work through the example study guide on p. 157. Ask others to do the same and compare responses.		X			
7. Construct, use, and evaluate a three level study guide, following the steps we suggest on pp. 158–161.			X		
8. Construct, use, and evaluate a pattern guide, following the steps we suggest on p. 164.			X		
9. Work through the concept guide for *The Outsiders* if you have read the novel.			X	X	
10. Construct, use, and evaluate a concept study guide, following the steps we suggest on pp. 170–171.			X		
11. Construct, use, and evaluate a combination study guide. (See pp. 174–175.)			X		
12. Try to develop a graphic post-organizer on one of the chapters in this unit.				X	

(continued)

	CONCEPTS				
	1	2	3	4	5
13. Design a cinquain on a topic related to this unit, using the guidelines suggested on p. 184.				X	
14. Work the vocabulary exercises and puzzles scattered throughout Chapter 12. Then try your hand at constructing ones similar to the examples we provide.				X	
15. List your favorite school subjects and teachers in school. Do they match?					X
16. List the two best and worst experiences of your life. Whom or what did they involve? (See p. 214.)					X

Selected Readings*

	CONCEPTS				
	1	2	3	4	5
1. Sanders, Norris. *Classroom Questions: What Kinds?*	X	X	X		X
2. Smith, Frank. "Twelve easy ways to make learning to read easy."		X			
3. Herber, H. L. *Teaching Reading in Content Areas, 2nd edition*	X	X	X	X	
4. Langer, Judith. "From theory to practice: A prereading plan."	X				
5. Stauffer, Russell. *Directing the Reading-Thinking Process.*					
6. Estes, Thomas & Johnstone, Julie. "Twelve Easy Ways to Make Readers Hate Reading."					X
7. Vacca, Richard. *Content Area Reading.*		X			

*Full bibliographic information for these items will be found at the end of the book under *References.*

CHAPTER 9 Prereading Anticipation

What the reader knows is more important to comprehension than is what the author says.

Overview

Comprehension depends on what the reader knows that can be related to what is being read. That is, the reader attempts to find in memory anything related to the author's message; success in this search for relationships is the primary determinant of comprehension. It would appear, therefore, that in preparing a student for a reading task we should strive to create an interaction which establishes information in the memory of the reader to which the content of the reading selection can be related.

Several techniques for accomplishing this are available. Each is a method of helping students to anticipate intellectually what they are going to learn. Set in the framework of a content reading lesson, prereading anticipation techniques help students to develop strategies and to understand what they are studying.

Something Old, Something New

Read the following paragraph and rate it on a scale of difficulty from 1 to 5, with 1 meaning very easy, 5 meaning incomprehensible.

Always begin from the left. Accomplishment requires balance, as well as the ability to stand on one foot cross-legged. You should, of course, hold on. The steps are these: push your left leg down, picking the right one up and over and down in one smooth movement. The propulsion which is caused will complicate the matter, so be careful!

If you are like most readers, you probably found the paragraph incomprehensible. But if we had said to you that the paragraph concerned mounting a bicycle, your comprehension would have been near perfect and on that basis you might have said the difficulty was 1 or 2, relatively easy.

A group of children were once asked to read the following paragraph, which they found very difficult. It is taken from a research article by Edward Thorndike (1917), entitled "Reading as Reasoning: A Study of Mistakes in Paragraphy Reading":

In Franklin, attendance upon school is required of every child between the ages of seven and fourteen on every day when school is in session unless the child is so ill as to be unable to go to school or some person in his house is ill with a contagious disease, or the roads are impassable.

You probably did not have difficulty with this item from a school board policy manual. In this case, and as was *not* true for the children in Thorndike's classic study, you could easily judge the topic of the paragraph and thus process the information. The readability levels of the two paragraphs, one about getting on a bike, the other about rules for attendance at Franklin School, are very similar. Why the difference in difficulty for the reader?

Perhaps a clue to the difference is found in Marvin Minsky's (1965) notion of "frames." He has proposed that whenever we try to understand anything, we do so by trying to relate it to a framework that we have previously constructed out of our experiences. Thus, if you had known that the earlier paragraph was about getting on a bicycle, you would have "pictured" certain expectancies for the paragraph before you began reading. Your "frame of reference," called to mind in anticipation of what the paragraph was to be about, would have given you a mental set for comprehension of what the paragraph said. Look again at the first sentence of the paragraph. Given a proper anticipatory frame, you would have known what you were to begin. As it was, you had no way to picture the event, and so you failed to understand the sentence. The same can be said for the second sentence; you couldn't picture what was to be accomplished. Your frame for getting on a bicycle was buried somewhere, and we weren't doing much to help you bring it into focus. A well written paragraph would be a help to the reader, and a good reader would constantly be modifying or adjusting his or her frame of mind on the basis of continually flowing information.

We confess we tried to write our bicycle mounting directions to *prevent* comprehension, done in fun and only to demonstrate a point. But for students

134

in school, reading incomprehensible paragraphs is not such fun, though unfortunately what happened to you in the bicycle example happens frequently to them. Too often, when students are reading, they either aren't properly cued to an appropriate frame of reference, or their experiences have not led them to construct the frame they need. In either case, they don't understand what they read because they have no way to relate the message of what they are reading to what they already know.

Among the more widely accepted and applied tenets of reading instruction is this: Prior experiences are a significant determiner of what a student will understand and remember from text. Recent research has clearly confirmed that one's prior knowledge directly affects the comprehension one generates during reading (see Anderson, Reynolds, Schallert, and Goetz, 1977).

Any time a reader, despite best efforts, does not comprehend what has been read, he or she has somehow failed to get the picture. It is possible that the vocabulary was too far removed from the student's experience, or that the logic of the writing was unfamiliar or too complex. It is also possible that the student didn't get quite the help needed in cueing to what was happening in the selection, didn't get quite enough help in "seeing" what the author was trying to say. The essence of reading instruction, we think, is to provide just such help as we will explain in terms of the content reading lesson and several specific prereading anticipation strategies.

The Content Reading Lesson

In our view, the most important thing that could be said about reading is that it is the application of reasoning in an attempt to understand what is being read. In the sense that comprehension is the object of reading, reading is reasoning. In teaching reading, the task is to lead students through the method and logic of reading as reasoning. In other words, it is to help them to call to mind a proper frame of reference built out of their previous experience and, by a process of reasoning methodically and logically, to modify the frame in the light of understandings gained from reading.

The content reading lesson is a strategy that allows teachers to guide and direct students' thinking about what they read. Designed on a plan similar to Stauffer's Directed Reading-Thinking Activity (1975), the content reading lesson is based on the notion that reading is reasoning *and* that students' ability to reason during reading can be increased through practice with a teacher's guidance and assistance.

A content reading lesson can be organized to incorporate three basic parts, each of which is essential to maximal learning. These parts also reflect the integral components of the reading process, and as such they represent concurrently the theoretical and the practical aspects of reading instruction.

135

These parts of the reading process and the content reading lesson are pre-reading anticipation, information search, and reflective reaction.

During prereading anticipation a reader actively seeks to remember all he or she knows relative to the topic of the selection to be read. Each of us knows a great deal about the world around us. What we know is stored in our mind, and it constitutes the frame of reference to which we must relate anything we try to learn. As we learn something new, we relate it to something we already know. The purpose of the prereading anticipation stage of a content reading lesson is to help students realize what they already know, and out of that to adopt an inquisitive mental set. Often students charge into a reading assignment without mobilizing their prior awarenesses. If they would first call to consciousness all that they know about the subject in a reading passage, they would vastly improve their chances of learning whatever new information they may find as they read.

Consider this concept another way. A student brings what he or she knows to a learning task, an entire cognitive structure. In this, there is little choice. There is much choice, however, about the degree to which that cognitive structure is organized and mobilized relative to the task at hand. If the student approaches a reading task without first thinking about what he or she already knows concerning the topic, learning will be minimized. On the other hand, if the student can have help in organizing his or her cognitive structure appropriate to the reading task, the chances of associating new information with prior knowledge will be maximized. Thus, comprehension will be much more likely to occur.

The purpose and value of the prereading anticipation component of a content reading lesson is to help students mobilize, call to consciousness, all that they have stored in their cognitive structure relative to whatever they are about to read. Without this component of a lesson, students will have to grope for bits and pieces of their cognitive structure as they encounter new information in their reading.

The second part of the reading process, information search, is unfortunately the only stage of the content reading lesson that students usually perform. Information search is, simply, reading. As you may have perceived by now, however, reading is not that simple. Different strategies for reading are required, depending upon the purpose of the reader and the nature of the material. Whatever the strategy, most students will benefit from guidance and direction. Exercises designed and used through the format of a content reading lesson will help students learn to choose appropriate strategies when reading on their own, will help in learning to form a proper frame of reference for questions.

The final stage of the content reading lesson, reflective reaction, is more elusive than either of the first two stages, but in some senses it is more critical. Passivity is the archenemy of comprehension. A very high percentage of what readers understand as they read is forgotten within a few hours. The exception often is that information to which the readers can react and upon which they can reflect. In effect, the purpose of this stage of the lesson is to help students reorganize their cognitive structure, adjust their cognitive framework, to assimilate the new information with the old information. That is why this stage is so crucial. Without it, new information may be only loosely attached in the cognitive structure and thus quickly forgotten.

A content reading lesson is often conducted in segments; that is, the students read a section, discuss it, read another section, discuss that, and so forth until the entire selection has been read. Segmented readings, however, are not essential in a content reading lesson. Students may read an entire selection, even as a homework assignment, and still benefit from the structure of a content reading lesson. The basic formula for such a lesson is: DISCUSS—READ—DISCUSS. Russell Stauffer provides the seminal discussion of this formula under the rubric "Directed Reading-Thinking Activity" in his book, *Directing Reading Maturity as a Cognitive Process* (1969). Along similar lines, we suggest the following guide for conducting a content reading lesson:

A. Anticipation (prereading discussion of any segment of the selection or for an entire selection):
   1. What do you know about the topic?
   2. Where have you learned those things?
   3. What do you expect, want, and/or need to learn about the topic?
   4. Why do you need to learn that? How will that be useful information?
B. Information Search (usually done by the reader individually and without interruption)
C. Reflection Reaction
   1. What did you find out?
   2. Pose specific questions after you have drawn as much information from them as possible.
   3. Pursue their answers with "Why do you think so?"

Begin the cycle anew; continue until the entire selection has been read and discussed.

To help you achieve a sense of the content reading lesson, we have included several examples of these activities in the four units in Chapter 16. The "script" for the lessons may help you experience this lesson as if you were a participant. We encourage you to turn now to those lessons and to examine them as they reflect the basic steps we have just delineated.

When implemented with confidence, a content reading lesson helps readers associate their previous experiences with the topic they are studying. The teacher has the opportunity to help students anticipate what they will learn and establish reasons for their study. After each appropriate segment, students will have a chance to clarify their understandings and to elaborate their conceptual awarenesses through discussion of the key issues being studied.

We hope this brief discussion and the examples in Chapter 16 have given you a perspective on content reading lessons: what they are, why they are necessary, their purpose, and their parts. In the remainder of this chapter and in the next two chapters we will focus on specific techniques that can be used during various phases of any content reading lesson. We want you to realize how to incorporate any of these specific activities into the context of a content reading lesson as well as how to use the strategies individually.

Building Anticipation: The Teacher's Role

What you do during any prereading activity must be based on what the students will be studying (e.g., what information is in the text and how is it structured) and on what the students know about the topic. It is appropriate, therefore, to devote the initial part of any lesson to determination of students' prior knowledge. Once you know what prior knowledge the students possess, you must decide whether it is sufficient for them to succeed with the assignment *if* you have also helped them establish a purpose and a desire for learning. If you believe the students lack certain requisite information, then provide that for them. We want to emphasize, however, that it is important *not* to give students a lot of new information. There is always a risk of preceding one learning task by another while actually facilitating neither.

One man who has addressed the problem of how to bring readers to a proper mental set in anticipation of the reading task is David Ausubel (1968; 1978). His idea is that we can best facilitate comprehension by helping readers realize the context for a new topic of inquiry rather than informing students about the specific information they are to study (hence, avoiding the likelihood of one learning task preceded by another while facilitating neither). The context is established, Ausubel suggests, by providing students with related information but at a higher level of generality. By helping students see the forest, so to speak, we make them more likely to find the trees as they study new ideas and issues. A higher level of generality affords students the chance to relate the new information they are studying to a broader context, a context they already understand. Hence, Ausubel suggests that if students are provided with some form of an advance organizer or broadened context for study, they will be better equipped to learn the new, unfamiliar information assigned for study. In this way, a teacher can implement Ausubel's instructional maxim: "The most important single factor influencing learning is what the learner already knows. Ascertain this and teach them accordingly" (1978, iv).

As you consider each of the strategies we describe, notice that the focus is on what the reader knows. If you find that the readers know little or nothing relative to the content of what they're about to read, you can take that as very good evidence that the reading is likely to be difficult, perhaps even frustrating, and may well be inappropriate, especially without some form of instructional intervention on your part. Properly, you will want to do something to make the assignment more appropriate before you require it of your students, and that begins by ascertaining what the students know. Notice, then, that within these strategies is a feature that helps you identify what students know and a component that helps students relate what they know to what they will learn.

The Structured Overview. This strategy is more a process than it is a strategy we can actually specify. It was first described by Richard Barron (1969, 1979) and Richard Earle (1976). An understanding of any instructional activity rarely requires any historical background, but this is one of the few that does. Dick Barron originally conceived of the structured overview as a solution to a problem. We'll let his words tell you more (Barron, 1979):

> Several years ago I became interested in studying ways to help students read the text materials required in subjects such as science, mathematics, and social studies. To identify the problems students encounter with these materials, I became involved as a participant in a high school biology class. At first this proved to be somewhat damaging to my ego. Because I had little background in the subject, I found myself actually struggling to keep up with the kids!
>
> One day, early in the semester, the teacher introduced a new unit by listing and defining a long list of vocabulary terms. I became quite confused by this presentation and my initial reaction was, "My God, how will I ever keep all this terminology straight?"
>
> Later that evening, as I attempted to read the chapters associated with the unit, a simple fact began to dawn upon me. *All the vocabulary terms were related in some fashion!* I started to arrange the words in a diagram to depict relationships, occasionally adding terms from the two preceding units. Gradually, much of the content with which I had been struggling became clear.
>
> Out of this came a procedure which was subsequently labeled the "structured overview." It was defined as "a visual/verbal presentation of key vocabulary in a new learning task, in relation to broader, more inclusive terms (presumably) understood by students." The device was incorporated into a larger set of instructional strategies under study at Syracuse University's Research and Demonstration Center in Secondary Reading and shared with a number of high school teachers. After they had used the structured overview for a period of time, most of these teachers reported positive feelings about its effects in helping their students to learn. (pp. 172–173)

What happened next may be one of the most important discoveries we can share with you. After conducting several studies to demonstrate empirically the value of the structured overview, Barron found that he could *not* find the support he hoped for. What had happened was that "we had been treating the structured overview as something teachers did *for* students" (1979, p. 173). To determine what had gone wrong, he talked with some students who had found the strategy helpful and he discovered that ". . . these youngsters took an *active* role in the reading/learning task, they attempted consciously to relate the new, specific information to the teacher's introductory presentation" (p. 173). The key was that students had to take an active role in the development of this "visual/verbal" graphic display. Those students who passively observed teachers present their structured overview gained little if anything from the lesson. The verification of the value of active participation by the students came shortly thereafter; it was the active thinking by the students that made the difference, for when students "... constructed their own structured overview during or following a reading/learning task (they) would achieve higher test scores than those who received one made by the teacher or none at all."

If you are anxious to see what a "structured overview" looks like, bear with us, for Barron subsequently changed the name of this visual/verbal display to "graphic post-organizer." Notice here a very important shift in focus. He called it a POST-organizer; so why are we discussing this in the context of pre-teaching? The answer to that question explains why we cannot easily specify what a structured overview is. We have learned, from Barron and others, that when teachers engage students in the activity of developing a graphic display of the concepts related to a given reading assignment, the students benefit only when they are actively involved in the activity. Let us now attempt to convey to you what we know as a structured overview. Remember, though, that it is the process, not a product that makes this strategy valuable.

As we now describe and use this activity ourselves, it is initiated by a brainstorming activity. The teacher either tells the students the topic of what they are going to read about or, if the text lends itself to this, lets them read just far enough to get an idea of the content of the selection. The teacher then stimulates the students to share whatever bits of information, feelings, or inclinations they may have about the topic. Perhaps it will be better if we show you what we mean, but we'll keep it light for the moment.

Read the following initial paragraph from an article entitled, "Cooking on a fireplace, dutch oven, and wood stove." While you are reading, think of all you know about cooking, particularly what you might do to cook dinner if you were lost on a mountaintop and stumbled across an old cabin.

> Today most people have fireplaces in their homes as an amenity rather than a necessity. Once, however, the fireplace was at the very center of home life, being used not only for warmth but also for cooking. Cooking over a fireplace may sound simple, but in fact it requires a great deal more time and effort than using a stove. Dry kindling is used to start the fire and green wood is cut and brought in to burn since seasoned wood burns too quickly and gives off less heat. For cooking, there must be a hot bed of coals—a process that takes a full hour for a new fire to produce. Then as the coals die down, more wood is added to maintain the temperature.

Now, think about what you know about cooking and how you'd begin to cook with firewood. In a classroom, as you and others gave us your thoughts and feelings about this task, we'd be frantically trying to write everything on the chalkboard as you came up with ideas. The conversation would go something like this:

We: What are some of the things you consider when you cook at home today?

Jamie: Nutrition. I'm always concerned about having a balanced meal.

Fred: Having it all come out on time. I never seem to be able to do that.

Marge: Making sure I have all the ingredients I need for what I want to prepare.

Jackie: Having the right utensils; I mean it's tough to fix poached eggs in boiling water but I know it can be done. The same goes for having the right kind of pan to fix a pound cake; you can't bake it in a skillet.

Harry: I guess you have to know the recipes; I can follow a recipe and get something to turn out ok, but without a recipe I never know what temperature to cook with or how long to let something cook. I mean, I just don't understand how somebody can say "Oh, throw in a snip of this and a thimbleful of that and then let it bake until it's done."

Maxine: You have to be able to figure out amounts and portions too; I don't like a lot of leftovers.

We: OK, now we could go on but let's stop and see what we have. At this point, our list on the board would look something like this:

Cooking Today at Home

nutrition — balanced meals

having things come out on time

need right ingredients at home

need proper utensils

must know recipes

cooking on right temperatures

knowing how much to fix

We: OK, now what about cooking on some of the type of things that were mentioned in the paragraph we read. What do you know or think about that?

Alex: Well, I can tell you from camping out, it's a different world. You can get used to it, but it's a lot more simple and basic, at least if this kind of cooking is anything like cooking over an open fire.

Susan: I don't see how anyone did it, or I guess I should say does it. The article has already said something about knowing what wood to use because one type gives off less heat than others. I can't tell an oak tree from a maple.

Marge: You'd sure spend a lot more time in the kitchen.

Billy: You'd also need to know a lot about natural herbs and spices and things. Too, you'd have to get your meats and vegetables from hunting and farming, I'd guess, because anyone who is going to use these older ways of cooking wouldn't be likely to be near a store to just drop in and buy some TV dinners or something.

Cindy: My grandmother used to cook on a wood-burning stove. I don't remember too much about it; her meals were pretty sparse, but they were great too.

Nathan: I bet the fireplace had to be a certain size and shape to be very effective for cooking.

Jane: I doubt that many people who cooked on a wood stove or in a fireplace used many recipes; I bet they just know how to cook from years of experience or 'cause their mother or somebody told them how.

We: Now, then, what have we said about what we know?

Joyce: It would be a whole lot different than what we are used to and I don't think we know much about it.

We: Seems so. Let's look at our list. At this point, the board would look something like this:

Cooking Today at Home

nutrition — balanced meals

having things come out on time

need right ingredients at home

need proper utensils

must know recipes

cooking on right temperature

knowing how much to fix

Fireplace Cooking, Etc.

different world, more basic, simpler

need to know woods, temperature

take more time

need to know herbs & spices

must get meats & vegs. nearby

no TV dinners

sparse meals

certain size of fireplace needed

not many recipes, mostly on experience

Notice now that what we would have on the board is lots of ideas, all from students in the class, like yourself. Our next step would be to categorize, or "cluster," all this information, *with your help.* This is a vital step since it would not only structure your understandings but provide a frame of reference you could use when you read the text. In this case, we would first ask you to create categories under each of the headings we have already placed on the board. You would probably come up with categories like "preparing the cooking place," "knowing your stove," "what ingredients can you use," "what utensils will you need," and "knowing how to prepare the meal." Of course it is difficult for us to predict how you and others might structure the ideas and feelings you have about cooking with wood heat. Joyce was right— if these were your answers, there seems to be a lack of prior knowledge about the topic to be studied, but there is plenty of information at hand about cooking in general and the context of cooking on these less modern conveniences. Because we know the text and know that it will not be difficult for you to comprehend, we'd proceed next to solicit reasons why you might want to read this selection, trying to get you to establish some anticipations of what you might learn.

Certainly, not all of what you predict you might learn would be in the selection; much may not even be mentioned. But your frame of reference will certainly be activated in the right direction to help you sort out the ideas you would learn if you did read the rest of this article. In case you do want to read the rest of this article or many others like it, you will find it in *The Foxfire Book,* edited by Eliot Wigginton, a book we mentioned in Chapter 1.

Now that you have experienced the process of a structured overview, we have only to tell you that after you and others have determined the categories for the information you had us put on the board, we could, again with your help, arrange that information into a graphic display that facilitates recognition of conceptual relationships. The display is what is often called a structured overview. If we designed a graphic display for what we listed on the board it could look like Figure 9.1.

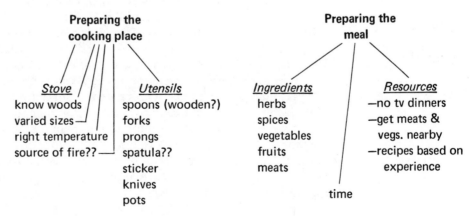

FIGURE 9.1
Structured Overview for Fireplace Cooking

We have one final comment to make about the structured overview. What we have described is the way we see it work in many content area classrooms. The emphasis is on student involvement that emerges from teacher guidance. If you were using this strategy and felt that important technical vocabulary should be introduced to the students before they read or if you knew that they had not mentioned some essential concept that could be difficult for them to grasp, you could supply that information for them after the structured overview had been constructed. To do this, you would simply say something like: "There are a few things I want to add to this overview. For example, you may not know what broiling is. It is a way to cook that is mentioned in the article and it means that the food is exposed directly to the source of the heat. So if you broil meat, you hold the meat directly over the fire." Of course, if you want, you can then add the term "broil" or any other concept to the graphic display. Other concepts can be added as well, but remember our caution about having to do too much pre-teaching of new concepts.

For those of you who might know structured overviews as a graphic display comprised primarily of key vocabulary terms presented to students and then discussed with them, we encourage you to read Barron's discussion of how to use a structured overview (1979). While we have modified his views somewhat to emphasize students' activation of their conceptual framework at the expense of a focus on new vocabulary terms, we are satisfied that what we have described here is in keeping with what works and what the teachers who use it find effective.

For you to become comfortable with this activity will necessitate practice and experience. We suggest that you develop, and implement if possible, several lesson activities using your own materials. Remember, you are seeking to build a bridge between what the students know and what the text says.

A Pre-reading Plan (PReP). As we have sought to emphasize, successful prereading instruction begins with identification of what students already know about a topic to be studied. Judith Langer (1981) has recognized this problem from first-hand experience and has developed a strategy, PReP, that combines both an assessment feature and an instructional component. Her intent is to provide teachers with a way to avoid making ". . . instructional decisions based on assumptions about students' knowledge," for when teachers plan prereading activities based on inaccurate assumptions, ineffectual teaching is almost certain to result. PReP resembles and is based on the structured overview, but it is more elaborate in that it is much more directly diagnostic. As Langer says, "PReP is a very straightforward teaching strategy (and) an understanding of why it works is essential to implementing it successfully." Let us proceed to explain why a strategy with such an easy-to-use format has consistently proven effective.

PReP addresses two issues, namely: (1) how knowledge is stored and accessed and (2) how new knowledge can be added to memory. Needless to say, these issues are rather complex. We will try to explain the basics, we hope without oversimplifying them too much. Factual, informational knowledge seems to be stored as ideas that are connected by links much in the same way that cities and towns are connected by roads. Presumably, a person's memory is composed of ideas and links. The ideas are interconnected by their association or relationships to one another, some directly (e.g., government—president), others indirectly (computers—manuscripts). Hence, when a learner is exposed to new ideas, the learner searches for a place in the network of ideas to fit the new idea. PReP is a technique that prepares the reader to anticipate what prior knowledge will be useful for understanding new ideas.

PReP consists of three stages built upon one another. In the first stage, the teacher seeks students' initial association with the topic. In the second stage, the students explain why they made those associations. In the third stage, the students reformulate their conceptualizations by adding associations that did not initially occur to them. As the students are proceeding through these stages, the teacher seeks to assess: (1) the amount of prior information the readers have about the topic *and* how this information is organized; (2) the language students use to express their knowledge of the topic (language used to express conceptual understandings can indicate sophistication of knowledge); and (3) how much additional information and vocabulary students might need before they can successfully comprehend the text.

To initiate a PReP discussion, you will need to give the students a cue that will elicit their associations with the topic. If students are to read about banks and the federal reserve system, you might begin by asking them, "Tell anything that comes to mind when you hear the word *banks*." You also might use a phrase or, in other cases, a picture, or even have students read the first paragraph of the selection if the text will cue the kinds of responses you are looking for. As students provide you with their associations, you can then add another cue, e.g., how do banks send money to one another? One caution is in order at this point; avoid using terms you suspect the students do not already know. That is, in this instance, it you used "federal reserve system" as a cue, you would probably inhibit student responses rather than encourage them. If students themselves mention the federal reserve system in response to your cues, then you get a sense of their knowledge, but your cues must be chosen to stimulate responses, not to restrict them. Recognize, too, that one student's response will trigger another student to say something that he or she did not originally think of. Encourage students to expand on each other's ideas.

Remember that you are trying to assess how much students know and how it will help them learn new ideas they will study. After you obtain a list of initial responses to your cues (and we recommend that you write the responses on the board as you would during a structured overview activity), you will want to have students reflect on their responses and elaborate the reasons for their responses. Ask students to explain "what made you think of that." So, if a student mentions home loans in response to banks, explore that response to find out why he or she thought of home loans. Your purpose here is to help students develop an awareness of the network that connects their associations. Students also have a chance to listen to each other's explanations, to interact, and to become aware of their developing ideas. They can consider, reject, accept, revise, and integrate old and new ideas. When asked what made him think of Christmas in response to banks, Chris replied, "I get a check every December from my Christmas Club account." When Becky, who had mentioned monthly statements, was asked about her response, she said, "I have a checking account at First National and every month I get a list of my checks and my balance." While Becky probably knows more about banks than Chris and even more than Franklin, who never said a word, both Chris and Franklin are given the opportunity to make associations with what others say and hence may come to realize that they know more about banks than they thought they did.

The next phase of PReP begins only when you have elicited a good sample of students' information and reasonings. If you have been listing students' responses on the board, you can ask them to examine the information and to suggest ways to cluster and classify it. If they seem to need help, you can suggest categories such as services, types of accounts, functions, and the like, depending of course on the information the students have provided. We're adding this dimension of the structured overview to Langer's PReP because we think it is important to help students recognize ways to organize the information they have. Such organization will help students perceive a framework for what they know; it will also help those who have learned about banks during the discussion to codify and arrange their new learning. In either case, students will have a frame of reference to guide their reading.

You should not proceed to the final stage of PReP until after the organizational categories have been established. Because you have helped the students organize their knowledge during phase two, they will now be likely to clarify and elaborate their initial responses. Encourage them with comments like, "Based on the way we've organized our knowledge about banks and banking, do you have any other ideas to add, anything that comes to mind about types of accounts? bank services? the way banks work?" Ask them about each category one at a time. You want to encourage students to verbalize associations and relationships. Because you provide an opportunity for students to elaborate and because the categories have been specified, responses during this phase will often be much more refined than the original responses during phase one. The real value of PReP is that it encourages students to think beyond their initial response which too often typifies a mere word-association task. When you observe students providing their more refined responses during this third phase of PReP, you will immediately realize why it is never enough merely to ask phase one kinds of questions. As a case in point, during this third phase, Franklin managed to offer, "I don't quite get it yet but I see that a bank can help me in lots of ways if I have money or if I need money."

146

When a PReP activity is completed and all the information and impressions that have been shared are pulled together, they will represent a good working sketch of the content that is likely to be in the selection, at least to the degree that students are able to anticipate it. It certainly provides them with a very clear framework of reference to use as they seek to learn about banks. Some lines of association will fade as students read and others will become stronger, but you can be sure that the students will understand far more of what they read than if they had approached the text without thinking about the topic. In fact, Langer (1981) and Langer and Nicolich (1981) have reported that the kind of prior knowledge we're talking about is more important than IQ in determining how much a student will be able to recall from reading.

Langer has extended our understanding of how to make prereading instruction more effective and, although it is not absolutely essential to your use of PReP, we would be remiss if we did not share with you her diagnostic perspective that makes PReP a significant improvement on the structured overview. Once you understand this diagnostic perspective, you will be able to apply it equally to PReP, structured overview, or any other diagnostic-instructional activity you might use, be it for prereading purposes or as an assessment of what readers have accomplished at any stage of learning.

Langer distinguishes three levels of responses that could emerge during a PReP activity. In effect, she makes qualitative categorizations of readers' knowledge that can help you understand the sophistication of students' understanding of concepts. The categories are not necessarily labeled, but can be described.

At the first and lowest level of sophistication, the students' knowledge is superficial and associations are often irrelevant. Asked "What comes to mind when you think of banks?" the student says, "people" or "big buildings" or "offices" or "drive-in windows." In some cases students might respond with a word that merely rhymes with the stimulus or has some structural feature in common, as in "penance—a necklace" or "binary—bicycle" or "despot—depot." Knowledge at this level may also include tangentially related experiential associations, as "My sister used to work at a bank." Too much information at this level should serve as a warning that students' prior knowledge may be insufficient for the reading task that is ahead of them. Such is not always the case, as in our example with cooking on wood fires; the key determiner will often be how well the text explains the new ideas and concepts and how well the new ideas are organized. That is why we say that such superficial knowledge *may* indicate that the reading will be difficult. If students know nothing about cellular structure and are to read a selection about the importance of nutrition for cellular growth, they will be in for a tough time. It is, of course, always possible that at a succeeding phase of discussion, such as during the third phase of PReP, the students' level of awareness and thinking will change for the better. This is particularly possible where students are simply unaccustomed to thinking about what they know in this way and really have more knowledge than they can indicate when they provide superficial responses during an initial discussion.

At the second and middle level of sophistication, students' awareness of a topic generally takes the form of examples, attributes, or features that are relevant to the topic. To a question about Congress, students might say "makes laws" or "representatives" or "House and Senate." To a question about banks, students might say "deposit money" or "make loans." These kinds of responses are quite good during the first phase of PReP or any other initial, off the top of the head discussion because they indicate knowledge which can easily be elaborated in a guided discussion.

The third and highest level or sophistication of knowledge is characterized by associations with more general concepts, more abstract ideas, complete and accurate definitions, analogies, or elaborations that include various components of a concept. "Congress is like Parliament in that . . .," or "Banks serve the public in various ways well beyond the checking and savings departments; for example, they serve as the economic base for a community," or "Holograms are three dimensional representations of a whole where every part is capable of reproducing the whole." This is the level you are working toward, especially after the students have studied the topic. If possible, bring the students to this level before the reading so that their thinking is in high enough gear that it stretches well beyond the level of simple associations, memories, and definitions. The object, then, is to mobilize the students' maximum reasoning skills as well as to provide them with a frame of reference relative to the topic.

As you judge the level of prior knowledge students possess, you can make on-the-spot instructional decisions. Is there enough there to permit comprehension? How should I try to channel their thinking? What sorts of expectations are they capable of? The knowledge you draw from them during any prereading discussion is your best clue to their potential success or frustration. "What you see is what you get," the expression goes. We'd add, though, that the important thing is what you do with it. Every learner has some knowledge that can be related to a new topic, since all knowledge is connected and interconnected. Students can be led to see how what they do know can be applied to what they will learn, although at times the relationship may seem to be stretched to make a fit. As students learn the new ideas, they will discover, as Richard Barron did, that these concepts are all related in various ways.

We will acknowledge, as you must, that the applicability of prior knowledge in a specific learning situation does vary from person to person within any given task. The specific knowledge, the potential of that knowledge to be accessed, the way it is stored, the degree of its sophistication, and the strength of the links that bind associations all contribute differentially to each person's ability to associate new learning to prior knowledge. The goal is not, nor can it realistically be, to create a common, convergent frame of reference for all members of a class. Instead, the goal is to help individuals in a group recognize the prior knowledge they have, evaluate it, organize it, and then use it actively as they seek new learning.

ReQuest. Any discussion of prereading strategies would be incomplete without inclusion of Anthony Manzo's ReQuest technique (Manzo, 1969). Like many similar techniques, ReQuest is a procedure that encourages students to question before they read and to base their purpose for reading on anticipatory questions. Unlike many strategies, however, ReQuest has a built-in feedback and modeling feature that gives the reader needed information. ReQuest is an acronym for reciprocal questioning, and the significance of its name will become apparent once you understand how it works. These are the steps one uses with this activity:

1. Both teacher and students read the first sentence in the first paragraph of a selection.
2. The teacher closes the book; the students keep their books open. The students may ask the teacher any question they wish that relates to that first sentence. The teacher must answer as accurately and completely as possible. Where it is pertinent, the teacher gives feedback to the students on the quality of the types of questions being asked.
3. The students then close their books and the teacher asks any questions that come to mind. These questions purposefully include (1) any that will help the students realize what knowledge they have relative to the topic and (2) the kinds of questions that students might emulate when their turn comes again.
4. The procedure is continued through a paragraph or two until students can be expected to project answers to the classic purpose questions, "What do you think you will find out in the rest of the selection?"

ReQuest has been validated as a strategy that helps students relate prior knowledge to new learning with both narrative and expository material. It is best used in small group or one-to-one activities, but it can also be effective with large groups when combined with the interaction similar to that included in structured overview and PReP activities. But there is more to ReQuest than building anticipation and teaching students how to prepare themselves for reading. The real value of the strategy, in our judgment, is that it provides a chance for feedback and modeling of questioning strategies.

With younger students, especially when they are just beginning to engage in this activity, we suggest that you follow the steps as described above. With older students, you may find it more valuable as a stimulus for discussion and interaction if you extend the amount of text that is read between each questioning. Often, one sentence just doesn't go far enough for your purpose. Remember, too, that your object here is not to evaluate students' comprehension; instead you are seeking to stimulate critical thinking and reasoning skills. ReQuest is a technique that can be used to build habits of thinking which make a technique like PReP work. Try it as a prelude to PReP where the level of sophistication of the readers' prior knowledge seems to be relatively limited. If you change the interrogative mind set of the students, you will often bring up the level of their thinking.

Questions: The Building Blocks of Anticipation

Each of the techniques we have suggested related to prereading anticipation has involved questioning. PReP is founded on questions much in the same way as structured overview. ReQuest engages students in questioning and helps them formulate an inquiry approach to learning. Whatever else one might do to build prereading anticipation, the following questions would seem essential:

1. What is the selection about?
2. What do I know about this topic?
3. What might I expect to learn of the topic from this reading?
4. Why might I want to learn more about this topic?

The importance of the purpose behind these questions cannot be over emphasized. The questions are, in fact, the first phase in the lesson format we have defined as the content reading lesson.

Allow Us to Share

Before this chapter went to press, Ronaldo Cruz[1] shared with us his experiences in using the following handout. We think it's an excellent way to introduce students to the idea of prereading. You might want to consider adapting it for use in your classroom.

Steps in Prereading

Prereading involves finding out what you are going to read about and making up questions that you want to answer when you read an assignment.

I *TEXTBOOK*
   A. Find out what the subject of the assignment is.
      1. Leaf through the pages of the assignment and find out what clues

[1]Our thanks to Ronaldo Cruz, of Adelante Institute, Tucson, Arizona.

150

the visual aids (maps, graphs, pictures) can give you. Read the captions.

    2. Look in the table of contents to put this assignment in context with the entire course. What has gone before? What will come after?

B. Study the questions at the end of the chapter or section to see what the author thinks is important in the assignment.

C. Look carefully at the bold face type in the assigned pages. From this, make up logical questions that you can answer when you read.

II *NOVEL OR PLAY (full length)*

A. Read a plot summary (synopsis)
1. *Masterplots*
2. *Masterpieces of World Literature*
3. *Oxford Companions*
4. Front matter of most study guides
    a. Barron's Educational Notes
    b. Monarch Notes
    c. Cliff Notes

B. Find a book in the library that contains critical commentaries about the book or the author. Look for something like *Twentieth Century Views Series*.

C. Look through *Book Review Digest* for the year the book was first published. (Use only as a last resort or if you need critical commentaries by critics—especially good for contemporary plays and novels.)

D. Use the study guide notes to preread each chapter or scene in the book.

E. Make questions to answer as you read each chapter or scene.

III *SHORT STORIES OR POETRY*

Read the entire story or poem through once to determine the plot or characters. Pose questions about the dramatic actions and anything else you may need to know.

IV *NONFICTION MATERIAL*

A. Look up subject in encyclopedia
B. Read the first and last sentences in each paragraph
C. Make up questions to answer

CHAPTER 10 Information Search

> In their search for information, students may find opportunities to practice a variety of reading strategies.

Overview

Information search, the second step in the content reading lesson, is closely tied to the comprehension process. How people *learn* bears heavily on how and what to teach them; what comprehension *is* bears heavily on how to teach it. Comprehension is not a skill, it is not a list of skills. It is a practiced strategy of adaptation and flexibility exercised with the intent of understanding an author's message sufficiently well to satisfy the reader. The information search step of the reading lesson provides an excellent environment in which students may develop adaptiveness and flexibility under guidance and direction of the teacher.

Study guides are often useful in providing students with needed guidance and direction, though discretion must be exercised in their use. A study guide should be employed where (1) students perceive its worth as a help to them in understanding what they are studying; and (2) the guide has the potential to develop students' sophistication in comprehension of similar material.

Several types of guides suggest themselves on this basis. The three-level guide leads the reader to see comprehension as both a process and an outcome, varying in sophistication which begins with a literal understanding of the author's message. The organizational guide leads the reader to see the pattern of thought and logic of the author and to use the same in an attempt

152

to understand. Concept guides are based on the idea that people remember what they can "chunk," or associate conceptually by categorizing within a cognitive structure.

What It Was Was . . .

Remember that football game we spoke of awhile back? What we said about it was that the object of the game is to move the ball and we drew an analogy between that and reading. Now, let's carry it one step further.

If we were to try to coach someone in how to play football, what would we need to know and how would we find it out? Offhand, several possibilities come to mind. We might view films of some of the great teams to analyze the way they work. We might talk to some football players, asking them how they play their position. We might play in a sandlot tag game at a picnic to get the feel of the game. But notice this: Football is a game understood only by an examination of the process of play. To know how to coach it, we would need to look closely at how it is done. Certainly, there are rules of football and strategies to consider, but they really only generally describe the play. They do not define it. Football is defined by its object, and knowing all the rules of football won't tell you how to move the ball or how to score points.

An almost precisely similar case can be made for the teaching of reading. And, as you will see, the content area classroom is the best place to teach reading, since the need to read is greatest there.

Consider this: What we know about reading is that its object is comprehension, and to teach people to accomplish the object, we must first look closely at what good readers do. It's like watching a great football player, a Jim Brown or a Gayle Sayers. By observing what they do, we can make conjectures about how they do it, about the way they do it. When we looked at Liz, Ron, Karen, and Mary, we asked ourselves what it was they accomplished when they read. Then we tried to make some qualitative judgments about their success in comprehending. Now, we want to look at what they actually seem to be doing as they try to accomplish the object of reading.

For example, the most important thing we know about how good readers read is that they read for different purposes. They seem hardly aware that they are constantly switching strategies. What's more, those purposes and strategies are highly individual and situational. And the essence of the strategies is not to be defined by a simplistic list of skills (reads for detail, reads for main idea, etc.) or by directives (skim, survey, etc.). Mature reading is best characterized by adaptiveness and flexibility, not by knowing the rules of reading. It is, among other things, a *creative* activity like any "languaging" behavior; it develops through practice and out of need.

In teaching reading, one must create situations in which maturing readers have a chance to explore and use appropriate strategies to suit different

153

purposes. In content areas, this means using different sources dealing with a similar topic rather than relying on the same book for all students. This is part of the reasoning behind units of study as a motif for content area instruction.

What other characteristics can we observe in the behavior of a good reader? For one thing, the good reader seems to sort material by what it says and what it means. He or she reads for meaning. Often the reader will say, "The author said _____, and by that I take him to mean _____." Or, "For *me*, the poet is saying _____." In both cases, the reader is reading beyond the literal message of the author. Robert Frost said, "Poetry is saying one thing in terms of another." The good reader knows that Frost did not mean *only* poetry.

Olive Niles, a luminary in the field of reading for many years, once said she thought there were three things that would distinguish the good reader. These were: the reader makes full use of previous understanding of the topic, reads with a definite purpose in mind, and, most importantly, looks for "various kinds of thought relationships which exist in reading materials" and uses these as an aid to understanding.

Yet another thing the mature reader will say he or she does is to process information by trying to understand and remember it in large chunks. Remembering a lot of detail is very cumbersome for most readers. What good readers try to do is to make groupings and associations based on concepts they are building. They deliberately sacrifice many details in the interest of deeper meanings.

In all of these strategies and behaviors, the student in the content area classroom can be helped. In giving that help, the teacher will be assisting the student in understanding what is being read and how to read better. The teacher does this when he or she identifies and provides strategies that facilitate the students' learning as they seek information in their reading. This is, in fact, the teacher's role in the second step of the content reading lesson, the step that we have called information search.

Before moving on, we feel compelled to repeat a particular point. What we have just done is to "diagnose" the reading act, examining the *general* behavior of good readers to determine what they do when they read. To teach reading, then, becomes a matter of creating an environment in which they have opportunities to practice good reading habits. But realize that *this step can be taken only when you know something about the specific reading behavior of your students*. Think again of the football coach. To teach football, he needs to know what good football players generally do and what his players specifically need to learn to do. He can know that only by looking at their specific behavior. Remember our earlier quote from Frank Smith's "Twelve Easy Ways to Make Learning to Read Difficult, and One Difficult Way to Make It Easy." The one way to make it easy is *"Respond to what the child is trying to do."* Let us now extend the quote, if we may:

Children learn to read only by reading. Therefore the only way to facilitate their learning to read is to make reading easy for them. This means continuously making critical and insightful decisions—not forcing a child to read for words when he is, or should be, reading for meaning; not forcing him to slow down when he should speed up; not requiring caution when he should be taking chances; not worrying about speech when the topic is reading; not discouraging errors . . .[1]

Now, how can we do that?

Guiding the Search

This is the familiar scene. We have a group of students. They have something to read, and a reason to read it. If the material is close enough to their grasp, if what they have to read is approximately suitable, the reading will provide the practice that will make them better readers. What we need to consider are the specific ways in which we *can* respond to what the readers are trying to do. In other words, we need specific ways to provide the help students need in accomplishing the object of reading. One way to help students as they seek to comprehend is through study guides, a reasonable alternative to textbook-accompanied worksheets. Study guides were introduced by Harold Herber (1970; 1978) as a viable activity to increase comprehension. Richard Vacca (1981) has extended Herber's pioneer efforts.

We will introduce three kinds of study guides which may be of value to students in different circumstances. We should emphasize, however, that what we are presenting are ideas, not prescriptions. The effective use of study guides in a classroom requires their creative adaptation to particular settings. Furthermore, study guides can be gratefully appreciated or resentfully rejected by students. Like Longfellow's child, when they are good, they are very, very good, but when they are bad, they are horrid. We therefore introduce study guides with the following cautions:

1. Study guides should not be used with every reading selection required of students. They should be reserved for reading selections that warrant careful reading and with students who need the special help a guide can offer.
2. Study guides should provide help in understanding specific content and should give direction in the application of appropriate reading strategies.

[1] F. Smith, 1973, p. 195

155

3. Format variety is essential. Don't let boredom with the procedure interfere with quality of the product.
4. Study guides must not be graded. To do so is to make tests of them when their purpose is to teach. They should, however, be checked and discussed with individual students when possible.
5. Study guides do not "run themselves." Certainly students may use them with relative independence, but guides work best when students share them in groups and are familiar with the way study guides work. Students feel better about study guides when teachers are available for help when needed.

Three-Level Study Guides

Among the characteristics of a good reader is the ability to go beyond what an author explicitly says to determine what was meant and how the message can be more generally applied. When diagnosing the quality of a reader's comprehension, a basic consideration is how well the reader can go beyond the explicit message to the inferential and applicative levels of understanding. Remember Liz, Ron, *et al.*? When guiding a student's search for information, teachers can use a three-level study guide to call the reader's attention to higher levels of meaning within a selection. At the same time, exposure to these guides will help a student explore the processes through which he or she can understand the same thing in different ways.

The three-level guide was conceived by Harold Herber (1970; 1978). He bases the idea upon a hierarchical relationship among what he has defined as the literal, the interpretive, and the applied levels of comprehension. That is, a certain degree of success with the literal level would seem requisite to interpretation, and likewise success at the interpretive level is requisite to application. For example, almost any literate person can know what the authors of the Constitution said simply by reading the document. What the authors meant, however, let alone how it applies in a given instance, requires a comprehension eluding most people. The Supreme Court sits in judgment of exactly such questions: What does it mean? How does it apply? By providing students with three-level study guides and helping them work through them, a teacher can lead students to seek higher levels of meaning. While their attempts may not always be successful, readers are never successful without the search. Remember how turtles make progress: by sticking their necks out. Only by seeking can answers be found.

As an illustration of the three-level guide, work through the one which follows and, if possible, compare your responses to those of one or more other persons. By the differences in response to such a simple story, you may see that reading is quite a creative process!

LITTLE RED RIDING HOOD[2]

Level 1 — What did the author say? (*check two*)

_____ a. Red Riding Hood met a wolf in the woods.

_____ b. Red Riding Hood visited her aunt.

_____ c. Red Riding Hood recognized the wolf immediately upon entering Grandmother's house.

_____ d. The woodsman killed the wolf.

Level 2 — What did the author mean? (*check two*)

_____ a. The wolf only wanted the goodies meant for Grandmother.

_____ b. The wolf appeared a lot like Red Riding Hood's grandmother.

_____ c. Red Riding Hood was a naïve little girl.

_____ d. Red Riding Hood was a trusting little girl.

Level 3 — How can we use the meaning?

_____ a. Don't walk in the woods alone.

_____ b. Don't speak to strangers.

_____ c. Look more carefully at sick grandmothers.

_____ d. All's well that ends well.

_____ e. Don't send a little girl to a nurse's job.

This particular study guide is much more structured than most designed for classroom use. However, it does illustrate the kinds of thinking the three-level guide may stimulate. An important feature of the guide is that the higher the level of reaction, the more individual may be the responses. That is, at level 1, reactions are limited since either the author said what is indicated or did not say, and the question is easily resolved. At level 2, however, the reader is required to think a little harder in making judgments and at level 3, there are virtually no limits to the applications that could be argued. The *use* of what an author said and meant is highly individual and students' reactions at this level are often exciting and creative.

Notice also that where statements in the guide are inconsistent with the story, it is for good reason. For example, it is *not* true that Red Riding Hood recognized the wolf immediately upon entering grandmother's house. In fact,

[2]Thanks to John Childrey of Florida Atlantic University for sharing this one with us.

her failure to do so is one of the problems on which the plot of the story turns. The same can be said at level 2. Note that the inference that the wolf only wanted the goodies is contrary to the intrigue and danger of the story. As any child could tell, Red Riding Hood is in big trouble and more than her goodies are in peril. It is precisely such judgment that is critical to inferential reading of any selection, whether it be a children's story or a treatise on a philosophical topic or scientific inquiry.

The idea of a study guide based on "levels" of comprehension is presented by Harold L. Herber in his *Teaching Reading in Content Areas* (1978) to which the reader is referred for a fuller description and many excellent examples. One of Herber's ideas is that the levels operate interdependently, that the applied level operates in relation to the product of the interpretive and literal levels, and that the interpretive level operates in relation to the product of the literal level. Furthermore, Herber suggests that greater sophistication is required of the reader at succeeding levels and that differentiation for varied ability levels may properly be made by requiring each student to respond only at the level(s) commensurate with his or her ability.

In our own experience, differentiation of instruction is more successfully accomplished by variation in material used than by variation in understanding expected. In other words, better a student be given material he or she can read fully (at all levels) than that the student be restricted by the material to lower levels of response. Recall the basis we take for organizing units of instruction: that all students come to different but individually better understandings of the same concepts through study in different materials and activities. Thus, with every student working in material that is appropriate to his or her needs and abilities, all individuals are allowed an opportunity to respond at equally sophisticated "levels."

The disparity of ideas we are exploring here leads us to a rule of thumb for the use of guide material. *Use study guides as aids to carry students' understanding to as high a level as the nature of the material and the ability of the students will allow.*

Steps in Constructing the Three-Level Guide

The construction of any study guide requires careful analysis of (1) the selection to be read; (2) the purposes of the lesson in which it is included; and (3) the needs of the students relative to that purpose. Construction of a three-level guide often begins at level 3. This is necessary where the underlying reasons for teaching the selection relate to the "transfer effect" the selection may have. The guide should build toward this transfer of learning, the application of new understandings to other settings. Thus, as the *first step*, you would consider possible generalizations of the basic ideas of the selection.

For example, a social studies teacher may be teaching a unit on *Practice and Principles of Democracy,* part of which includes the study of suffrage. The general application of the concept of suffrage leads into participatory government, equal rights of minorities, responsibilities of citizenship. Level 3 of a guide to comprehension of a selection on suffrage might focus on ideas of this type. By initiating his or her own thinking at the most general level, the teacher creates a mind set which tends to focus thinking at other levels on ideas that lead in the right direction, i.e., toward reasonable transfer and application of ideas.

The construction of a three-level guide moves from the general to the specific. This is necessary because the importance of a specific idea is derived from its relationship to a more general idea. Detail, or what the author said, will be judged important in terms of the inference it can generate, or in terms of what the author meant. Thus, when the purpose of the lesson is to foster an ability to generalize, the *second step* in constructing a three-level guide is to devise level 2. Think of level 2 as comprised of the possible inferences which might be drawn from what the author said. Include inferences that lead directly from the literal level to applications. In other words, allow inferences to stem from what the author said, but think simultaneously in terms of level 3, the application level.

Referring again to the example of the social studies selection on suffrage, perhaps the author has said much about suffrage for various groups—landowners, freemen, blacks, women, teenagers, other groups. What the author has *said* is that these groups gained suffrage at various stages of our history. What he or she might have *meant* to imply could be that "suffrage is earned, not given," or "people's right to vote is an inalienable right," or "those who can vote, should vote." Such inferences lead to *applications*— "persons' rights often must be fought for," or "participatory government requires participation of the governed," or "civil rights, like muscles, require exercise for their maintenance." Inferences that bridge the way from the literal to the applied levels are the ones you should include in a guide.

Part of the purpose of a guide is to help the student "tie things together," to see relationships of ideas within and without the context of what is being read. This interrelatedness of the levels of the three-level guide is critical to proper understanding.

The *third step* in constructing this kind of guide is to examine what the author said and to select only those details that are essential to making the inferences included in level 2 of the guide. Detail is important primarily as the foundation of inference. Part of many students' reading problem stems from an inability to sense the relative importance of general ideas and specific detail. Naïve readers lack the ability to separate the chaff from the grain, the important from the irrelevant, in the face of the incredible detail of many textbooks.

Often as not, it will be necessary to vary the procedures we have outlined for three-level guide construction. The primary reason for teaching a particular selection may be to lead the student to "see" the author's implications. In such cases, the focus of concern will be on level 2, the inferential level of comprehension, and so construction of the guide would begin there. That is, you would begin your thinking with this level and balance the other levels on it.

Take a look at the guide on cigarette smoking, for example.[3] What the teacher intended was to get the students to realize what the data on smoking are telling us, beyond mere facts and figures. You might think at first that the applicative level (level 3) was most important in this guide, especially where the interest was in getting high school pupils to take action about their own habits. On second thought, though, we know that no one just *quits*. People only quit smoking when something about the *meaning* of smoking finally overcomes their desire to smoke. Because the force of the article on which this guide is based is in the inferences which can be drawn from it, its construction would center on level 2.

We have found it convenient here to discuss the steps of construction of a three-level study guide in a one-two-three fashion. Actually, we do *not* mean to imply that one completes construction of one level, then moves to another and another. In practice, you will probably find yourself working on all parts at once in constructing a guide. Our point is that the product of your work will be best if your thoughts carry you, in general, from either level 3 or level 2, depending on your major purpose in the lesson. But, for example, you will often find that what you perceived to be a reasonable line of thought (in level 2 or 3) is not adequately supported by the facts (level 1). So you switch tactics midstream. Likewise, as you examine the literal level of the selection, you may be led to applications and inferences you hadn't before considered. So what you must do is to work back and forth between and among levels of comprehension, searching for a clear and precise guide which will lead students to understandings and thought processes which they can eventually take as their own.

"100,000 DOCTORS HAVE QUIT SMOKING CIGARETTES"

I. Answer these:
   1. How does smoking one cigarette affect these body functions:
      a. circulation
      b. respiration
      c. temperature
   2. How do death rates and morbidity rates relate to smokers?
   3. How many doctors have quit smoking?
   4. Is the damage done to the body by smoking reversible? How?

---

[3]Thanks to Juanita Hutton, health and physical education teacher at Sahuaro High School, Tucson, Arizona, for permission to use this guide as an example.

II. Explain why you agree or disagree with each of the following:
1. Smoking is directly related to lung cancer.
2. There are more heart attack victims among smokers than non-smokers.
3. The more cigarettes smoked per day, the higher the death rate.
4. Cigarette smoking is an expensive habit.
5. There is no excuse or reason for smoking.
6. Smoking is a detriment to the quality of the smoker's life.

III. You may find it interesting to answer the following questions:
1. Does your family doctor smoke?
2. Does anyone in your family smoke?
3. How many of your teachers smoke?
4. Why do you smoke (or not smoke)?

We hope you realize that study guides are intended to provoke thought and thinking. In Chapter 16 (p. 274), we include a three-level guide by Julie Stockwell for Act Two of *Macbeth*. That guide exemplifies the basic form for this type of study guide. Examine, too, Mark Emshwiller's three-level guide on biological compounds (pp. 309–310). By having students think initially about applications, Mark guides students from somewhat familiar generalizations to eventual consideration of important specific, factual information. Thus, study guides can take various forms and be modified for varied purposes as these several examples indicate.

One final comment about this kind of study guide. The question often arises of how guides can be used without unduly limiting students' thinking. The paradox is one of how to stimulate thinking without telling people what to think: How can we teach but not tell, instruct but not indoctrinate? At the risk of oversimplifying an answer, we would say that guides should be as structured as necessary to stimulate thinking. As their familiarity with the procedure increases, students will adopt the process, will gradually stop looking for "right" answers, and will start thinking much more creatively. As this happens, loosen the structure of the guide. Let students have more freedom for open-ended response, at the application level at first but at all levels later. What you will see is that students themselves can write guides, can use the procedure, for example, as a notetaking system, as a motif rather than a model of thinking. When that happens, the guides will have served their ultimate purpose, to habituate in students the process of comprehension they originally sought to stimulate.

Pattern Guides

Often it is true that the manner in which a reading selection is organized is its most salient and useful characteristic. That is, where a reading selection has been written in a clearly discernible pattern, that pattern may help the reader understand in the same way it helped the writer compose. For the pattern to help, however, the reader will require, first, a knowledge that organization exists in composition and, second, practice in utilizing the organizational pattern of the text to good advantage.

There are several thought relationships an author may use. Most commonly, these are comparison-contrast, cause-effect, sequence (chronology), and simple listing. Also possible are other patterns such as categorization and taxonomy, logical argument (induction and deduction), general idea/specific detail and spatial arrangement. In fact, any form which a writer might employ could be included under the idea of "patterns of organization." What the good writer tries to express by the form chosen is the relationships among the ideas expressed. These relationships are as valuable to the reader as to the writer.

Let's consider now four ways in which students can come to know patterns of organization. Following this, we will offer suggestions for practice in using the patterns in reading.

First, perhaps the best way to teach what organizational patterns *are* is to show pupils various examples taken from their textbooks. Texts generally do have an overriding pattern in their organization, but within that will be embedded various other patterns used by the author to organize "single sentences, . . . paragraphs, . . . selections of various length," to use again the words of Olive Niles. Often these patterns are evident in the author's use of "signal" words which you can call to students' attention. For example, where an author is setting up a contrast, he or she will often use the conjunction *but*. A comparison calls for the conjunction *and*. A simple list may use the terms *first, second, third,* or *first, then, last.* Similar terms are used when an author has begun with a main idea and is listing supporting details. A cause/effect pattern will often be cued by terms like *because, as a result, if/then,* and *consequently.* Temporal organization is commonly distinguished by such terms as *after, before, by, within, since, until,* and *finally.* Students need help in seeing these terms and in using them as an aid to comprehension. Providing that help is often a matter of scanning the text with the students, searching for "organization words" which might be used in reading.

Second, with regard to teaching, it is almost always helpful, even necessary, to "walk" students through the process of inspecting what they are about to read as an assignment, somewhat in the vein of a prereading anticipation activity. As students perceive the logic of the organization of their book, chapters within that book, and key sections within those chapters, students' understanding of organizational patterns is facilitated and their reading ability enhanced. As students begin to read any assignment, it would be helpful for them to answer two questions about the selection, "What is the structure of the selection?" and "What are its parts?"

A third technique of teaching patterns of organization is to have pupils look for examples of various patterns in newspapers, magazines, and other sources they may find. One teacher's idea was an attractive bulletin board, entitled "How Do You Say?" and containing examples of different organizational schemes of sentences, paragraphs, and short selections. The examples were supplied by the students. It is also possible to construct games for learning centers on organizational patterns, where students compete in time and accuracy of categorizing examples of patterns.

From time to time almost all content teachers require writing assignments of their students. These may be short essays, term papers, observational records, extended answer exams, and so forth. When it is required, instruction in composition provides one of the best possible opportunities for teaching logical organization. Writing and reading are in some ways mirror images of one another. Organized writing is generally good writing, mainly because it is easy to follow and comprehend. But when you read a composition written by a student, what are you looking for and what have you done to help that student write? Anyone who makes writing assignments should at the very least remind and explain to students that he or she expects an introduction, a body, and a conclusion. Surprising as it may seem to some, however, the skills involved in outlining, arranging ideas before writing, revising before final copy, in short, the rudiments of composition are not the strict domain of English classes. They are a part of "languaging" and instruction in them is imperative wherever they are required. The pity is that so many opportunities for teaching writing and reading simultaneously are ignored! Our fourth and final suggestion of how to make pupils aware of organizational patterns is to give them help in organizing their own writing. Help them use organization words themselves, to organize from topic sentences, to arrange details in logical fashion, to "clinch" their ideas with a snappy ending. The result could easily be better writing and reading for everyone concerned.

When students have at least a basic understanding of organizational patterns, study guide material which guides practice in using the patterns in reading will be useful. (Following ideas from Olive Niles and others, Harold Herber originally conceptualized guides for organizational patterns. Reference is again made to Herber's books as a source of further explanation and examples.) The pattern guide might be no more than a skeleton outline listing main ideas under which the students fill in detail. Other pattern guides might list causes and have pupils fill in effects, or list both causes and effects and have pupils match them as they read. List one half of various comparisons or contrasts, let students fill in the other halves.

In Chapter 16 (pp. 295–296) we have included a pattern study guide developed by Noreen Wang for a geometry unit. In that example, she sought to guide students to a better understanding of how to prove a proof that is written as a sentence. Using that example and the ones that follow here, with help from the suggested steps listed below, you may wish to try your hand at constructing a pattern guide to accompany a textbook selection you are using.

Steps in Constructing the Pattern Guide

The *first step* in constructing this guide, as any, is to carefully analyze the purpose of the lesson and the nature of the reading selection. Look for the overriding logic the author has chosen. Underline key words the author has used, if any. If you can classify the organization of the material, you may proceed to construct a guide based on that pattern. Not all writing yields easily to such analysis, however, TAKE CARE: use patterns guides only for material in which a clear organizational pattern exists.

The *second step,* once the pattern has been identified, is to look for key statements that reflect that pattern. At times, these key statements will have to be created from inference since they may be implied rather than stated. For example, consider this passage from Grace Halsell[4] in which she sets up a comparison between the way of life of modern man and that of the American Indian:

> You sleep on dirt floors, on sheepskins. When you wake up, you don't need to get dressed, because you have slept in your clothes. There are no windows in the hogan; it's dark as a dungeon. (*Excerpted from an address by Grace Halsell, reprinted in the* Washington Post, July 29, 1975.)

The comparison/contrast pattern in this paragraph is implied. When *you* awoke this morning, you were probably in a bed covered with soft sheets. You got dressed, having slept in night clothes. And so forth, the comparisons and contrasts are implied.

Within the same selection, however, other comparisons may be stated directly. Examine the comparison in the following passage, from the same source:

> We've been taught the work ethic; we've been taught to want the good things in life, as we define them: good salary, good house, good car, a good carpet on the floor. None of us really wants to go back to sleeping on dirt floors.
> But the Indian, if he remains Indian, is tied to the land, which he calls his Mother Earth. He never attempts to conquer nature, but to live in harmony with it. He wishes to be like a fish in the sea, a bird on the wing: to pass by without leaving a trace of his existence. *Being,* not achieving, is important. (Grace Halsell, *ibid.*)

Now, examine part of a simple study guide for this selection. Grace Halsell's intent is to help the reader see how the life of the Indian is different from the life of the modern person. The guide will be set up to help in this.

---

[4]Grace Halsell is author of *Bessie Yellowhair,* an account of life among the Navajos. Social studies teachers would find this sensitive book an excellent source in a unit on American Indians.

LIVING AS A NAVAJO

Directions The selection entitled "Living as a Navajo" on p. 164 contrasts the lifestyle of Bessie Yellowhair with the lifestyle we have. Listed below in *Column A* are things that apply to our life. Read these. Then read the selection and beside each item in *Column A*, list in *Column B* a contrasting aspect of Navajo life. Number 1 is done for you.

Column A	*Column B*
1. We sleep on beds.	Navajos sleep on dirt floors.
2. We wake up in light.	
3. Achieving is important.	
4. We want a good salary, house, car, etc.	
5. Etc.	

In the example, we have completed the *third step* in constructing a pattern guide. This step is to construct the guide in a way that reflects as clearly as possible the pattern you hope students will see. The best rule here is not to assume too much; give students all the help they may need. The pattern guide can be as simple or as complex as the nature of the selection, purpose of the teacher, or needs of the student may demand. The guide we began here, for example, gives the implied half of comparisons, asks for the stated half. More thinking would be demanded (and more creativity) if the opposite were true. A third or fourth column might be added which would set up a structure for syntopical reading with reference to previously studied cultures. Still more creativity and skill might thus be required. How much to demand and how much to assist with a guide is impossible to decide outside the context of a given situation. As you construct guides, however, attempt to make them as challenging as possible and as helpful as need be in reference to the abilities and needs of the pupils who will use them.

There is one more example we'd like to share with you before moving on to a third kind of guide. In some materials, the pattern of organization of material is absolutely critical to comprehension. This would call for extraordinary care in understanding the pattern, as many a home economics teacher knows.[5]

[5]Reprinted from *Improving Reading in Every Class, a Sourcebook for Teachers, Second Edition*, by Ellen Lamar Thomas and H. Alan Robinson. Copyright 1977 by Allyn and Bacon, Inc.

165

READING RECIPES

If the oven is to be used, locate temperature required.

Think ahead! And at the appropriate time preheat your oven. Light your oven before assembling your ingredients. It will take about 10 minutes for it to reach the temperature desired.

<u>PART I MATERIALS</u>

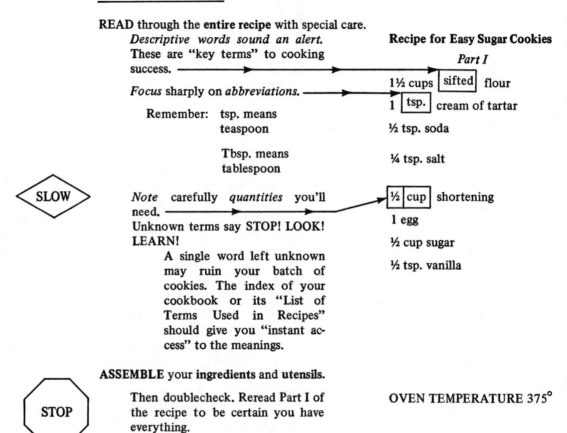

READ through the **entire recipe** with special care.

Descriptive words sound an alert. These are "key terms" to cooking success. ───────────►

Focus sharply on *abbreviations.* ────►

Remember: tsp. means
teaspoon

Tbsp. means
tablespoon

Recipe for Easy Sugar Cookies

Part I

1½ cups sifted flour

1 tsp. cream of tartar

½ tsp. soda

¼ tsp. salt

SLOW

Note carefully *quantities* you'll need. ───────────►
Unknown terms say STOP! LOOK! LEARN!

A single word left unknown may ruin your batch of cookies. The index of your cookbook or its "List of Terms Used in Recipes" should give you "instant access" to the meanings.

½ cup shortening

1 egg

½ cup sugar

½ tsp. vanilla

STOP

ASSEMBLE your **ingredients** and **utensils.**

Then doublecheck. Reread Part I of the recipe to be certain you have everything.

OVEN TEMPERATURE 375°

<u>PART II METHOD</u>

Carry out all the steps one by one in the **order given.**

Notice that the ingredients are conveniently listed in the order in which you'll use them.

Watch for special *action words,* for example:

Sift	Beat
Cut in	Mix

and perform the technique called for. Remember that specific words are used for a purpose. Though some words may *seem* to differ only slightly, there is a *decided* difference in the action called for and a world of difference in the way your cookies may turn out!

Focus on *descriptive words.*
"Zero in" on *amounts, timings, temperature.*

Quantitative directions are "danger spots"

Carry out each step **with great care!** For example, add the egg mixture to the flour, **not** the flour to the egg mixture.

Reread as often as necessary.

A single error in any step may make your cookies not a delight but a disaster.

Then *time* precisely.

Note the description of the finished product.

Part II

1. Sift together flour, cream of tartar, soda, and salt

2. Cut in shortening until like fine crumbs

3. Beat egg with sugar and vanilla.

4. Add egg mixture to flour mixture and mix well. Dampen hands with water and roll into balls the size of walnuts.

5. Place balls 1½ inches apart on an ungreased cookie sheet.

6. Flatten first cookie with bottom of dampened glass tumbler.

7. Dip tumbler into the sugar and then press all the cookies.

8. Bake in a moderate oven 375° until pale brown, about 6-10 minutes

---

TAKE TIME for Precision Reading!

SAVE TIME When things Go Right!

Concept Guides

Concept guides are a third type of guide that often stimulate students' understanding. These guides are based on the proposition that for learning to occur, one must first be aware of an idea and then associate it with something already known. In other words, concept guides are based on a theory that learning is a two-step process. First, the learner becomes aware of an idea. The trigger step in successful learning is cognitive awareness. Second, the learner must categorize awareness by relating it to previous experiences or ideas. That is, once awareness is achieved, learning occurs when the idea is associated with something familiar through a categorization process. In that way, the learner places the new idea into cognitive perspective. Thus, stimulated by concept guides, learning occurs in somewhat the following way:

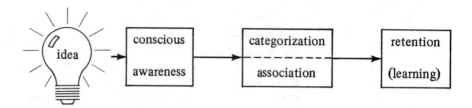

The theory behind concept guides is related to a psychological process called "chunking." Derived from information theory, "chunking" is presumed to be what the human brain does to compensate for limitations in processing and storing bits of information. Consider this example. Say the following numbers aloud, one at a time: 194114921215. Repeat them several times, so that you might remember them two days from now. You will likely find, however, that it will be almost impossible for you to remember them in two days unless you saw that there are only three, not twelve, things to remember; the dates of Pearl Harbor (1941), Columbus' discovery (1492), and the Magna Carta (1215), all of which you probably know or could likely remember. What you would do with this information is to "chunk" the twelve numerals into three dates.

To retain information, then, a learner "groups the input events, applies a new name to the group, and then remembers the new name rather than the original input events" (Miller, 1967, p. 38). Ausubel (1968) has defined chunking as the "process of rearranging the stimulus input into a more efficiently organized 'sequence of chunks' " (p. 59). Thus, the concept guide is designed to make the learner consciously aware of discrete bits of information and then help chunk the facts, inferences, and ideas into more meaningful conceptual units through categorization and association. It is awareness that triggers learning; it is association that synthesizes it.

This theory of learning seems to hold true for much more complicated information than the list of numbers we used in the preceding example. People remember what they can associate into higher order categories. Students in a social studies class, for example, might find it easier to remember the conflicts between the North and South leading to the Civil War if (1) they studied characteristics of the North and of the South, and then (2) were guided in categorizing the information in terms of similarities and differences between the two cultures. Thus, they would be more likely to conceptualize the idea of conflicting ideologies as they chunked the bits of information about each.

Similarly, in teaching a unit on the parts of the body, a biology teacher would be particularly concerned that students understood the relationship of the various parts to one another and to the roles each play in the process of

168

living. By constructing a concept guide, these understandings can be fostered. For example, the first part of such a guide might be concerned with identifying the proper terms relative to their specific job. Thus, the first part of the guide might look like this:

PARTS OF THE HUMAN BODY

Concept Guide

I. As you read the assigned pages, fill in the right word from choices below.

1. The _____ controls reactions of all parts of a human body.

2. The _____ surrounds the pupil of the eye.

3. The _____ is a part of the brain.

4. An _____ pumps away from the heart.

5. The _____ is a bone located in the leg.

6. The end of the nose is composed of _____.

7. The _____ is a large muscle inside the mouth.

8. _____ protect the eye.

9. _____ protects the lungs.

10. The entire human body is a mass of _____.

1. artery	9. cartilage
2. tongue	10. bone
3. iris	11. femur
4. vein	12. eyelashes
5. muscle	13. pupil
6. cells	14. ribcage
7. cerebrum	15. skin
8. brain	16. cells

Having provided the students with a conscious awareness of the key "bits of information" in the selection, the next step might be to help them relate these "bits" to the higher order concepts of internal and external parts of the body. Thus, a second part of a concept guide might be:

II–B: Group each of the body parts which you used to fill in the blanks in Part I under one of the two categories below:

Internal Parts	External Parts

This will enable the students to associate the specific parts of the body to one another and to begin to associate each with their respective roles in the total process of living.

To extend the students' learning to the specific functions to which each body part is related, a third part of the guide could be designed.

II–C: Write each of the ten body parts under one or more of the following senses with which they are associated.

Sight	Touch	Taste	Hearing	Smell

Steps in Constructing Concept Guides

Construction of a concept guide follows the same process inherent in the learning theory that it represents, except the construction process is the reverse of the theory. Briefly, the construction steps are:

1. Analyze the reading passage to determine the major concepts the students should acquire. List each in a word or phrase.
2. Reread the passage and select statements that underlie the major concepts chosen for emphasis.
3. Arrange the guide so that the statements from the selection become Part I of the guide and the categorization component becomes Part II.

The first step in constructing a concept guide is to analyze the selection *and* your purpose for having students read it. Determine the major concepts you want the students to learn. (Your unit objectives should provide some guidance in this determination.) List each concept in a word or, at most, a phrase. This will form Part II of the concept guide, the higher order categories under which informational bits may be organized and associated. The number of such categories should be limited, as the purpose is to facilitate learning, not tax it.

When the major concepts overriding the information in the selection have been determined, the second step in constructing this kind of guide is to reread the passage so that you can select (or reword) statements from it that underlie those concepts you want to highlight. Those statements you choose to use must be directly related to the concepts on which the selection focuses.

The statements from the selection form Part I of the guide; the categories, or overriding concepts, form Part II. In format, they occur as headings for columns. The first two steps completed, there remains only to arrange the guide's physical format. As the third step, then, place the information generated in step two (notice: *step two*, not Part II) in a format similar to the format used in level I or level II of a three-level guide. Insertion of distractors is sometimes advisable, but the distractors should be deliberately worded to be in error for good reason. When using true-false items in Part I of a concept guide, students can be asked to reword false statements to make them true, thus avoiding the danger of students' remembering a distractor as truth.

Now, consider the following example of a concept guide based on the novel *A Patch of Blue*. The teacher chose prejudice, love, intolerance, sincerity, and fear as the concepts the students might acquire. The quotations in Part I were then chosen because they, or part of them, would lead to an understanding of the concepts. A reminder: The form of activity in Part I is limited only by the imagination of the teacher, but care must be taken to make the activity accurately reflect the content of the reading selection. In the example here, italicized portions of the quotations were used as the basis for transferring items to the concepts in Part II. Often the whole item would be used. In completed form, a concept guide derived from *A Patch of Blue* might look like what follows. (You might want to work through it yourself, if you've read the book or seen the movie.)

A PATCH OF BLUE

Concept Guide

Part I   In the space provided, identify the speaker. For the moment, disregard the italicized portions of each quotation; they will be used later. You will probably not remember who said these particular words directly, but thinking about what is said should help you determine the speaker.

_____ 1. *"I wear them* (dark glasses) so I will not have to *show people my true feelings."*

_____ 2. "Without *tolerance* there can be *no friendship."*

_____ 3. "I can *never be like you."*

_____ 4. *"I got to come home and clean up* after the *biggest slut of all."*

_____ 5. "You are not only beautiful, you are *brave and beautiful.* I never saw a braver one than a *blind girl sitting under an oak tree in a park."*

_____ 6. "You are my *much sinned against baby."*

_____ 7. "Leave Sleena be. You *God damned nigger."*

_____ 8. *"Pearl,* I love you, Pearl."

_____ 9. *"Niggers is black.* You want to have a *black friend?"*

_____ 10. "It was crazy to be *out of the room."*

Part II   Below you will find five terms related to this novel. Take each of the italicized words or phrases from Part I and write them under the term(s) to which they apply. Be prepared to justify your choices.

Prejudice   Love   Intolerance   Sincerity   Fear

Once a concept guide is designed, how might it be used? First, have the students respond by:

1. Identifying the correct responses to the items in Part I (in this case by identifying the speakers).
2. Categorizing the statements or parts of statements from Part I under the proper concept(s) in Part II.

Second, provide the students with feedback. This may be accomplished in teacher-led discussions with the entire class and/or in student-directed, small group discussions. The students should be encouraged to express their own ideas and to support their opinions with references to the text wherever possible. They should also be urged to explain their responses to the guide.

Another example of a concept guide may help to illustrate its flexibility and possible extensions. In this case smaller bits of information, vocabulary, serve as the initial activity and the interrelationship of characters and concepts serve to extend the thinking process. This guide is divided into three parts, but each is based on the dual concept of cognitive awareness and association. (You may also wish to work through this one if you've read the novel.)

THE OUTSIDERS

Concept Guide

Part I From the list of words below, choose the one that best fits the definitions given.

conscientious	vulnerable	lonely
tolerant	bitter	empathetic
sensitive	understanding	responsible
straightforward	naïve	prejudiced
charming	amicable	haughty

_____ 1. responding or feeling acutely

_____ 2. standing apart from others; being isolated

_____ 3. attractive; fascinating; delightful

_____ 4. involves knowing right from wrong

_____ 5. sympathetic awareness

_____ 6. a fixed notion or conception based on prior experiences

_____ 7. direct; honest; open

_____ 8. easily hurt

_____ 9. ability to share another's feelings or emotions

_____ 10. readily assuming obligations; dependable

_____ 11. feeling and acting superior

_____ 12. friendly

_____ 13. not suspicious; foolishly simple; childlike

_____ 14. being free from bigotry or prejudice

_____ 15. a strong feeling of hatred, resentment, cynicism

Part II "If the shoe fits . . ." If the words in the left column apply to the characters below, put a check in the proper box. Be prepared to justify your answers.

	Pony	Soda	Darry	Johnny	Dallas	Randy	Cherry
conscientious							
vulnerable							
lonely							
tolerant							
bitter							
etc.							

Part III   Below you will find several major concepts which were included in *The Outsiders*. List each character in the book according to the concepts with which they are associated. Be prepared to justify your choices.

> *Brotherhood   Prejudice   Sensitivity   Maturity*

A concept guide can be used whenever it will help students understand the concepts in a passage and/or will lead to an improvement of students' conceptual skills. However, to maximize the potential success of concept guides, they should never be used as tests. The students should not be threatened by being "wrong," as it is the thought process that is right, not the answers themselves. In many cases, more than one answer can be "right." The *process* must be the focal point of the feedback.

Having done all this, you are probably ready now to construct a concept guide for trial and evaluation. Pick a selection in which there are certain but limited concepts being developed by the author.

Combinations, Permutations, Adaptations

An understanding of the three different guides we have discussed is only a bare bones beginning. The true value of study guides in learning is in the creation of them to fit the specific needs within a classroom, not to force the format of any one of them to a passage. Often a selection that you want your students to read does not lend itself to the purposes or format of any one of the specific guides we have discussed. Instead, you will discover that you need to pick and choose elements of two or all three of these specific guides if you are to provide the most appropriate guidance for your students.

Once you become comfortable with each of the guides separately, you will almost certainly feel the constriction imposed by each, and you will recognize the need to become more flexible and adaptive in creating guides. When that happens, you will have reached a milestone in becoming adept at using study guides for both diagnosis and instruction. Since combination guides must evolve from direct instructional needs, we suggest that you examine the combination guide developed by Mark Emshwiller included in Chapter 16 (pp. 310–311).

As with the construction of each of the other types of study guides, we urge you to begin any construction of a combination guide with an analysis of your instructional objective and the overriding concepts in the selection. From there, the format and content of the guide should be limited only by the students' needs and your imagination. Happy permutating!

Study Guides: An Afterword

It is important for you to realize that study guides are but a part of a total lesson framework. Because it is important, we beg your indulgence with what may seem like repetition. The lesson framework we refer to includes pre-reading anticipation, information search, and reflective reaction. A study guide is neither necessarily nor sufficiently the central substance of any one of these parts. A particular danger with study guides of which you need to be aware is that they may be oversold and overused. They absolutely must be *adapted* to a set of circumstances, not *adopted* as a motif of instruction. What we have been able to present here and what you may find among the examples provided in the units included in the final section of this book will be useful as it can be modified to suit the purpose of a given setting. The guides that will work best for you are those you create, and that's why we believe that good teaching is dependent upon imagination and creativity.

TEXTBOOK QUESTIONS vs. STUDY GUIDES

Textbook Questions	*Study Guides*
1. Assume reading skill	1. Develop reading skills
2. Emphasize questions	2. Emphasize content/skills interrelationships
3. Tend to ignore individual differences	3. Can compensate for individual differences
4. Tend to test	4. Tend to facilitate learning
5. Focus on recall	5. Focus on conceptualization
6. Foster passive learning	6. Foster activity
7. Emphasize product of learning	7. Emphasize process as well as product (*how* as well as *what* was learned)

Textbook Questions	*Study Guides*
8. Promote memory	8. Promote problem-solving
9. Correct answer is the solution of differences	9. Reasoned premises and conclusions explore differences in search of understanding
10. Create dependence	10. Build independence

Textbook Questions as an Aid to Information Search

We do not intend to leave you with the impression that textbook questions are necessarily negative in effect. They are not, any more than study guides are a cure-all. It is quite possible that if the textbook being used is reasonable in terms of students' ability, then the questions at the end of a chapter or section can be of value. Their main value may be, however, in prereading anticipation. Not their answer, but the *asking of* good questions fosters comprehension. Thus, in discussion before and after reading, textbook questions can be used as guides to the germane parts of the textbook selection. If used in this way, they may act to guide students' reading in the sense of helping them see what to remember or consider most carefully.

CHAPTER 11

Reflective Reaction

> The opportunity to reflect and react to what one
> has read solidifies learning.

Overview

The purpose of reflective reaction is to allow readers to examine relationships between what they know and what they have read. People remember what they can relate; people comprehend what they can integrate into their cognitive structure. Students need to understand that reading comprehension, if by that we mean understanding what is read, does not stop with the end of the act of reading. It continues as understandings are deepened in reflection.

Small groups of students are the logical classroom entity for reflective reaction. Most groups will require some teacher participation and direction, unless the problem for which the group is constituted is very clear to group participants.

Guide material used in the information search phase of the reading process can be a good stimulus to small group reflection. Students often need and appreciate the opportunity to explain and defend their reactions to guide material while seeking to understand others' differing reactions.

Students can also locate selections of broader generality to be used as a successive organizer or develop graphic post-organizers to depict the conceptual relationship among concepts under study. Cinquains are also creative means of reflective reaction, the essence of which is summarized as,

Reflection.
Retrospective thinking
requiring cognitive reorganization,
demanding a rewarding, growing
reaction.

Memory, Comprehension, and Reflection

As the queen said to Alice, "It's a poor sort of memory that only works backwards." Those of you who are also friends of Alice and the queen, like us, will know that no one has the power of the queen to "know" the future. She, of course, could determine it in many ways. But so can readers when it comes to determining what they will learn. As the queen continued, good memories "work both ways." For the skilled learner this is certainly true. One of our recurring themes is, therefore, that what one knows determines what one can learn. That is, knowledge that can be transferred from one cognitive setting to another serves as the anchor for new knowledge. The pre-eminent concern of education should be to help students become learners, to help them develop skills and knowledge on which to base future understandings and attainments. Good learners need two-way memories.

The value of anything learned and remembered is determined by whether it (1) relates to and modifies or supplements previous understandings and (2) nurtures future learning by providing scaffolding on which memory and understanding may be built. As we have been saying all along, success in the search for relationships between what is known and what is read as new information is the major determinant of comprehension. This search, however, does not commence and cease simultaneously with the act of reading. The search begins in anticipation and continues through reflection, both of which involve tying what is being learned to what is already understood.

Comprehension is constructive. To understand, even to remember the most trivial fact, human beings must integrate what they learn into their cognitive structure. Comprehension is not to be confused with simple memory, however. Indoctrination requires only memory and belief; education requires, in addition, comprehension and understanding. Presumably, schools are in the latter business, that of education, of developing comprehension and understanding. If so, students must be given opportunities to carefully and critically construct those understandings which are appropriate to their individual cognitive needs and abilities. One of the best times for this is while one reflects and reacts to what is read or experienced.

Mature readers often seek the opportunity to reflect and react with others about what they have read or learned. Discussion and criticism of the current bestsellers is common fare of conversations among adults. People can be heard everywhere talking about news stories they have read. This need to share and discuss is ubiquitous in a literate society, and it should be in-structive to those of us who teach reading. When they are sharing, mature readers are reflecting and reacting, and are saying, in effect, "This is how it seems to me; how does it seem to you?" By comparing their reactions and reflections together, two or more people usually gain a deeper understanding than any one of them could accomplish alone. Because of its importance to them as mature readers, a major part of teaching reading to young readers should include opportunities to develop and exercise the habit of reflective reaction.

The Value of Small Group Interaction

There are several reasons for our continued recommendation of small groups as the prevalent organizational pattern for teaching subject matter and read-ing skills. In the context of reflective reaction, perhaps we should address this topic most directly. We will discuss post-reading activities in this chapter with the assumption that students will have an opportunity to discuss what they are studying. We will further assume that the setting of the discussion will be in small groups involving five to ten students only.

The primary value of the small group is that it allows differentiation of assignment by interest and ability. By teaching a class of pupils in three or four subgroups, flexibly arranged with different individuals comprising the groups at different times, it is much easier to individualize with effi-ciency. A good rule of classroom organization is to teach to the largest sub-group possible given the nature of the subject and the needs of pupils. With the variation that inevitably exists within a class of pupils, most reading as-signments will necessarily be made to subgroups of the class. Put another way, it is hardly possible that everyone in the same class will need or be able to read the same thing. Fortunately, it is not necessary that they do so, given proper classroom organization.

If discussion groups are to work well, it is recommended that the teacher exercise control over who is in the group and that he or she participate with the group. This is easiest to accomplish where individual students receive assignments in the form of a weekly log, as described in chapter 9. This places the teacher in rather direct control of group composition. Students can quickly learn a routine of gathering in a small group activity as a part of the content reading lesson. This activity commences with prereading anticipation under teacher guidance; from there proceeds to information search, done by stu-dents more or less independently; and culminates with reflective reaction, again under teacher guidance for at least part of the time.

There are some conditions under which small groups may function well without direct teacher guidance. Such groups are those formed for solution of specific problems. In a classroom setting, these problems characteristically involve such activity as investigations in science, simulation exercises in social studies, problem solving in math and related subjects, and role playing or dramatization in literature. Many other examples might come to mind, but the problems that are best solved by self-directed groups are those with the following three characteristics: (1) the problem requires multiple-step solution, where each member can offer something to the solution and no member is likely to have all the steps at his or her command; (2) every member of the group understands the problem and values the group in the sense of believing that the solution will more likely be reached by the group than by an individual; and (3) the resources for solution of the problem are readily at hand.

Whether or not under direct supervision of the teacher, small group work is usually the best setting for reflective reaction. It provides the opportunity for pooling ideas, providing the basis for new associations that one person might never come to alone.

Reflective Reaction to Study Guides

Where used as a part of the information search stage of the content reading lesson, study guides can easily serve as the stimulus for reflective reaction. For example, having completed a three-level guide, students can compare their individual responses to the guide in the setting of the small group, seeking to follow one another's reasoning through the levels of comprehension. Similarly, for other sorts of guides, students can compare and discuss their reactions in the context of reflective reaction. The teacher's purpose in this small group setting is to moderate the discussion, seeking to involve as many individuals as possible.

Students should not get the idea that the reaction group is formed to "check" or "grade" the study guide. The guide is a catalyst for thinking and discussion. It is not a test of comprehension. Every student in a discussion group does, however, have two major responsibilities. First, each should be able to explain and defend his or her reaction to a reading selection. Second, all students have a responsibility to understand their peers' opinions and reactions. They needn't accept contrary interpretations, nor should they be expected to. But if people can dare to be different from one another, they must feel that others will try to understand.

Therefore the rules for reflective reaction are:

1. Disagree with reason, not disputation.
2. Everyone deserves understanding, but no one should demand acquiescence.

Where everyone understands the meaning of these rules, discussion may be fruitful and reflective reaction productive.

180

Think back to your own reaction to the study guide for Little Red Riding Hood, for example. If you compared your responses to those of others, you may have found differences. In effect, this particular guide asks the reader to decide on the best use of the meaning of the story, forcing a qualitative decision. Your decision may have been different from another person's since people seldom see exactly the same meanings or applications of the same story. But many positions are arguable, many are understandable. The point is that having taken one or another position, each person has the responsibilities of (1) defending his or her own choice with reason and (2) understanding alternative choices made by others. The reflective reaction stage of the lesson is designed to let students do these things.

Successive Organizers

Typically, the lesson plan of the textbook includes suggestions for "extension" activities, activities appropriate as "follow-up" to a reading selection or group of related stories. Unfortunately, this part of the lesson is often given short shrift as time runs out on the teacher's best plans. One reason the suggestion is made for follow-up activities is to provide students the chance to reflect on and react to what they have read, especially in light of new but related activity and reading. Often, the suggested follow-up is for additional, topically similar readings that students complete individually and discuss in a small group.

It is possible that David Ausubel's theory of advance organizers bears implication for post-reading reflection as much as for prereading anticipation. That is, readers may profit as much from a "successive" organizer as an advance organizer, as much from an organizer that "succeeds" as an organizer which "precedes."

For example, suppose a group of students in an earth science class has completed reading a chapter or selection on minerals in which the major emphasis was mineral identification. As it happens, minerals are defined by such features as luster, hardness, color, crystal, streak, and cleavage, all of which are related concepts. For example, hardness is measured in terms of whether one mineral will scratch another, color varies along a continuum of values, luster is reflected light judged against other materials regarded as standards, etc. A grasp of the idea of relational comparisons is prerequisite to fuller understanding of mineralogy and mineral identification. Following the reading about minerals, therefore, students might be asked to read a short selection on relational concepts and to move from that to discuss their reading of the selection on minerals.

Another idea, and this might be more appropriate for less advanced students, would be to succeed the selection on minerals with a shorter organizing selection on rock formation. Minerals compose rocks. Therefore,

181

some understanding of rocks could lend perspective to the study of minerals. Discussed in the perspective of their occurrence in nature, minerals might be more easily understood. The successive organizer, the selection on rocks, would lend such perspective.

Graphic Post-Organizers

The structured overview, introduced earlier as a stimulus to prereading anticipation, may find its most flexible and creative use in the setting of reflective reaction. There are several forms that the structured overview idea may take as a catalyst for reflective reaction.

In most cases, the structured overview may display graphically the interrelationships of concepts. It can provide a framework for interim discussion in the progress of a unit. Furthermore, it may serve different groups of students in their reflection over different readings related to similar concepts. This is possible because when units of study are organized around concepts for emphasis, all reading and study required of pupils by the unit is related to one or more of the concepts. It is these concepts that have served as the basis of the unit and that should serve as the focus of any reading selection in the context of the unit. Therefore, in their reflective reaction to a particular reading selection, students often find it helpful to try to relate what they have read to what they have anticipated *vis à vis* an overview of the unit or some part of it. In effect, they are thus setting what they have read in the context both of what they know and what they are studying.

The research of Richard Barron (Barron and Stone, 1974) who, as we mentioned before, first proposed the structured overview concept, bears directly on the question of using the structured overview *after* rather than *before* reading. His suggestion is that students may construct their own overview (now called a *graphic post-organizer*) by arranging and rearranging 3 × 5 cards on which have been written terms related to the concepts underlying the reading selection. The attempt would be to devise an accurate, graphic account of interrelationships of ideas understood from the reading. Having done this, a group of students can then easily compare their display with that of other groups and with the overview of the unit. An example based on the reading of a selection about the banking system is provided to help you visualize a graphic post-organizer. (See Figure 11.1.)

As you can see, a graphic post-organizer is an attempt to graphically depict key concepts and to relate them to one another in a diagram. This strategy is not, however, learned quickly; practice is required to understand its intricacies and more practice is needed to master its potentials. Allow students to share with others their different versions of graphic post-organizers. Or, allow students to work in groups with 3 × 5 cards of ideas they think must be included in the array. Having done this, students can then compare their display with that completed by other groups. The comparison and the dis-

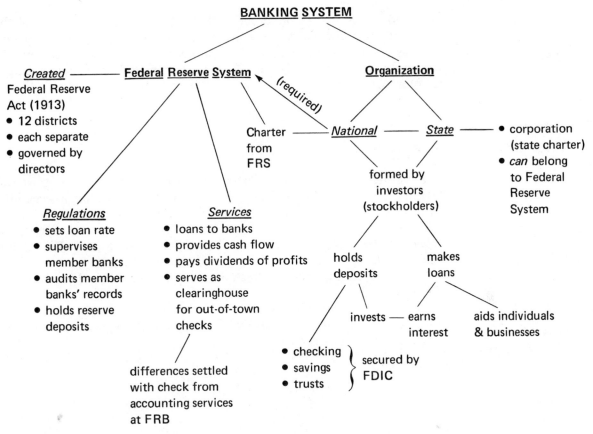

BANKING SYSTEM

Created ——— **Federal Reserve System**

Federal Reserve
Act (1913)
- 12 districts
- each separate
- governed by
  directors

(required)

Charter
from
FRS

National ——— *State*

Organization

- corporation
  (state charter)
- *can* belong
  to Federal
  Reserve
  System

formed by
investors
(stockholders)

Regulations
- sets loan rate
- supervises
  member banks
- audits member
  banks' records
- holds reserve
  deposits

Services
- loans to banks
- provides cash flow
- pays dividends of profits
- serves as
  clearinghouse
  for out-of-town
  checks

holds
deposits

makes
loans

invests — earns
interest

aids individuals
& businesses

- checking
- savings
- trusts

} secured by
FDIC

differences settled
with check from
accounting services
at FRB

FIGURE 11.1
Graphic Post-Organizer for Selection on Banking System

cussion is essential as students learn to manipulate concepts into meaningful
proximity to other ideas.

A way to link the structured overview idea with graphic post-organizers
in an effort to stimulate reflective reaction was suggested by the work of a
group of high school teachers in Petersburg, Virginia. As an introduction to
a unit of study, these teachers assign a general reading to all groups, a reading
that surveys the major concepts in the unit. The reading might, for example,
be a chapter in the textbook. Group members read the selection the best they
can in the setting of the content reading lesson. Following that, each group
discusses the selection in terms of what seems to them to be its major concepts. In the form of a structured overview, they seek to graphically display
the concepts and their interrelationships, and the relationships of the concepts to other ideas. Each group submits its overview for review by the
teacher, who makes passing comments. At the next class session, each group
is given ten minutes to display and defend its overview to the rest of the class.
Discussion is lively! The result of all this is that students have a chance to

read and reflect and to build out of that reflection an anticipation of the content of a unit of study. The concepts of the selection are the concepts for emphasis in the unit as a whole. What these teachers have done is to combine creatively the strengths of both reflective reaction and prereading anticipation through the use of student-constructed structured overviews.

Cinquains: Synthesizing

The synthesis which may come from reflective reaction is a most powerful learning experience. Time spent reflecting about the meaning of something learned will often establish it in the learner's cognitive structure. We have tried to suggest ways in which to provide an environment conducive to that reflection. In closing, we want to make one further suggestion. We think it has unlimited possibilities and are excited about sharing the idea with you. It is certainly among the most creative techniques we've seen for getting students to reflect and react.

A cinquain (pronounced: sing' • kān) is a short, simple poem. It is a creative outlet for reflecting on the meaning of a concept. Here is one that might strike a familiar chord:

Remembering
Simple, Difficult
Learning, Participating, Giving
Exciting in every way!
REFLECTING

And here's one from an experienced colleague of ours:

Teaching
Complex, Tough
Challenging, Invigorating, Rewarding
Tying New to Known
Educating

Have you noticed that cinquains have a definite form? Here are the guidelines for writing cinquains:

1. The first line is a one-word title (usually a noun).
2. The second line is a two-word *description* of the topic (usually two adjectives).
3. The third line is three words expressing *action* about the topic (usually three "ing" words).
4. The fourth line is a four-word phrase showing *feeling* for the topic.
5. The last line is a one-word synonym that *restates the essence* of the topic.

Another example is based on students' reading of the geological concept of folds:

Folds
Rocky, layered
Moving without moving
Heat and pressure's result
Waves

And a younger student reflects on geological disturbances:

Volcanoes
RED HOT
Erupting from within
Nature's furnace of fire
Inferno

Notice that both of these examples deviate slightly from the rigid guidelines we mentioned, but the essence of each line is maintained.

You try some now. Think of a topic, any topic. Say, someone you love. Your parents. Your children. Now, fill in the blanks:

Title (usually a noun)	_____		
Describe (usually adjectives)	_____,	_____	
Action (usually "ing" words)	_____	_____	_____
Feeling (phrase)	_____	_____	_____ _____
Restatement of essence	_____		

Next, do one on the subject of some concept you teach in school. Try it out on your students. Then, ask them to do and share some with the whole class. First do one about any topic, then about school, then about something they've enjoyed learning.

To write cinquains requires thought and, usually, the deeper the thought, the better the cinquain. The deeper the reflection, the more permanent the image.

What we like to do is have individuals do cinquains on a common topic and then combine their thoughts into one poem. These group poems can then be shared on bulletin boards, or read to the class for discussion. The power of cinquains in reflection is axiomatic. The beauty of them is that they *require* the reflection they are supposed to stimulate. Their use knows no limit of content area, or intelligence level, or reading ability. Kids love them, and they work.

185

CHAPTER 12   Developing Meaningful Vocabularies

Knowledge of vocabulary reflects a stage of understanding.

Overview

Vocabulary development, like vocabulary diagnosis which we discussed earlier, is intimately tied to conceptual development. It is not a matter of teaching words but of providing the opportunity for students to develop understanding. Then, the expression of those understandings will require vocabulary to which students are systematically exposed as a part of vocabulary enrichment.

The major thrust of vocabulary development activity in content areas should center on understanding and meaning. Meaning exercises, recognition exercises, and word study exercises must be coordinated with one another and timed appropriately with students' growing conceptualizations. Matching exercises, categorization activities, and various word puzzles may focus on meaning. Word games such as cryptograms and word hunts, so popular with people of all ages today, are appropriate for building word recognition. Word sort activities, as we describe them, are useful for word study; basically, these activities involve exploration of *how* words mean.

Perhaps we could best introduce this chapter by saying that language is *essentially* ambiguous. What a word means to any two people must be different, for if it were exactly the same, their experiences and hence their conceptualization associated with the word, would need to be the same. *Exactly* the same. And that is both impossible and undesirable if language (or anything else) is to work. Thus, the meanings which students have for words (notice that words don't have meaning; people have meaning for words) are essentially different. The purpose of vocabulary development is to allow people to share their individual experiences and to provide them opportunity to have common experiences out of which may grow a richer meaningful vocabulary for every person involved. Thus what they study may come to make better sense and find better expression in the students who come to understand it.

The Möbius Strip, a Circuitous Enigma

No one would deny the importance of vocabulary to understanding anything. Much of what is written about reading suggests that the first step in teaching concepts is to teach vocabulary. Common practice in elementary schools is to "preteach" the "new" vocabulary before reading. Secondary materials often follow the lead and list important vocabulary at the beginning of each selection. So why don't we just take up the cadence and go directly to a discussion of ways to build students' vocabularies? Well, we think we hear a different drummer and want you to listen with us for a moment.

Vocabulary facilitates learning; it is neither a requisite for nor the final product of learning. It is inseparable from conceptual development, and to try to make the separation is to get trapped by the paradox of the chicken before the egg. At the risk of oversimplifying, we might say that a word is merely the label for a concept; without understanding the concept, students have little need for the label. As Lavoisier, the father of chemistry, said, "It is impossible to dissociate language from science or science from language, because every natural science always involves three things: the sequence of phenomena on which the science is based; the abstract concepts which call these phenomena to mind; and the words in which the concepts are expressed." (Antoine Laurent Lavoisier, *Traité Eléméntaire de Chimie*.)

The vocabulary/concept paradox creates problems for students and teachers alike. First, to think abstractly and to communicate effectively about content area subject matter, students need to know the labels (i.e., vocabulary) for the concepts. Second, before they can meaningfully assimilate the labels, students need to associate those labels with the concepts they represent. Thus, it appears that we've come full circle. Can we escape from this Möbius strip?

The thrust of what we are saying is that vocabulary instruction is not the teaching of words but the teaching of meanings. Perhaps even that oversimplifies it, because meaning is of a variety of sorts, parts, and stages—always in stages, never a matter of fact. At any rate, what we are suggesting is no more than what James Michener was saying in *Centennial* when he described Potato Brumbaugh's acquisition of two words important to him,

He was only a peasant, but like all men and seminal ideas, he found the words he needed to express himself. He had heard a professor use the words *imprison* and *replenishment* and he understood immediately what the man had meant, for he, Brumbaugh, had discovered the concept before he heard the word, but when he did hear it, the word was automatically his, for he had already absorbed the idea which entitled him to the symbol. (p. 678)

Can you hear that drummer yet?

Vocabulary Development in the Classroom

Plans for a unit of study should include specification of concepts, description of phenomena to be experienced, and delineation of the vocabulary that may come to have meaning for students. The question this raises, then, is: What vocabulary should you specify for emphasis in a unit?

In some instances the question of what vocabulary to highlight in activities seems easily answered. In math and science, for example, technical terminology is often highlighted by textbook authors. But is this a good way for a teacher to identify vocabulary for emphasis? Actually, we think not. Our own rule of thumb is this: *Vocabulary important enough to teach is vocabulary required for students to understand the concepts being taught.* Since a single textbook provides only one avenue for learning major concepts, highlighted vocabulary in a text provides only a general clue to the words that should be emphasized.

The best way to determine the vocabulary for emphasis in a unit of study is to form a list of all the possible terms that you consider relevant to each of the concepts to be studied. In doing so, you can include terminology at various levels of sophistication. In effect, what we are suggesting is that you make a concerted inspection of the vocabulary of each unit of study. From that inspection, choose the vocabulary that should be included.

For example, when designing a unit on forms of government, a social studies teacher might list this and similar concepts for emphasis: "Democracy is government 'of the people, by the people, for the people.' " What are the important words that come to mind when we recite this idea? Equality, representative government, constitution, self-government, home rule, vote, Congress, law, populace, people, public, majority rule, common man, silent majority, plebian, proletariat, democrat, republican, etc. Dozens of words can be listed. In effect, a thesaurus can be built for the unit as terms relevant to each concept are listed. From this can be selected those words that, at various levels of sophistication, represent the kernel or basic ideas underlying the concept. Certainly not all the vocabulary relevant to a concept will come to have meaning for all students. However, from such a broadly inclusive list, a teacher can select words of varied sophistication and incorporate them into a variety of exercises designed to enhance vocabulary development for students of varying ability.

Introducing the Labels

In our discussion of the content reading lesson, we emphasized that prior knowledge is a major contributor to new learning. It stands to reason that this principle would apply to learning new vocabulary as well as to anything else. Thus, when new vocabulary is introduced, it should always be done in the context of familiar ideas. Perhaps that means that structured overviews would be most appropriate where students actively participate in their creation. Perhaps word association activities or an informal discussion about a topic should precede students' initial encounter with new vocabulary. The most effective, hence appropriate, strategy would necessarily be determined by the situation, but the principle holds true for almost all cases. Teach vocabulary and concepts as if they were part and parcel of the same thing *and* keep both in close proximity to ideas and terms with which students are already familiar.

Vocabulary Activities

Like Potato Brumbaugh, students will naturally "pick up" some of the vocabulary of anything they come to understand better, much as young children acquire words to express relationships that they come to understand. Through their experience with activities related to concepts, they will find some meaning for the words in which the concepts are expressed. Experience with words in specific vocabulary activities is essential, however. Vocabulary cannot be left to chance without considerable risk: risk either that words may have little or incomplete meaning for learners or that learners lack the proper terminology in which to express their understandings. Vocabulary activities must be designed to allow systematic exploration of words in relation to concepts, to phenomena, and to other words.

Vocabulary we will use to mean recognition and understanding of words and meaningful word parts. One may at times, in other contexts, see *vocabulary* used to refer rather loosely to word recognition and analysis skills, namely phonics, structural analysis, and use of context. Such skills, though necessary for reading, are only indirectly the concern of the content area teacher. Not only that, but each of the skills, phonics included, *presupposes* meaning. In other words, meaning is the primary object of vocabulary development viewed from any perspective. It would therefore probably be helpful to reserve the term vocabulary for reference to the idea of under-

189

standing and using words. Certainly, as students develop understandings of words, their skill at recognizing those words is enhanced by familiarity. But that skill and familiarity is incidental to an increase in understanding of word meanings. While there are recognition practice activities, which students may enjoy and from which they may profit, the major thrust of vocabulary development activity in content areas should center on understanding and meaning.

It is too often the habit, if not the intent, in content area instruction to incorrectly do one of two things in the name of vocabulary development. It is only too easy either to assume students have or will learn meanings for words "on their own" or to require that pupils look words up in the dictionary and "copy the meaning and use the word in a sentence." Meaning is not copied from a dictionary. Valuable as they are, dictionaries are notoriously circular in their definitions: their stock in trade is the synonym. A dictionary's main worth is realized only when the person who uses it already possesses a firm grasp on the concepts and phenomena to which a word is related. Where this is so, the dictionary can be a great help in refinement and nicety of *definition*. It is only definition, i.e., preciseness, and not meaning, however, which the dictionary can provide.

How many students have heard the terms sine, cosine, tangent, cotangent, secant, cosecant, and yet have not now or ever understood the concept of trigonometric functions? How many have learned to spell and copied definitions for terms like tragedy, climax, denouement; or sonnet, epic, meter, verse, cadence, metaphor? It would have been possible for these same students to have understood the concepts to which these words are related and to have only then met the words. Lacking the concepts, the words remain hollow shells in the recesses of the memories of most people who once "learned" them.

To insure that students do acquire the meaning of vocabulary in a way that honors the natural way in which meaning grows for individuals, the following principle must govern: Provide students the opportunity to explore word meanings concurrently and as a complement to their conceptual development. That is, where they are most effective, vocabulary activities are appropriately integrated and timed with concept development and experience of phenomena. Several different kinds of activities and exercises may be utilized, each of which we can now present with explanation and example.

The three kinds of exercises that we will present may be classfied roughly as meaning exercises, recognition exercises, and word study exercises. These labels are similar to those used by Herber (1978) and several of the exercise types we discuss have their origin with him. Each will be described in its turn, but by way of introduction we should emphasize that our classification is more convenient than real. Perhaps they are seeds for a program of vocabulary development in content areas. Rooted firmly in the ground of meaning, we believe they can be developed into valuable learning exercises.

Meaning Exercises

These are exercises aimed directly at helping students firmly attach words to concepts. Their purpose is to expand the vocabulary of the learner to fit an improving conceptual framework, to provide the vocabulary demanded by a capacity for nicer distinction. This means that the words they focus on must be seen by the learner in the context of the phenomena under study. The observation, experiences, discussion, reading, writing, and all other activities designed to enhance students' conceptual development form the context in which meaning exercises may be effective.

Meaning exercises bear an important relationship to other vocabulary activities which we call recognition and word study exercises. These latter two should, as a rule, be followed by meaning exercises. Recognition and word study exercises may focus on dimensions of vocabulary other than meaning, or, that is, focus on meaning only indirectly. They will need follow-up, therefore, with meaning exercises if the primary goal of vocabulary activity is to be honored.

Perhaps it won't be taken as redundancy to make the point that meaning exercises can be difficult and inappropriate unless students are well on their way to understanding the concepts on which the terms in the exercise focus. If students do not have some grasp of the concepts, vocabulary exercises of any sort can be so difficult that they become mere drill, impossible to relate to anything. Any exercise must be simple enough for performance by most, if not all, students and must not assume the strength it seems to build. Furthermore, specific and detailed directions and examples should be provided regarding the proper performance of the exercise. This will usually guard against confusion.

Matching Exercises

This type of meaning exercise seems very simple, and in fact it is little more than a recognition exercise. It does, however, concern meaning and is so categorized. Vocabulary items are listed in two columns on a sheet, in random order. They may be synonyms, antonyms, roots and derivatives, terms and definitions, etc. The task for the learner is to match the items in one column with those in the other. The form is familiar:

```
_____   1. ..........   a. ..........
_____   2. ..........   b. ..........
_____   3. ..........   c. ..........
_____   4. ..........   d. ..........
              etc.
```

Students are asked to place the lower case letters in the blanks before the arabic numerals to indicate a match between the items. Consider this exercise:

_____	1. diamonds	a.	lowest suit
_____	2. spades	b.	one suit higher than clubs
_____	3. clubs	c.	one suit higher than diamonds
_____	4. hearts	d.	highest suit

The novice bridge player who works this exercise may become more familiar with the relationships among suits. Notice that the exercise tends to be self-correcting. If a mistake is made, it is apparent in the failure of a subsequent match. In other words, a person can reason his or her way to the correct answer even if he or she has only partial understanding of the terms. This is a desirable feature of such exercises since it allows relatively more teaching and less testing. All exercises should have this feature built in whenever possible.

Here is another exercise of the same type, again set up so that errors are somewhat self-correcting. Match the symbols on the right (lettered a., b., c., etc.) with the definitions on the left (numbered 1., 2., 3., etc.) by placing letters in the blanks before the numbers. If you come to a definition that you cannot at first match with a symbol, skip it and go on. From those matches of which you are sure, you may be able to figure out the ones of which you are unsure.

	Definitions	*Symbols*
_____	1. identical with	a. $>$
_____	2. not identical with	b. $=$
_____	3. not greater than	c. $\equiv$
_____	4. equal to	d. $<$
_____	5. is to; ratio	e. $\neq$
_____	6. greater than	f. $\geq$ or $\geqq$
_____	7. greater than or equal to	g. $\approx$
_____	8. not equal to	h. $\not>$
_____	9. less than	i. $:$
_____	10. congruent to	j. $\not\equiv$

Some of the symbols in this exercise may be unfamiliar to students, but almost all will know at least the equals sign. By deduction and elimination the others may be reasoned out if the student has even the vaguest idea of how the definitions and symbols fit. For example, if = means equals, the best guess for not equal might be ≠ which is correct. By deduction, | must mean not. If the student couldn't remember > and <, he could deduce it from ≯, not greater than. Notice that ≮, not less than, is not included since to have done so would have been to require complete knowledge of the symbols being taught.

Many exercises of the matching type are, unfortunately, better tests than teaching tools. It is admittedly more difficult to build the self-correcting (i.e., teaching) feature in, but it is that feature more than any other that makes such exercises worthwhile.

Categorization Exercises

One of the best and most flexible of meaning exercises, the categorization exercise may frequently serve as a good follow-up to matching the other types of exercises. The basic form of the exercise is the categorical column head based on concepts to which terms are related. For example, an exercise related to a unit on nutrition might look like this:

Directions   The basic food groups are carbohydrates, proteins, and fats. Certain foods are known for their particularly high content of these substances. List the foods given below under the group with which each is associated. Then add other foods you think might be closely related to one or another basic group.

Carbohydrates	*Proteins*	*Fats*

cheese, butter, cereal, fruit, corn oil, fish, shortening, flour, bacon drippings, eggs, sugar, milk, vegetables, olive oil

Students should be allowed to discuss their categorizations in small groups following completion of this sorting exercise. The categorization exercise will be most effective when:

193

1. Students have completed reading something that discusses the concepts used as column heads.
2. Either before or after the reading, but preceding the categorization exercise, students have completed a recognition or word study exercise (to be explained presently) that used vocabulary similar to that in the categorization exercise.
3. As they complete their categorizations, students can refer to the reading selections in which the vocabulary and ideas used in the exercise appear.
4. Students are allowed to compare their responses to the exercise in small groups. The task of the group is to resolve any differences and to present the group's completed categorizations to the rest of the class or to submit it as a group effort.

In the atmosphere described by these conditions, the pressure for the "right" answer may be relieved. In fact, there may often be no right answer, only various defendable choices. Being able to make, defend, and *relent* choices in the face of good and better reasoning is the most important lesson anyone can learn about vocabulary. The categorization exercise can demonstrate this and that is its strongest asset as a vocabulary development tool.

Crossword Puzzles

Long a favorite of word hounds of all ages, the crossword puzzle can be found on almost any topic through educational supply houses. Many people enjoy working them and there can be little doubt that they foster curiosity about words.

For classroom use, especially where the objective is to build students' familiarity with particular words, the teacher-made crossword may serve best. It allows the teacher opportunity to use words most closely related to concepts under study and to associate the words with most appropriate definitions. Despite their complicated look, they are also rather easy to construct. Using either graph paper or a scrabble board and tiles and working from a list of conceptually related terms, a crossword can usually be worked out in less than an hour. What it may lack in professional appearance will improve with practice and is more than made up for by the appropriateness of the activity for the context in which it is used. Let's look at some examples.

In her fifth grade unit on oceans, Peggy Donaldson has developed a crossword puzzle that does more than provide her students a chance for vocabulary reinforcement. Notice that this one includes several multiple meaning words that also extend students' word knowledge, for example the clues one across and eleven down.

194

ACROSS

1. a shellfish; to *shut* up

2. periwinkle; s-l-o-w

3. very well "armed"

4. flat, tasty fish; struggle

5. has a "pearly" shell

11. Jaws; a tricky person

DOWN

1. an 8-legged shellfish; a grouch

2. the giant is deadly

7. is caught in a pot

8. a very "bright" fish; You may see it in the sky!

9. has many stingers; Great with peanut butter.

11. small, curved shellfish; a puny person

10. underwater mammal; huge

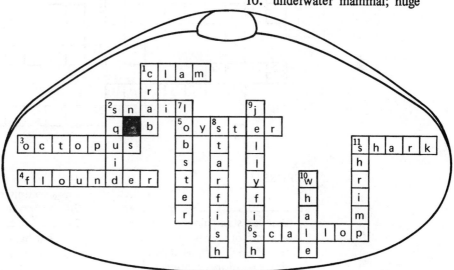

Adelia Leath shares an example from an eleventh grade unit on grammatical elements related to composition skills. We'll let you try your hand at this one.

Individuals or groups of students often enjoy making their own crossword puzzles. The reading and discussion necessitated by this activity is usually very productive. It can require a very close examination of the concepts under study and the terminology in which those concepts are expressed. More than this, if other students have a chance to work the puzzles their peers construct, chances are that the level of difficulty of the puzzles and the words in which definitions are expressed will be appropriate. In fact, we have found that student-made puzzles are often more effective learning activities than

CROSSWORD PUZZLE

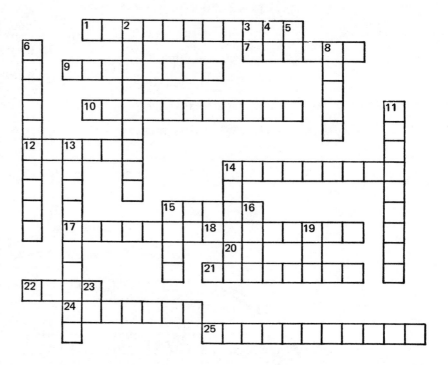

ACROSS

1. _____ Clause: A clause that can stand alone.
7. A group of words without a subject and verb, used as a single word in a sentence.
9. Two or more simple sentences joined by a coordinating conjunction.
10. A word that connects sentences, clauses, phrases, or words.
12. Part of a sentence, with a subject and verb.
14. _____ Clause: A clause used to modify nouns and pronouns.
15. Enthusiasm: energy; vigor.
17. _____ Sentence: A sentence with only one subject and one verb.

18. A group of words that expresses a complete thought.
20. Abbreviation for *road*.
21. _____ Phrase: Phrases that have no grammatical connection with any part of a sentence but are related in meaning.
22. _____ Clause: A clause that can stand alone as a sentence.
24. Verb forms that are used as nouns, adjectives, or adverbs.
25. _____ Conjunction: connects a subordinate clause with a main clause.

DOWN

2. _____ Clause: A clause that depends on another clause in the sentence.

3. Tap dancer Eleanor Powell's initials.
4. Abbreviation for New Hampshire.
5. Theodore Roosevelt's initials.
6. A verb form that modifies nouns and pronouns.
8. The person or thing about which a verb asks a question or makes a statement.
11. _____ verb: A verb that does not use *ed* or *d* in the past participial.
13. A noun or pronoun placed be-

side another noun or pronoun to explain it more fully.
14. _____ Clause: A clause used to modify verbs, adjectives and adverbs.
15. A word or group of words used to express action or being.
16. A period is used when a sentence_____ .
19. _____ Clause: A clause used in any way that a noun may be used.
23. A direction.

those made by teachers. Making puzzles may be more instructional than working them.

A word of caution, however, on student-made puzzles: it is critical that you take the time to instruct students in exactly how to make them. The time you spend to model this activity will pay off in the long run with less confusion on the part of your students. We have found that the following simple instructions can be used to launch students on this project:

1. Start with the concepts to be reinforced.
2. List the words that reflect those concepts. They become the answers in your puzzle.
3. Arrange the words into a crossword puzzle configuration. Use either graph paper or a scrabble board to simplify this task.
4. Create clues or descriptions to go with each word.
5. Set the clues up into "down" and "across" categories to correspond to the puzzle design. Number the clues and boxes in the design to coincide.
6. Transfer the outline of the squares for the crossword puzzle onto a ditto or paper for duplication.

Once you have collected your student-made puzzles you can either duplicate the best ones for class use or merely have students exchange and work each other's puzzles. We have found that students benefit greatly from the time they have spent wrestling with concepts and meanings in their creation of a crossword puzzle and their final products often outshine ours!

Magic Squares

The magic square is another popular puzzle format with an unusual twist. This puzzle has a self-correcting aspect because students are not only matching words and meanings, but are also looking for a "magic number" as well.

If the correct meanings are matched with the terms, the numbers in each straight row (not diagnonal row) will add up to the same total.

As with most matching type puzzle formats, this one can be made more difficult by adding foils, or extra clues that will not be used. Here's an example taken from an earth science lesson:

5 geologist	3 fold	7 strata
9 crustal movement	4 sediments	2 pressure
1 decompose	8 fault	6 salt domes

Directions Put the number of the clue below in the square with the appropriate term. Check your answers by adding the numbers to see if the sums of all rows both down and across add up to the same "magic number". The Magic Number is ___15___ .

Clues:

1. To decay or break down the original parts.
2. A bearing-down or squeezing.
3. A wave-like tendency seen in rock formations due to pressure and heat.
4. The fragments and solutions of decayed and crumbled rock.
5. One who studies the history of the earth as recorded in its rocks.
6. Formations caused by masses of salt in the earth reacting to heat and pressure.
7. Layers.
8. A break in the continuity of a rock formation.
9. The shifting and settling of the earth's strata.

Given below are some additional numerical combinations that add up to a magic number. Those that do not include all consecutive numbers 1-9 or 1-16 include foils in the definitions.

7	2	9
8	6	4
3	10	5

5	7	9
12	8	1
4	6	11

10	8	6
2	9	13
12	7	5

3	2	16	13
10	11	5	8
6	7	9	12
15	14	4	1

12	18	7	2
15	11	5	8
3	6	17	13
9	4	10	16

Central Word Puzzles

A variation and simplification of the crossword is the central word puzzle. These are very easy to construct and simple to work, but they are appropriate for students who might be unable to work the more complicated, traditional crossword.

As an example, you might work the following puzzle. The central word expresses the major concept under consideration.

1.   M _ _ _ _ _
2. _ _ _ _ A _
3.   _ _ _ _ M _ _ _ _
4.   _ _ M _ _ _ _ _ _ _
5.   _ A _ _ _ _ _ _ _ _
6.   _ _ _ L _

1. small powerful burrowers (pl.)
2. rabbit-like, small, and almost tailless, also called conies (pl.)
3. the order that includes monkeys, apes, and humans
4. probably the oddest mammal, it carries a plate of armor
5. meat-eating
6. the largest animal ever to inhabit the earth.

199

Quite a variety of these puzzles is possible, all related to one general subject. For example, carnivore could serve as a central word, around which would be arranged different members of this zoological order (raccoon, bear, otter, hyena, lion, civet, badger, and seal, for example).

Karla Rice, a junior high school music teacher, offers a variation on the central word puzzle.

THE SCALE AND KEYS

Directions   For each of the numbered blanks, use the corresponding clue to identify the word. Select from the following list:

sub-dominant	dominant
sub-mediant	cadence
chord	leading tone
triad	mediant
broken chord	scale
tonic	supertonic
flat	pitch
key	

In every item there is a circled blank. Take the letters that fall in each blank (in order 1-16) and write them on the staff. They should form a melody that you recognize!

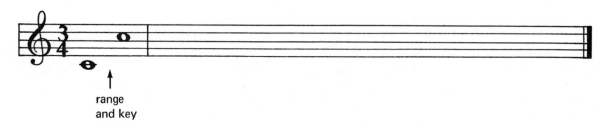

range
and key

1. 𝅝 _ _ _ _
2. _ _ _ _ 𝅝
3. _ _ 𝅝 _ _ _ _
4. _ _ 𝅝 - _ _ _ _ _ _ _
5. _ 𝅝 _ _ _
6. _ _ 𝅝 _ _ _ _
7. _ 𝅝 _ _ _ _ _ - _ _ _ _
8. _ _ _ 𝅝 _ _ _ _ _

9. 𝅝 _ _ _ _
10. _ 𝅝 _
11. 𝅝 _ _ _ _ _ _ _
12. _ _ _ _ 𝅝 _
13. _ _ _ _ _ 𝅝
14. _ _ _ _ _ _ _ - 𝅝 _ _ _ _
15. _ _ 𝅝 - _ _ _ _ _ _ _
16. 𝅝

Clues:

1. A combination of three or more notes
2. The first step of a major scale
3. The ending point of a chord progression
4. The sixth step of a major scale
5. An organized pattern of eight notes
6. The third step of a major scale
7. The seventh step of a major scale
8. The second step of a major scale
9. When placed by a note, it lowers it one-half step
10. A group of related tones with a common center or tonic
11. The fifth step of a major scale
12. Intonation
13. Three notes played simultaneously
14. A triad played separately, notes in succession
15. The fourth step of a major scale
16. What would you think is the logical ending note?

For those of you who, like us, could use some help, we share with you Karla's answer "key":

1. c h o r d
2. t o n i c
3. c a d e n c e
4. s u b - m e d i a n t
5. s c a l e
6. m e d i a n t
7. l e a d i n g - t o n e
8. s u p e r t o n i c

9. f l a t
10. k e y
11. d o m i n a n t
12. p i t c h
13. t r i a d
14. b r o k e n - c h o r d
15. s u b - d o m i n a n t
16. C

And the staff should look like this:

And what is the answer? "My country 'tis of thee, sweet land of liberty, Of thee I sing!"

Here's another central word puzzle for a geometry class designed by Wayne Shelton.

201

CONGRUENT TRIANGLES

Directions   Use the clue provided to complete each word below.

```
 1.    C _ _ _ _ _ _ _
 2.    O _ _ _ _ _ _ _ _ _ _
 3.    _ N _ _ _ _ _ _
 4.    _ _ G _ _ _
 5.        R _ _ _ _
 6.    _ _ _ U _ _
 7.            E _ _ _ _ _ _ _ _ _
 8.    _ _ _ _ _ N _ _ _ _ _
 9.        _ _ _ T _
10.    _ _ _ T _ _
11.    _ _ _ R _
12.        I _ _ _ _ _ _ _ _
13.        A _ _
14.    _ _ N _ _ _
15.            G _ _ _ _
16.    _ _ _ L _ _ _ _
17.    _ _ _ _ E
18.        _ _ S
```

Clues:

1. When one figure (triangle) is physically placed on top of another like figure (triangle).
2. When two triangles lie partially in the interior of each other.
3. A part of a triangle used in proving triangles congruent.
4. A triangle is a geometric _____.
5. A type of triangle that contains an angle by the same name.
6. Same clue (different answer) as #5.
7. A triangle with all three sides equal.
8. A triangle with all three angles equal.
9. A type of triangle containing all three angles of the same kind.
10. A special point in an angle.
11. Equal angles and segments come in _____.
12. A type of triangle with only two angles and two sides equal.
13. The method of proving triangles congruent that involves two angles and the included side.
14. Segments have _____.
15. The first step in a "proof."
16. A type of triangle with all three sides of different lengths.

17. The last step in a "proof."
18. The method of proving triangles congruent that involves three sides.

Beginnings and Endings

In this last meaning exercise we will discuss, a beginning or ending element
is listed that is common to many words or to words that are conceptually
related. Definitions for the words are listed in one column, the words in another, with blank spaces for all but the common element. Try this for an
example:

LOGY QUIZ

1. The scientific study of man. — — — — — — — — —logy

2. The study of fossils. — — — — — — — — —logy

3. The ethnology of early man. — — — — — — — — — —logy

4. The study of ancient animals. — — — — — — — — —logy

5. The study of the influence of
heavenly bodies on human
events. — — — — — —logy

6. The study of weather. — — — — — — —logy

7. The study of the evolution of
language etc. — — — — —logy

Another version of the same game lists common beginnings and asks for
endings. You may find this easier:

ANTHRO QUIZ

1. The scientific study of man anthro— — — — — — —

2. Attributing human
characteristics. anthro— — — — — — — — —

3. Resembling man. anthro— — — — —

4. Of or pertaining to man. anthro— — —

5. Study of the origin of man. anthro— — — — — — — — —

Or, try this one:

Par one, two, three, . . .

1. To peel   par __

2. A hooded fur jacket   par __ __

3. Equality in amount   par __ __ __

4. A model of excellence   par __ __ __ __

5. Being equal distance apart at every
   point   par __ __ __ __ __

6. A distinct division of written work   par __ __ __ __ __ __

7. Oval protozoans etc.   par __ __ __ __ __ __ __

Recognition Exercises, Games, and Puzzles

When followed by the use of the word in meaningful context, simple word games may be useful. Basal reader manuals have traditionally called for recognition exercise in the recommendation that the teacher write "new" or "unfamiliar" words on the board and pronounce them with children. Seemingly, a bond between the sight (look) and sound (say) would be established by this look-say technique. The problem is that the technique teaches something else, that reading is saying words.

An alternative to the show-and-tell method of building word recognition is the variety of word games and puzzles that students like to play. Newsstands are full of examples that can be copied, and students who enjoy working them are usually happy to try their hand at building games and puzzles. When they are centered on vocabulary related to a unit of study or area of concern to the course, such word exercises may have real value, particularly to the student who makes them up! They cause and reinforce genuine curiosity about language, just as traditional crosswords have done for so many years.

Two common and popular examples of word games that can easily be adapted for class use are the cryptogram and word hunts.

Cryptograms

These are coded lists of words which may be related to the same topic. The code is such that letters stand for something other than themselves. In the same puzzle, however, letters are substituted for one another consistently.

An example from the puzzle is given as a clue to the other words. Our sample cryptogram will strain your memory of history:

CIVIL WAR GENERALS

Example: Grant

M D L E V R Q

— — — — — —

P H D X H

— — — — —

J U D Q W

— — — — —

O H H

— — —

V K H U P D Q

— — — — — —

M R K Q V W R Q

— — — — — — —

Z R U U H V W

— — — — — —

Word Hunts

This is one of the most popular puzzles of the day, known by a variety of names—ring around the word, seek-a-word, search and find, etc. News-stands carry multiple sources for word hunts, and too they are almost as easy to make as to find.

FAMOUS ARTISTS

```
A R T I R E M I N G T O N A
R E M B R A N D T I I S U W
E B P S D E G A S N J U D Y
Y M I C H E L A N G E L O E
N U C V E S A L N R P L B T
O S A L E B U V W E E Y O H
L E S R O B T I S S A N B C
D I S M O N D R I A N V L N
S S O E F G C E Z A N N E W
V T H D E L A C R O I X Y Z
```

If you want to convert word hunts from a recognition task to a meaning exercise, consider the following example.

READING IN THE CONTENT AREAS

Directions   Find and circle the words that appropriately correspond with each of the following:

1. author of a readability formula
2. should be used as stimulators rather than evaluators
3. a purpose of prereading
4. with label, it comprises "a word"
5. knowledge isn't static, it _____
6. reflective-reaction focuses on this
7. information search is really a search for this
8. Wigginton is almost synonymous with this

9. the essence of reading in the content areas is "_____ in every class-room"

10. the first principle of interpersonal relations is the ability to be this

Reminder: the words can be backwards, diagonal, or upside down as well as horizontal or vertical.

```
I L F O X F I R E Q
E I A P O R M N U M
V T L K D Y R E A L
O E A V L R S E I J
L R A P A T Z H P S
V A T U I Y G B M X
E C C O N C E P T Y
S Y N L C U I D T F
E S T D A R C T D W
Q G R M E A N I N G
S I S E H T N Y S A
```

And here's one designed by Joyce McAndrew for an ecology unit in her bi-ology course.

```
D E R T F G I O L O G B J E R E T T I K O E
N O R Y E T O P C W H I C H N T Q U I C K R
M I O H P R T I F R O A D I T O P W E C E E
O P C T O T E R R E S T R I A L O O N C S H
S V E Y E M C I E L U A N O I T A L U P O P
B O O G O C O N S U M E R S O I T D X C Y S
T I E O I P S M H Q M P L A N T O E Q R S O
R O W L N E Y E W O E F I S H R E C O E N C
I I I O T R S A A T R U E D P O B O I E X E
N V N C E O T W T W A T E R H O N M W E N T
I N T E R D E P E N D E N C Y R O P S N O W
T I E C V I M C R E M N E X S O E O R G E Z
C C R P E N M A E N O V C N I O T S E P S O
W H V N N I T I R I C I N H C D W E Y B C D
B E E O T O W N M C W R O C A K L R T Y I T
J O N B I O L O G Y E O M O L B T R E E T S
P O T E O W Q K N C F N E N V I I T O Y O X
K L I V N Y T I N U M M O C O E M T O U I S
I R O J A C K L E R P E S T O L T Y A D B V
R E N Y G O L O G Y E N R F C B G Y N T I M
N M P E R S I S T E N T C H E M I C A L S U
W H Y D O Y O U T H I N K I A S K E D Y O U
```

The words defined on the following page are hidden in the puzzle. Can you find them and place them in the line before the definition?

_____ relying upon each other for existence and support of the sea

_____ that niche that is larely composed of plants

_____ the total role of an organism in the ecosystem

_____ those chemicals which do not readily decompose

_____ ecosystem that includes ponds and streams

_____ natural surroundings

_____ all ecosystems on earth

_____ study of the relationships between living things and their environment

_____ group of organisms of one kind in a given area

_____ that niche that is composed of bacteria

_____ ecosystem that includes forest and deserts

_____ group of populations in given area

_____ interference

_____ where an organism lives

_____ study of life

_____ composed of physical environment and living organisms

_____ they eat producers

_____ substance that combats disease

_____ one that destroys

A Pause for Perspective

The same purpose as that served by word puzzles and games can be served by the teacher in directing the content reading lesson. A part of the introductory moments of the lesson can be spent examining with students the words that are italicized in the selection, listed at the beginning or end of the selection, or otherwise highlighted by the author. As an initiating step, students can be directed to look at the words, answering questions such as these, posed more or less informally: Do any of these words look familiar? Who can pronounce the first word? the second, etc.? Does anyone know of other words that look the same as the third (or other) word? Who can find a sentence on the first page of the selection which contains the fourth word? Questions can be asked in this manner to stimulate students to examine closely the vocabulary items that will be important to their understanding of the selection.

Of course, alternatives to a conversational format can be used for this. The purpose of the exercise, in whatever format, is to lead into an examination of word meanings.

Thus, as the introductory comments proceed, the meanings of some of the words may be brought to the fore with questions which begin to focus on meaning. ("Does anyone know a word with the same meaning as _____?" "What other words have the same stem as _____?" etc.) In this way a nice transition between recognition and meaning can be made. This strategy will also provide a good lead into purpose setting and hypothesis formation which are the purposes of the initial part of the content reading lesson.

Word Study Exercises

The third category of vocabulary exercises which we will discuss includes some features of both the meaning and the recognition varieties just discussed. The major difference is that the word study exercise, as we will define it, is never limited to only the words taken from a selection or unit. Other exercises are limited in that way in order to focus directly on the vocabulary of the phenomena and concepts under study.

Word study exercises may be completed in a variety of formats. The common characteristic of all, however, will be a concentration on word "families" of various sorts. Students are asked to work with words of similar stem, specialized meaning, similar phonetic properties, similar affix, similar derivation, or other particular features. The choice of feature is based on the likelihood that its understanding might lead to increased sophistication with respect to the language of a particular content field.

The basic format of the word study exercise is called "hunt and sort." The exercise gives students a guiding pattern or model and asks them to find and sort other words with the same pattern which match the model. This must, of course, be varied to suit the task.

One such exercise gives the student a word that is described by its meaningful parts, and asks him or her to search in newsprint, texts, reference sources, and other printed matter for words that are related to the model word. The relationship will be found in similarity of the meaningful parts which occur in other words of the same "family." To take an obvious example, the word "biology" divides into "bio" and "logy," "life" and "study of." Words of this family can be categorized into two columns suggested by the two parts. (The format is similar to the categorization exercise discussed before.) There are many such words to be found in common speech, among them the popular "bionic," which students will know on at least one conceptual level.

To take another example, a similar exercise, though perhaps a bit more erudite, would have students explore and categorize the examples they found of words related to sine, cosine; tangent, cotangent; and secant, cosecant. These words have a variety of interesting relationships to one another and to other words. Given a rudimentary understanding or trigonometric functions, it is helpful to see that the "co-" in each paired word means "complementary," which itself is an interesting word. Further hunting, properly structured, will reveal to students that "sine" is related to sinusoid, sinus, sinusoidal projection, and sinewave, among others, and that all are related to fold, curve, and hollow. Tangent, it can be found, is in the "tag" family, words whose relationship is related to "touching," such as "contact," "tact" (i.e., just the right touch), "tangible" (i.e., capable of being touched), and so forth.

The study of any new field opens wide the door for an exploration of how words are related. Rhyming words can be sorted easily, which can be shown to relate to poetry. Various meanings of the same words can be sorted to highlight their special meaning in relation to a given concept. "Similar," for example, means something different in biology and social studies and math. Part of any content area study is study of the specialization of vocabulary. The number of "families" that are possible is determined by the number of ways in which words have come to have a place in the study of any concept. The word study or hunt and sort activity is a way of giving students part of the opportunity they need to have words come to have meaning for them.

CHAPTER 13 — Changing Attitudes

Attitudes toward school are changed by experiences in school.

Overview

Schools seem to exist for the cognitive domain of learning. The affective domain, students' attitudes, beliefs, interests, and values, is often a weak stepsister to other objectives. The irony of this is that attitudes toward what they learn are strong determinants of what students choose to study or learn in the future. (If schools, for example, were to teach people to read but to hate reading, need they bother?) As Karl Menninger has said, "Attitudes are more important than facts." Or skills, we would add.

There are several things we do know about attitudes and their change and development. We know that attitude and achievement are not synonymous, so that to assume good attitudes will result from high achievement, or the reverse of this, is a mistake. On the other hand, grades based on achievement do tend to reflect attitudes. At times, this can be unfair unless proper attention to attitudes has been given. Classroom climate and the teacher are critical factors in attitude development. Somehow, children's attitudes toward school grow worse with successive years in school.

The implications of what we know about attitude change are none too clear. However, certain factors are both important and amenable to change. These include curriculum factors, the physical setting, pupil characteristics, and teacher characteristics. With attention to the details of these factors, directions of pupil attitude change may become more positive.

Attitude Change as an Educational Goal

We wonder how many people have ever considered the implications of this: Research studies on attitudes in the world of business and politics outnumber those in education 100 to 1. The businessman and the politician depend for their professional lives on how people *feel* about what they have to offer. They seek what they call AIDA, which stands for *attention, interest, desire,* and *action.* If a product or political idea can get AIDA, it will survive. Otherwise, it will be rejected and forgotten, and when people aren't buying, somebody's going to want to know why! Why aren't people buying? Find out and change it and you've got a success on your hands. Ignore it and you've got an Edsel. We think there's a lesson in this somewhere.

Are schools looking for AIDA? It's hard to imagine a curriculum guide which doesn't include affective objectives: interests, values, attitudes, and the like. The question is whether schools are investing heavily enough in the things that cause good attitudes, or whether they are sacrificing attitudes for knowledge by caring more about what kids learn than about how kids feel.

Think of your own experiences. Most people sooner or later come up against a teacher whose philosophy seems to be "I don't care whether you like it or not; I know it will be good for you to learn this and some day you'll thank me." But the idea that learning in school need be painful is at best anachronistic and at worst damaging to the future learning experiences of students. The affective result rather than the cognitive product of learning will likely determine those experiences.

A case in point: For reading to become a lifelong habit, a person must *know how* to read and must *like* to read. A similar argument would hold for any content area. And in this light, students' attitudes toward what they study are more important than what they learn. "No profit grows where is no pleasure ta'en,"[1] and Shakespeare was right again; people study what they learn to like.

Suspicions Regarding Attitude Change in Schools

There simply isn't a great deal known for sure about why students' attitudes toward school and school subjects form or change. There are, however, some firm suspicions about attitudes which experience and common sense would suggest. Before we get to specific suggestions about what can go on in school to make attitudes better, let's look at these points:

1. *Attitude and achievement are not the same thing*, which means that learning and feeling good about school don't fit quite like the hand and glove people sometimes take them to be. Many of you were probably very good

[1]*The Taming of the Shrew,* Act I, scene 1.

students, yet it would come as no surprise to us if many of you have strong negative feelings about school. Knowing that you were a good student simply wouldn't say much about your attitude toward school. (You see, even being a good teacher doesn't mean you like school. Why, some of our best friends abhor school but love kids, and they're excellent teachers!) So, if anyone wants to change students' attitudes for the better, he or she will have to take that as a specific goal and do things to make it happen rather than hope that attitude will slide along on achievement's coattails.

2. *Teachers allow students' attitudes to influence grades.* We noticed this when we were studying attitudes and achievement and found their relationship to be weaker than the relationship between attitudes and grades. On the surface, that may seem reasonable; any humane teacher would tend to give better grades to cooperative class participants than to hellish troublemakers, even if the achievement of both were the same. It's a way of rewarding good behavior, which counts in school. But it is also a way of punishing bad attitudes. Below the surface of things, though, one could ask whether it is fair unless everything possible had been done to change the attitude of the troublemaker.

3. *Classroom climate is a very important factor in determining pupil attitudes.* Have you read the introduction to *Foxfire 2* yet? Remember Carlton and what Eliot Wigginton had to say about him?

I was in the office and Suzy was in the outside room and I heard her laughing—as usual—except she was really cracked up this time, and so naturally I had to go out and see what was happening, and she said just be quiet and listen. And Carlton, one of the tenth grade kids, had been in the darkroom alone for an hour and I had forgotten—and God he was missing his English class—and this string of muffled swear words suddenly drifted through the darkroom door. Yep. Carlton was still in there—oh, hell, that English class—trying to make a double exposure print for Karen's and Betse's burial article. And he was trying to figure out how to do it and burning up all this printing paper and coming closer and closer to getting it just right and talking to himself explaining what was wrong like there were seventy-eight people watching. And Suzy had been listening to the struggle, laughing, when—Bam—out he came with a dripping wet print and a *There how does that grab you*—and it was beautiful, and we used it on the cover of the magazine that had that article in it (and in the book). And Suzy and I were both laughing, and then Carlton cracked up, too. And we laughed some more. And then he went to English.

And when he got to English, he had to write five hundred times, "I will not be late to class any more."

And the teacher read some poems aloud that nobody listened to, so she spent the whole hour reading to herself while the kids hacked off—or slept. Sort of like us in church five minutes into the sermon. You know.[2]

[2]Wigginton, Eliot. *Foxfire 2*, p. 9.

4. *Student's attitudes toward school get worse the longer they're in school.* Somehow, for many pupils the longer they're there the less fun school gets to be, until they finally drop out one way or another. (For evidence of this, see research by Johnson, 1965; Neale, 1969; Anttonen, 1967.) For one thing, what they are required to read may appeal less and less as their tastes in reading enter the adolescent phase of development. As Robert Carlsen put it, ". . . this is the crucial period when many potential readers stop reading. Paradoxically this is also the period when the young person may devote more time to reading than at any other period of his life, provided his interest is not killed."[3] We think the quote would be equally justifiable if you changed the word "read" to "learn" in all three places. In the interest of "quality," schools have in the last few decades moved more and harder subject matter into earlier grades. The result is not only that pupils may understand set theory but not know how to do long division, but schools can become nonsense to them. Why the furor to teach everyone everything in twelve years? After the loss we suffered in Sputnik, we won the race to the moon, but some people are wondering what the prize was to begin with. The effect on schools was not altogether healthy, especially where we forgot that

"To everything there is a season, and a time to every purpose under heaven."[4]

5. *The classroom teacher affects attitudes of students more than does anything else in school.* College students especially find this little activity interesting. First, write on the left-hand side of a sheet of paper your favorite subject (or subjects) when you were in school. Then, on the other side, list the teachers who were your favorites. (Do they match?) Next, list all of the things you think made those subjects and teachers your favorites. (If possible, compare your list of reasons with someone else who has done the same activity.) We think the results will tell you a lot about the effect of teachers on attitudes in school.

Here's another one. Think about the two best experiences in your life and describe them briefly. Now, by "best" we mean experiences that affected your life, your personal development, in a positive way. Then, think about and describe the two worst experiences in your life, ones that retarded your personal development, experiences you had to overcome later.

If what you put down in this activity is anything like that found in a study by Banan (1972), the overwhelming number of experiences (86 percent according to this researcher) involved other people. And that 86 percent, the largest group of other people were teachers. Banan asked only for negative experiences, but our experiences in replicating the study suggest that results hold for positive experiences as well. Teachers have a lot to do with the attitudes of students.

[3]Carlsen, Robert, *Books and the Teen-Age Reader*, p. 23.
[4]Ecclesiastes, 3:1.

In the eyes of the student, it is the teacher who is democratic or authoritarian, interesting or boring, fair or unfair, student-centered or subject-centered. And those eyes make the student feel whatever he or she feels about what is happening to him or her in school. What the student sees is up to the teacher.

Implications for Classroom Practice

What is known or supposed about affect is useful only if it can be translated into practical implications and suggestions. "Practical" means "capable of being put into practice" and we will limit our discussion to suggestions that have practical possibilities. (For example, if parents have bad attitudes toward school, so will the children, more than likely. But changing the parents' attitudes is all but impossible, and it might serve little purpose to discuss the problem and its unlikely solutions by teachers or schools.) Factors that are under control of the teacher and that have bearing on student feelings may be divided into four categories: (1) curriculum factors, (2) classroom setting, (3) pupil characteristics, and (4) teacher characteristics.

Curriculum Factors

The term "curriculum" may be taken to mean, collectively: what is taught, how it is taught, and what is used to teach it. Generally speaking, if what is taught is taught in a way that is appealing to students through materials that are appropriate for them, the chances of their liking it are increased. If learning is pleasant and successful, then students' attitudes toward what they learn are likely to be positive. Conversely, if learning is unpleasant, students will reject what they are taught. They simply won't buy.

There are always determinations to be made regarding curriculum, particularly what to teach. Whatever the choice, one result will be that students' attitudes will be touched. Therefore, choices of what to teach should relate to consideration of interest, appeal, and usefulness to students. In other words, what is taught in a course should relate in some way to students' present or future needs and be taught at a time appropriate to those needs. In no course can *everything* be taught about *anything*. To better the chance that students may continue to learn more of what they can be taught, what they are taught must be chosen to emphasize what is potentially interesting and useful.

Not only what is taught, but how it is taught must be considered in relation to affective change. For example, attitudes are likely to be more positive where students are allowed to express their thoughts freely. A class-

215

room characterized by an open and honest atmosphere that stimulates creative and critical thinking is conducive to positive attitudes. Students, like all people, feel good when their ideas are considered worthy. They tend to feel bad when the atmosphere of their learning is autocratic and threatening. The outcome is practically axiomatic: if students associate good feelings with what they learn, they will likely continue to learn more of it; if they associate negative feelings, they will likely avoid learning of it. Classroom atmosphere plays a big role in this outcome.

The manner in which assignments are made to students is another example. To be successfully completed and for students to feel good about their assignments, directions and purpose for the task must be made very clear. Where they see little reason for what they must do, students' attitudes suffer. However, where assignments are made very clear, with the purpose explained and suggestions given for efficiently completing the task, students will more likely enjoy their accomplishments. And attitudes toward what is accomplished will be better.

The materials of the curriculum, what is used to teach whatever is taught, also bear on students' attitudes. Textbooks selected for a course should be carefully chosen for a pleasing, readable style. Moreover, a variety of texts and other materials should be used in a course. Surely an economist must have invented the single-text approach; teachers know that no textbook can serve all pupils equally well. We might also add that big books with hard backs tend to be intimidative rather than elucidative to many students. Materials of teaching are tools of learning and if the tools suit the needs of learners, their attitudes toward what they experience will be more positive.

Classroom Setting

The effect of physical surroundings was the object of study in the classic "Hawthorne Experiments," from whence derives the term "Hawthorne effect" heard so often. Actually, these were industrial experiments conducted by the Western Electric Corporation. One of the significant findings of those studies was that variety and change in surroundings had a positive effect on workers' production. All people seem to react badly to boredom and sameness in their surroundings.

Some characteristics of the physical surrounding may be out of the teacher's control. The thermostat for the room may be in an office down the hall, lights may need replacing but budget won't allow proper upkeep, desks may be old and dilapidated. Nevertheless, there are always so many factors about the teaching setting that *can* be controlled or changed that those that can't are made bearable. There are many striking exceptions, but the brightness, the activity, the receptiveness of so many classrooms of grades one through three are often a contrast to typical classrooms of grades ten through twelve. (By the way, those striking exceptions of high school classrooms invariably contain students whose attitudes are also exceptional.)

Wall space and bulletin boards can be used creatively for instructional and aesthetic purposes at any grade level. Where possible and appropriate, facilities and settings other than the classroom can be used for instruction. Within the classroom, desks and other furniture can be arranged and rearranged in a manner to serve a variety of instructional needs. (Straight rows of desks are good for two things: listening to lectures and sweeping between. Avoid lecture and seek custodial blessing, and your life in school will be easier.) These suggestions are meant as examples of the kinds of features of the learning environment that affect moods and attitudes toward learning. Learners invariably associate attitude toward what they learn with attitude toward how and in what surroundings they are asked to learn.

The classroom setting is defined not only by physical surroundings but also by that intangible element called "atmosphere." For example, where quiet is maintained at high expense, the atmosphere can be oppressive. Where the classroom is active and buzzing with purposeful activity, the atmosphere is stimulating. To hold interruptions to classroom activity to a minimum is to pay respect for the importance of what kids are doing. Conversely, if, and this by recent actual count, the interclass P.A. system interrupts thinking and learning fifteen times a day, students may believe that there are very many things much more important than their study and learning. The effect on students' attitudes is painfully predictable.

Pupil Characteristics

If it were possible in schools to teach young people what they can learn instead of what they should learn, they would learn more and feel better about it.

Pupils might, for example, be allowed to group themselves on the basis of interest in topics relevant to the course curriculum and then to pursue those topics under the aegis of the course. For example, a group of social studies students could put together an interpretation of the early 1900s through music, focusing on Scott Joplin. The research they do on the time period would bring them to an understanding that is expert. Contrast their resulting attitudes with those of pupils who read a small portion of their dry text with a drier title like "America Turns the Century."

Individuals in a class can and should be given freedom to choose a maximum depth to which they will study. So many texts and so many courses are superficial surveys from which pupils learn little. But school can be a place to study in depth under teacher guidance, even inspiration. Where this is so, pupil attitudes flourish.

The most important pupil characteristic to consider, however, is the

217

"self" each student brings to the learning setting. What education comes right down to is *kids,* young people. If they are given a voice in the decisions affecting them, if the "system" seems to care for them, if they are helped to see their needs in perspective of the needs of the larger group, then they will often return the respect in the form of cooperation. The curriculum of a course, and the way it is "taught," can be cooperatively chosen by pupils and their teacher. The result will assuredly be more positive attitudes on the part of students.

Teacher Characteristics

As we discussed before, ask a person to name his or her favorite subject and favorite teacher in school, and chances are very good the two will go together. The overwhelming influence of the teacher on pupil attitudes can hardly be overstated. There is no more potent force in the classroom; the teacher above all other factors affects student attitudes and achievement. This is true, we believe, because of the influence the teacher has on various dimensions of the school experience. But it is also true because of the teacher as an individual, the things he or she is or seems to be to students.

For example, a teacher's effectiveness in influencing attitudes toward a course is undoubtedly related to that teacher's own interest in the course and his or her conviction regarding its value in the curriculum. If the teacher approaches a course with enthusiasm and excitement, the students will often catch the feeling and begin to share it. Pity the teacher (and pupils of) who is assigned a course no one else wanted and doesn't like simply because no one else would take the assignment. The price of such expediency is staggering. Whatever the course, whoever the teacher, the image and practice of the teacher is an important determiner of pupil attitudes. Pupils need a resource in teachers, not a taskmaster. They appreciate fair grading and discipline, realistic expectations, adequate attention to detail. It is all of these characteristics that cause students to judge a teacher as good, and the corollary to that judgment is a better attitude toward the course and, in turn, learning.

In closing, we are reminded of the king of asteroid 325 whom the little prince met on his journey. The prince has just plucked up enough courage to ask a favor of the king:

> "I should like to see a sunset. . . . Do me that kindness. . . . Order the sun to set. . . ."
>
> "If I ordered a general to fly from one flower to another like a butterfly, or to write a tragic drama, or to change himself into a sea bird, and if the general did not carry out the order that he had received, which one of us would be in the wrong?" the king demanded. "The general, or myself?"

"You," said the little prince firmly.

"Exactly. One must require from each one the duty which each one can perform," the king went on. "Accepted authority rests first of all on reason. If you ordered your people to go and throw themselves into the sea, they would rise up in revolution. I have the right to require obedience because my orders are reasonable."

"Then my sunset?" the little prince reminded him: for he never forgot a question once he had asked it.

"You shall have your sunset. I shall command it. But, according to my science of government, I shall wait until conditions are favorable."[5]

[5]de Saint-Exupéry, Antoine. *The Little Prince.*

UNIT 4

Organizing for Instruction

Conceptual Objectives

1. Organization is the key to effective teaching and learning.

2. Many sources are available for the selection, location, and use of instructional materials in learning activities within the content classroom.

3. Content instruction and literacy development can be organized concurrently.

Activity key

Suggested Activities

	CONCEPTS		
	1	2	3
1. Keep a log of learning activities in your classroom for a week. Classify the activities by major categories in Figure 14.2, p. 226. Redraw Figure 14.2 to picture the way you teach. (If you are not teaching now, think back to the way you were taught and do essentially the same thing.)	X		
2. Make a preliminary examination of one of the units of study included in Chapter 16.	X		X
3. Rank various learning activities that we list on pp. 234–235, in the way suggested on pp. 233–234.	X		
4. Examine carefully the materials described in Chapter 15 and identify sources that fit the subject(s) you teach.		X	
5. Make a list of the professional journals in your content field.		X	
6. Locate sources that frequently review materials for your subject field.		X	
7. Try to contact the publisher's representative for the textbook(s) you use for any supplementary ideas or activities you might secure. Also try to contact representatives of competitors to ask for a professional (complimentary) desk copy for examination. If you succeed, compare texts (see Chapter 3).	X	X	
8. Examine the units in Chapter 16 for varied ways to organize content and literacy study.	X		X
9. Design a unit of instruction that integrates content and literacy study.	X	X	X

CHAPTER **14**   Guiding Students' Learning

> Organization is the key to effective teaching and learning.

Overview

Diagnostic instruction incorporates all the elements of instructional demands relative to the students, the teacher, and the curriculum. It provides for the process of learning without slighting the content to be learned. When these factors are merged within an organizational framework, the task of creating a stimulating learning environment is greatly simplified.

For a summary of the organizational framework that can mobilize learning through diagnostic instruction examine Figure 14.1. As depicted in this figure, the goal of diagnostic instruction in a content classroom is the successful learning of both content and process. Such learning is accomplished when the teacher structures the classroom and designs daily lessons on the basis of instructional needs. When identifying these needs, the teacher must take care to account for the implicit interaction among students' needs, the teacher's goals, and curricular demands. Once all these needs are identified and made compatible, the classroom must be organized to allow learning to occur through a structure of total class, small group, and individual activities. In addition, daily lessons should be clearly designed in terms of the concepts to be emphasized, materials to be used, and appropriate activities that will precede, support, or reinforce the learning. The focal point of the overview in Figure 14.1 is instructional needs. As you consider the other

223

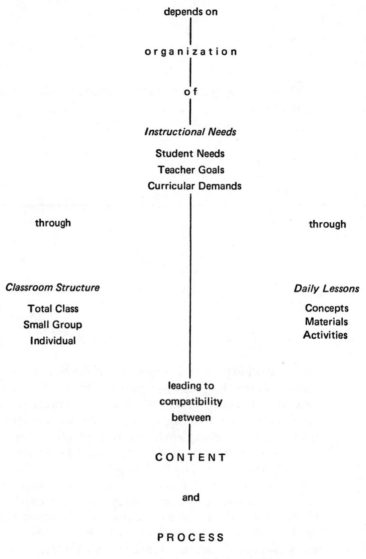

LEARNING THROUGH DIAGNOSTIC INSTRUCTION

depends on

o r g a n i z a t i o n

o f

Instructional Needs

Student Needs
Teacher Goals
Curricular Demands

through   through

Classroom Structure   *Daily Lessons*

Total Class   Concepts
Small Group   Materials
Individual   Activities

leading to
compatibility
between

C O N T E N T

and

P R O C E S S

in units

FIGURE 14.1
Organizational Framework for Process Instruction in Content Classrooms

parts of this organizational framework, bear in mind that its parts are dependently related.

Classroom Organization

The education to which most of us have been exposed was conducted in a setting of large group instruction. This is almost certainly true beyond the primary grades, although the practice is now changing. Though the reading we have done and the "projects" we completed may have been accomplished individually (meaning with little help), in colleges certainly, in high schools and junior high schools likely, the *modus operandi* is typically whole class instruction.

It has been said that this is because teachers tend to teach the way they have been taught; perhaps so. Perhaps also, however, few teachers have been convinced that it could be otherwise. "How can I break the class into groups? For that matter, why should I? They all have to learn the same things anyway and I would multiply my job and divide their learning time." Such a comment reflects a common misunderstanding of alternatives to large group instruction. It may be true that we would want all pupils to learn *of* the same things, but never could all students learn the same amount in the same way. As for the learning time of pupils, one would hope that students can learn at times other than when in direct contact with the teacher.

Consider the purpose of diagnostic instruction in content area classrooms: that the students' conceptualizations of what they study and their ability to read and learn will show concomitant growth. This is most feasible where opportunities for individual and small group instruction are provided as alternatives and supplements to total class instruction. Examine Figure 14.2, an overview of classroom organization presented to suggest types of activities appropriate to three instructional motifs. Total class activities are appropriate for some purposes; small groups may be best suited to other purposes; for yet other purposes, individual instruction may be best.

Total Class Activities

Under this heading are included three suggested purposes. Certainly there are more than these, but consider the *type* of activity that may be appropriate. Screening tests are easily and efficiently given to an entire class, be they of a standardized or an informal nature. The value of these tests stems from the necessity to ascertain what pupils know before specific instructional and learning strategies are planned.

Likewise, a total class setting is often appropriate for an introduction to the rudiments of concepts to be emphasized. The purpose of units of study,

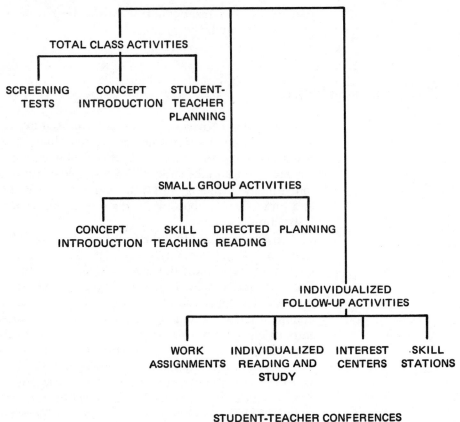

FIGURE 14.2
Classroom Organization

explained subsequently in this chapter, is to allow all pupils to come to different, but individually appropriate, understandings of similar concepts through different activities. At one level of instruction, however, the entire group or class may need to see the "big picture" of what they are studying. This picture would be necessarily sketchy but nonetheless important for the whole class to understand before proceeding to small group or individualized study.

Consider, for example, a familiar concept in the study of literature: "The short story is distinguished by unity of characterization, theme, and effect." A whole class discussion in a high school English class might, over a span of one or more class periods, bring into focus (for all pupils) the meaning of this rather erudite but essential concept. It would not be necessary, however, that everyone had read the same short story or, for that matter, any short story prior to such a discussion. The purpose of this discussion, to introduce the concept, would be to allow exploration of the terms *unity, characterization, theme,* and *effect*. Deeper individual understandings, made richer by a general introduction of the concept, would be developed in other organizational settings.

The third example of total class activities in Figure 14.2 is student-teacher planning. This is especially important. Much planning of time, space, and materials is necessary for the individualization desirable for effective instruction. Many problems of discipline and order are solved when everyone concerned knows when, where, and how individuals are expected to learn and what the consequences are for inappropriate behavior. This knowledge can best be introduced to the whole class at once and reiterated for small groups and individuals as necessary.

There are many other activities appropriate for the whole class setting. For example, films or guest presentations are often appropriate in such a setting. In some schools, trips to the library as well as field trips must be scheduled for whole classes at one time. Figure 14.2 is by no means definitive, nor is it meant to suggest that total class activities are undesirable. It should suggest, however, that activities other than in a total class setting may often be appropriate and necessary.

Small Group Activities

Four activities are listed in Figure 14.2 as appropriate for small group work. Again, think of the type as well as the specific activity suggested. For example, the concept of the short story having been introduced to the total class at a previous time, the idea can be refined to a level appropriate to a smaller group. In the organizational framework we are building, the small group may occupy the majority of the teacher's time. With roughly three groups, which constantly change according to purposes and needs, the teacher might spend approximately two-thirds of his or her time with groups made up of a third of the class or less. At a given moment, then, the remaining two-thirds of the class must be engaged without direct teacher contact, working either in groups or individually.

To elaborate, let's examine how this type of instruction can be applied to a discussion of the elements of a short story. Pupils who have read a story can form a small group to discuss characterization, theme, and effect with reference to that story. As this is done, the individuals in the group are to clarify their understanding of the element of unity in relation to the story. They can thus come to a better understanding of the concept than they did from the whole class discussion, and they can then proceed to read other stories, individually or under teacher direction, as in a content reading lesson. In other cases, a group may be more advanced and have read several stories which, with a teacher's help, can be compared and contrasted with respect to defined elements. In each case, the discussion in the small group may be made more meaningful for the individuals in that group than would be possible in a large group discussion.

This kind of discussion is the kind which realizes the greatest potential of small group work. Small groups need specific purposes, and these purposes are often most effectively defined by activities already completed by individuals. An individual's completion of a project is, in effect, his or her ticket to the small group. For example, notice the way Julie Stockwell handles her three level study guide included in her unit on *Macbeth* (Chapter 16, pp. 274–284). In our experience it is *not* usually effective to have small groups complete a group project. The only way this will work is in instances where (1) the task or problem under consideration requires several steps for completion, and each group member can offer something to the solution, no member having all the steps at his or her command; (2) every member of the group understands the problem and values the group in the sense of believing that the task will more likely be completed by the group than by an individual; and (3) the resources for completion of the task are readily at hand.

We've also placed the content reading lesson in the context of the small group. In Chapter 9 we defined this lesson as an organizational plan for helping students reason through reading. The plan will work for groups of various sizes, depending on how many students in a class are reading the same thing at the same time. As we conceive it, most classroom instruction will *not* focus on one reading for the whole class, and so the content reading lesson will necessarily apply to subgroups of students. About eight to twelve students is the number we've found most effective for directing students' reading. Here's a rule of thumb—the group should be large enough to insure a lot of sharing of ideas but small enough that everyone who wants to can share her or his ideas.

Planning is as important a component of small group work as it is of total class activities. While total class planning may be directed to general operating procedures, small groups may plan their common work together, even without the teacher's guidance. In this setting, plans may be made more specific than was possible in a total class setting. Indeed, often the small group may work with the teacher to plan certain activities that can be carried out while the teacher works with another group.

Individualized Follow-Up Activities

The final element in the organizational paradigm presented in Figure 14.2 is individualized work. It is in this setting that students may spend as much as two-thirds of their time. One of the major purposes of the organizational plan is to allow for the most appropriate setting in which individuals may work at their own pace toward common goals. Realistically, the purpose of education, and let us emphasize that we might be speaking of any content area, is to allow all students to achieve individual levels of understanding of similar concepts. Individualized work is therefore essential as an extension of whole class and small group work.

In the individualized setting, pupils may complete assignments that have been explained in another setting. The number and kinds of activities which might be completed individually by pupils in a class are limited only by the teacher's, and, for that matter, the students' imagination. Reading and study may be individualized through teacher assignment or self-selection by students. Every classroom should have a quiet library corner where one can find interesting things to read related to the study at hand. Some teachers have found it convenient to label this the "time-out" corner where students may retreat from pressure or frustration on days, or at times, when things are not going well. All of us need to get away or take a break now and then; students in a classroom are no exception.

Interest centers and skill development areas are other places of focus for individualized work. In the small group setting, students will often mention special interests in a topic. Individual follow-up to this is valuable in allowing these interests to be developed. In like manner, skill instruction in the small group may require follow-up (e.g., map reading). Such work areas need not be elaborate; a place to work alone on individual deficiencies or areas of interest is all that is required.

Overriding all individualized work are student-teacher conferences. Because of the provision for self-directed and individualized work, the teacher is left free to engage with pupils in cooperative evaluation, guidance, and planning. The teacher who can manage up to two minutes of individualized time with each pupil in each class each week can accomplish at least two critical goals of instruction. First, there is the possibility of doing a lot of teacher "homework," reviewing work folders and performance on school time and in a meaningful setting for pupils. Second, any individual contact with pupils may enhance the possibility of greater learning. In a world driven to impersonalization by sheer numbers, the classroom environment can be set up to avoid impersonalization despite the numbers. This effort in itself may often result in more positive feelings on the part of individuals, leading to a more stimulating and rewarding classroom environment for all.

Organization of Units of Instruction

The unit is the ultimate organizational consideration in diagnostic instruction. As we will define it, a unit is a system of teaching and learning in which the teacher coordinates time, space, and activities around key concepts and understandings that the students are to acquire. It provides an atmosphere for the varying abilities and needs of all students and seeks to create the best possible opportunity for learning for each student. The effect of the organizational system in the unit is to allow students of varying abilities and background to come to better understandings of similar concepts through individually tailored combinations of activities and learning experiences. That is not only a mouthful of a sentence; it is the desideratum of education! It can, however, be translated into practical terms.

Examples of units of study in various content areas appear in the appendix of this book. You might choose one of these examples, preferably one most appropriate to your content specialty, and examine its parts as we discuss the parts of units in more general terms.

There are four essential parts to the framework of any unit of study:

1. a definitive title
2. conceptual objectives
3. materials and resources
4. learning activities

The Unit Title

The title of the unit is important since it should describe in briefest terms the specific domain of inquiry that the unit will cover. While it is impossible to say how general the domain might be, this generality will determine the breadth of other parts of the unit, namely the concepts, materials, and activities. A title like "Biological Science" or "U.S. History before 1865" would probably be too broad since it is doubtful that such topics could be compressed into manageable form. More likely, some part of these would have to be chosen, such as "Amphibian Life Forms" or "The American Revolution."

One clue to the definition of a unit will often be provided by the textbook in use for the course, given that the book is reasonably appropriate for the grade and class with which it is used. Many texts in current use are divided into units, and often this is well done. In cases where the text is well organized, the definition of a unit's scope is facilitated, as the text can suggest the scope while the teacher defines the content of the unit. In effect, the text can be used as a baseline, and the other major components of the unit (concepts, materials, and activities) can be organized by the teacher to develop and individualize that content baseline.

Conceptual Objectives

Composing the list of conceptual objectives for the unit is the second step in its development. The ideal number of concepts for a unit is impossible to define, but the actual number should rarely exceed ten. The assumption is that all students will be exploring the various concepts in sufficient depth to acquire reasonable understandings within a limited period of time. If too many concepts are projected, the depth of learning will certainly be diluted.

We do not want you to confuse what we are calling conceptual objectives with the more common notion of behavioral objectives. Conceptual objectives are related to ideas and understandings. This is not to say we think that many objectives don't result in changed behavior, but rather that in many instances, behaviors seem of secondary importance. A behavioral objective, as you probably know, can be written in answer to the question, "What will the learner be able to *do* as a result of his or her new understandings?" Our question seems to us the prior one to ask: "What is it that students will *understand* as a result of their study?" The first emphasis of instruction has to be on ideas and concepts to be developed. To reduce this to behaviors runs the risk of sidestepping the more important issue of what it is students will understand, i.e., conceptualize, as a result of their reading and study.

So, a conceptual objective is the statement of a general concept in complete sentence form and in language familiar to the students for whom it is intended. The content of a conceptual objective is the understanding you hope learners will retain for many years beyond their first encounter with it. So, for example, for a study of "The Origin of New Groups," a topic often explored in biology, an appropriate conceptual objective might be, "A species is a group of organisms which are able to interbreed and produce fertile offspring under natural conditions." The corresponding behavioral objective would be "The student will be able to list the criteria which define a species," which anyone who did understand the concept would be able to do, but it is the understanding rather than the ability to list which we think is important to emphasize in instruction.

The choice of specific concepts to be included rests on two basic considerations. First, the concepts should be reasonably appropriate in sophistication and interest appeal for the students. To a degree, this must be determined by the level at which the unit is to be taught. In any case, it is a diagnostic decision the teacher must make in trying to match the sophistication of the students' thinking and their interests to what they are expected to learn. The information on which such decisions must be based can be obtained from simple, informal observations through daily contact with the students as well as through formal and informal pretesting. In such pretesting, when items are keyed to concepts being considered for inclusion in a unit, a rather good profile of students' existing understandings can be compiled. Those concepts about which the students seem to know least should be dealt with at a low level of sophistication, if at all. Conversely, concepts in which the students have a firm grounding can be treated at higher levels of sophistication.

Second, concepts should be chosen for their relative importance to an understanding of the overall topic of the unit. With respect to any topic, there are many concepts that might be understood. Those that are most basic and essential for understanding the essence of the unit topic are the ones from which choices must be made. It is the choice of a limited number of appropriate concepts that will form the foundation of a good unit of study; five or six is often sufficient. The object is to focus study, not to elaborate it to the point of dilution or confusion. In Chapter 16 where we have included several examples of units, you can examine other examples of conceptual objectives in the context of those unit topics.

Materials and Resources

Following the list of concepts comes the list of materials and resources. The textbook used in a course is often one good source to include, especially if divided into short sections rather than presented as a set of chapters. Textbooks, however, often tend to be rather limited in their breadth of appeal and suitability of difficulty. One major advantage of the units we are describing is that students are often freed from textbook limitations, freed from the fact that the textbook is insufficient in meeting either their needs or the goals of the teacher.

Other materials and resources may include supplementary readings, both fiction and nonfiction; films, filmstrips, and records; guest speakers and field trips; encyclopedias and other library resources; pamphlets and brochures; materials for use in making collages, dioramas, displays, and the like; charts and maps; and the list goes on, limited only by imagination. The key to determining whether a source is appropriate is simply its value in helping students seek understanding of the concepts within the unit.

Each piece of material is then keyed to the concept(s) to which it bears relevance. As such a key is constructed, the teacher insures that sufficient materials for each concept will be available. Where they are not, for whatever reason or resource limitation, the teacher must reconsider including the concept in the unit. No concept for which little material is available can be well taught to students; thus, the materials and concepts can be manipulated against one another as additions and deletions are made.

Learning Activities

The unit title, the list of concepts, and the list of materials then form a definition of what is to be learned and what means will be used for learning it. The next element, the list of activities for the unit, will define *how* the content of the unit will be learned.

A question that frequently arises is, "How many activities do I need?" Arbitrarily, the number of activities for a given unit can be set at three to five times the number of teaching days to be devoted to the unit. For a three-week unit, excluding one day for pretesting and one for postunit evaluation, one could think in terms of thirteen teaching days and, thus, thirty-nine to seventy-five activities. While that number may not be realistic for a unit of study being created and used for the first time, each time a unit is taught, a backlog of materials and activities will tend to build. With a few years, thirty-nine will seem almost insufficient and seventy-five will begin to loom as almost necessary. The object of a lengthy list of activities is to provide every student, regardless of background or ability, an appropriate combination of activities related to the concepts being stressed. Very likely, no two students would engage in exactly the same combination of alternatives for study. Not all would read the same textbook; not all would write term papers; not all would see the same film. But all *would* come to a better understanding of the same concepts through the means most appropriate to their individual needs and skills. That this might happen is the object of any unit of study.

As activities are listed, they are keyed both to materials and to concepts to which they are related. This, in a similar manner to the materials/concepts key, provides a visible account of the scope of the activities, across the various concepts. Thus, it can be assured that each student engages in a combination of activities that covers the range of conceptual content within the unit. There are always different means (i.e., activities) to accomplish any instructional end (i.e., objective). In fact, different activities are necessary for different pupils to achieve better understandings of the same concepts. At the outset, then, we are assuming that any unit plan will incorporate a range of different kinds of activities from which students may choose or be assigned. Our first question is, therefore: What are the types of activities that might be used in schools and what are their pertinent characteristics? From the answer to the question, we will be able to proceed to the question of what types of activities are preferable among those possible. Eventually, a third question emerges in the classroom, concerning which activities are best for the accomplishment of a given objective for a given pupil. That question is addressed to a circumstance where pupil and teacher are relatively free to choose among many types of activities. This will help insure that the quality of a specific activity is appropriate to the developmental needs of the learner.

Now, let us return to our question regarding types of activities and their characteristics. We sought an answer by consulting teachers and textbooks, and over time we were able to compile the following list of twenty-five categories of activities commonly (and uncommonly) used in schools. As you study the list, we want you to partake of an activity we have used with many other teachers. Following that, we will discuss results we have obtained previously so that you can compare your ideas with those of other teachers.

Think of the activities listed here in terms of children of upper elementary and secondary grades. Your task is to rank the activities on the basis of your judgment of their effectiveness. The following steps should make this easy to do.

First, place a I in the spaces before the five most effective activities. Place a V in spaces before the five least effective.

Second, for the remaining fifteen activities, place a II in the spaces before those which are the most effective of these. Place a IV in the spaces before those which are least effective of this group. The remaining five activities are in the middle range of effectiveness in your judgment and should be marked III.

Third, sort each of the groups of five activities from most to least effective, indicating this in the spaces to the right of the activities. Number your I activities 1, 2, 3, 4, 5; number your II activities 6, 7, 8, 9, 10; etc. When completed, you should have all twenty-five activities ranked from most effective to least effective, 1 through 25.

ACTIVITIES

Use these
spaces to rank
I, II, III, IV, or
V.

Use these
spaces to rank
1–25.

_____ 1. Watch a demonstration. _____

_____ 2. Do an experiment or put on a demon- _____
stration.

_____ 3. Take part in role play or dramatization. _____

_____ 4. Answer questions as the teacher calls on _____
you.

_____ 5. Construct artifacts, models, diaramas, etc. _____

_____ 6. Complete vocabulary activities: matching, _____
puzzles, sorts, etc.

_____ 7. Listen to a record or tape. _____

_____ 8. Write a report or research paper. _____

_____ 9. Read a selection and answer questions at the _____
end.

_____ 10. View a film or filmstrip. _____

_____ 11. View still pictures. _____

_____ 12. Listen to reading or lecture. _____

_____ 13. Use a study guide as an aid to reading and _____
skills practice.

_____ 14. Find pictures or other examples to illustrate _____
a concept.

_____ 15. Participate in discussion led by teacher. _____

_____ 16. Participate in a debate. _____

_____ 17. Take part in content reading lesson. _____

_____ 18. Look up vocabulary words in dictionary. _____

_____ 19. Go on an organized field trip. _____

_____ 20. Do something (cook a meal, dissect an ani- _____ mal, etc.) in class.

_____ 21. Listen to a guest speaker. _____

_____ 22. Participate out of class in some concept- _____ related activity (clean-up campaign, community committee, etc.)

_____ 23. Participate in simulation of experience in _____ class.

_____ 24. Do an exercise in which you sort and catego- _____ rize ideas, words, etc.

_____ 25. Join a group to construct a structured over- _____ view.

Now we would like you to do one more thing. Reflect on the reasons for your decisions. What is it that you think distinguishes effective from ineffective activities? If you think this question through before going on to see what other teachers have thought, you'll probably see that your ideas are similar to other teachers'.

When other teachers have evaluated this list of activities and ranked the items on effectiveness, we have noted that four major categories of activities emerge:

1. Those involving physically and mentally active participation.
2. Those involving mental activity of a creative nature.
3. Those involving solely watching and/or listening.
4. Those involving mental activity of a rote nature.

The rankings of effectiveness of activities tend to be highest for activities involving both physical and mental participation and successively lower for each of the other types of activities in 2, 3, 4 order, as listed. In other words, we can list the activities from most to least effective across major categorical placements. This is generally how the picture looks to most teachers with whom we have worked on the problem:

CATEGORY: *Physically and Mentally Active*

Out of class concept-related activity

Do something

Construct artifacts, models, diaramas, etc.

Simulation

Do experiment, investigation, or demonstration

Role play or dramatization

Join a group to construct a structured overview

Field trip

CATEGORY: *Creative*

Participate in debate

Complete directed and independent readings with various study guides

Illustrate concept with pictures or examples

Content reading lesson

Participate in a discussion

Write a report or research paper

Categorization exercise

Complete vocabulary activities

CATEGORY: *Watching and Listening*

Watch a demonstration

Guest speaker

View still pictures

View films or filmstrips

Listen to a record or tape

Listen to oral reading or lecture

CATEGORY: *Rote Mental Activity*

Question-answer session

Read and answer questions

Look up vocabulary words

MOST EFFECTIVE

LEAST EFFECTIVE

What this means is that within each of the major categories, which we labeled when we saw how the activities were "grouping" themselves, the activities tended to be ranked close together in effectiveness. However, looking at activities in one category and comparing them to activities in another, we find clear qualitative differences. Grouped as they are, there is no doubt in most teachers' minds that the more physically and mentally active, the better; the more passive and rote, the worse. Does this ring true with the kinds of thoughts you were having as you ranked the activities?

Aside from consideration of the major categories of activities, there seem to be three other general considerations, each of which implies several subquestions, which are undoubtedly a part of the judgment of effectiveness. These form a sort of checklist when listed as questions:

1. Is the purpose of the activity apparent?
   a. Are activities logically related to objectives?
   b. Are activities thematically related to each other?
   c. Does the activity allow development of skill and understanding of content?
2. Does the activity provide opportunity for student involvement and participation?
   a. Does the activity demand thinking?
   b. Does the activity require creativity?
3. Does the activity possess inherent appeal?
   a. Does it appeal to student interests?
   b. Does it appeal to students' personal and intellectual needs?
   c. Is the activity likely to be enjoyable to students?

In conclusion, we should comment briefly on one more point. The qualities of activities we have gathered in research with teachers do distinguish

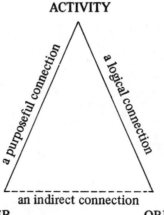

ACTIVITY

a purposeful connection

a logical connection

an indirect connection

LEARNER   OBJECTIVE

FIGURE 14.3
The relationship between learners, activities, and objectives.

activities on the basis of *general* effectiveness. Effectiveness, however, is not inherent in an activity as such; the success or failure of an activity is determined by the relationship among the learner, the activity, and the learning objective. With the possible exception of rote drill, but perhaps including even that, the *specific* effectiveness of an activity depends on a delicate set of connections between learners, activities, and objectives, as we illustrate in Figure 14–3, modeled after the semantic triangle of Ogden and Richards (1923). We hope learners as well as teachers can see the purposeful connection between what they need and what they are doing. The learner should also see the relationship between what he or she is doing and the objective of that activity. Both of these connections are direct. But notice that the connection at the base of our triangle is indirect. Learners achieve, that is *connect with,* objectives in school through the activities they engage in. *If a given activity provides a proper connection between a learner and an objective, that activity is effective.* In other words, effectiveness is a general term which takes on various definitions in specific instances.

CHAPTER 15 Sources for Instructional Materials

Prepared by Betsy Anthony,
Education Librarian, University of
Virginia.

Many sources are available for the selection, location, and use of instructional materials in learning activities within the content classroom.

Instructional Materials

All kinds of activities can be used in a unit of study, but activities must be designed so that each student will develop the desired learning skills as well as content understandings. Since different activities are necessary for different students to achieve these desired instructional objectives, responsibility rests upon the teacher to select quality instructional materials and guide their use in an activity.

Instructional materials and activities may be teacher-produced, student-produced or produced by an outside source. These can be almost anything from a simple folktune or a leaf to an expensive commercially-produced product introduced effectively into the teaching situation. Regardless of the kinds of instructional materials, the product must be in the right hands, at the right time, and in the right learning activity.

The task of planning, developing, and locating appropriate instructional materials can be quite difficult at times for teachers and students. New materials, new methods of use, and new knowledge are being produced at an unprecedented rate which can be quite overwhelming for librarians and teachers. The librarian and media personnel are faced with the task of classifying and organizing these many resources in an effective way in order to help teachers successfully identify and use quality selected materials of instruction.

239

All too often librarians feel that teachers are not fully acquainted with the resources available in the professional library or school media center. Most are eager for teachers to consult with them in planning their units, to explore the selection tools, and to use the newly acquired materials that are available in the library media center. Librarians spend a large amount of money acquiring these resources and therefore are anxious that the materials be used to the fullest by teachers and students.

This chapter is included to acquaint you with some basic sources which will help you in selecting, locating, and using instructional materials and activities necessary for implementation of specific teaching strategies. These sources may be used as a means for looking beyond the school system's adopted curriculum guides or resource units. They will provide you with a sampling of the resources available and give you an idea of the kinds of materials that do exist and others that can be identified as you begin your search in selecting instructional materials.

The Library Catalog

The search for sources must begin in the library. The key to the library's resources and their location is the library catalog, whether the format be the traditional card or a more modern computer-produced catalog. Your approach to the catalog is through the author, title, subject, or added entries. Whatever the approach, full bibliographic information with subject headings assigned is given for each source. If you have difficulty locating subject headings in the catalog, consult the *Sears List of Subject Headings* or the *Library of Congress Subject Headings*, whichever is used by the library. If still unsuccessful, ask the librarian. Always note carefully the call number and location designation such as Reference Collection, Juvenile and Young Adult Collection, Periodical, Film, etc. As you begin using the sources, you will find yourself consulting the catalog many times to check for additional sources as one source leads you to another.

The ERIC Collection

A very useful source of educational information which is not covered in the library catalog is the Educational Resources Information Center (ERIC) microfiche collection. The ERIC system is a national information system designed and developed by the former U.S. Office of Education in 1966 and currently supported and operated by the National Institute of Education, U.S. Dept. of Education. The system is comprised of 16 clearinghouses located at universities and professional organizations. Each clearinghouse collects, screens, organizes, and disseminates reports and prepares interpretive summaries, research reviews, and bibliographies on critical topics in education. The system is also an archive of education literature.

Each of the sixteen clearinghouses in the national network system is responsible for a major area in the field of education. Materials such as current research findings, project and technical reports, speeches, unpublished manuscripts, bibliographies, curriculum guides and materials, statistical data, legislation, proceedings of meetings, directories, tests, questionnaires, books, and monographs are screened according to the ERIC selection criteria. Each item is then abstracted, indexed, and put into the ERIC database. Complete information on addresses and telephone numbers of the clearinghouses can be located in any of the ERIC reference tools.

ERIC Clearinghouses

ERIC Clearinghouse on Adult, Career, and Vocational Education. Ohio State University, Columbus, Ohio.

ERIC Clearinghouse on Counseling and Personnel Services. University of Michigan, Ann Arbor, Michigan.

ERIC Clearinghouse on Educational Management. University of Oregon, Eugene, Oregon.

ERIC Clearinghouse on Elementary and Early Childhood Education. University of Illinois, Urbana, Illinois.

ERIC Clearinghouse on the Handicapped and Gifted Children. Council for Exceptional Children, Reston, Virginia.

ERIC Clearinghouse on Higher Education. George Washington University, Washington, D.C.

ERIC Clearinghouse on Information Resources. Syracuse University, Syracuse, New York.

ERIC Clearinghouse on Junior Colleges. University of California at Los Angeles, Los Angeles, California.

ERIC Clearinghouse on Languages and Linguistics. Center for Applied Linguistics, Washington, D.C.

ERIC Clearinghouse on Reading and Communication Skills. National Council of Teachers of English, Urbana, Illinois.

ERIC Clearinghouse on Rural Education and Small Schools. New Mexico State University, Las Cruces, New Mexico.

ERIC Clearinghouse on Science, Mathematics, and Environmental Education. Ohio State University, Columbus, Ohio.

ERIC Clearinghouse on Social Studies/Social Science Education. Social Science Education Consortium, Inc., Boulder, Colorado.

ERIC Clearinghouse on Teacher Education. American Association of Colleges for Teacher Education, Washington, D.C.

ERIC Clearinghouse on Tests, Measurement, and Evaluation. Educational Testing Service, Princeton, New Jersey.

ERIC Clearinghouse on Urban Education. Teachers College, Columbia University, New York, New York.

People who use the ERIC system are teachers, school administrators, researchers, information specialists, professional organizations, graduate and undergraduate students, and others interested in education. Teachers are able to obtain the latest information on preservice and inservice training, learn about new classroom techniques and materials, and discover how-to-do-it projects for personal and professional development.

The information placed in the computer database is announced through two major publications, *Resources in Education* (RIE) and *Current Index to Journals in Education* (CIJE). The user has accessibility to the ERIC system by means of a computer search or manually searching the two publications.

Resources in Education (RIE)

RIE is a monthly abstracting publication announcing recently added documents of educational significance, indexed by subject, author, institution, and publication type. Each document resume is assigned an ED (ERIC Document) number and arranged by clearinghouse. Most abstracted documents are found in the library's ERIC microfiche collection and filed by the ED number. Documents may also be purchased on microfiche or paper from the ERIC Document Reproduction Service in Arlington, Virginia. Some are copyrighted and entered into the ERIC system for identification purposes only.

ERIC ACCESSION NUMBER — ED 176 284   CS 205 116 — CLEARINGHOUSE ACCESSION NUMBER

AUTHOR(S) — Heirzmann, William Ray

TITLE — The Newspaper in the Classroom. What Research Says to the Teacher.

ORGANIZATION WHERE DOCUMENT ORIGINATED — National Education Association, Washington, D.C.

DATE PUBLISHED — Pub Date—79

Note—31p. — PAGINATION & DESCRIPTIVE NOTE

ALTERNATE SOURCE FOR OBTAINING DOCUMENT — Available from—National Education Association, Order Department, The Academic Building, Saw Mill Road, West Haven, Connecticut 06516 (Stock No. 1048-5-00, 50. 75)

Pub Type—Information Analyses (070)— Guides · Classroom · Teacher (052) — PUBLICATION TYPE

ERIC DOCUMENT REPRODUCTION SERVICE AVAILABILITY (mf denotes microfiche, pc denotes paper-copy) — EDRS Price · MF01 Plus Postage. PC Not Available from EDRS.

Descriptors— •Content Reading, •Educational Research, •Elementary Secondary Education, English Instruction, •Newspapers, •Reading Instruction, •Reading Skills, Social Studies, Teaching Techniques, •Urban Education — DESCRIPTORS & IDENTIFIERS

This review of the research on using the newspaper in the classroom offers suggestions to aid teachers in incorporating the newspaper into their class activities. Ways in which the use of the newspaper improves classroom discussion and reading skills and ———— ABSTRACT motivation (in inner-city schools especially) are discussed. Suggestions for specific activities are given for elementary grades, social studies, English and communication arts, and other subjects. Suggestions are made as to how to begin using newspapers in the class classroom, and a list of resources is provided. ABSTRACTOR'S (MKM) ———————————————————— INITIALS

An Example of a Document Resume in *Resources in Education* (RIE)

Current Index to Journals in Education (CIJE)

CIJE is a monthly guide to the periodical literature indexing more than 800 journal titles. The annotated entries are indexed by subject, author, and journal title. One advantage of this periodical indexing system is that journals in other disciplines are selectively indexed when an issue contains education-related articles. Each article is assigned an EJ (ERIC Journal) number and arranged by clearinghouse.

ACCESSION NUMBER ——— LI 196 006   CS 711 032 ——— CLEARINGHOUSE NUMBER

ARTICLE TITLE ——— Using Comic Books to Teach Reading and
                  Language Arts ——— JOURNAL TITLE
AUTHOR ——— Swain, Emma Halstead *Journal of Reading:*
           v.22, n3, p253-58, Dec 1978 (Reprint UMI) ———
VOLUME NUMBER ——— *Descriptors:* •Comics (Publications); Elemen-   AVAILABILITY
                  tary Secondary Education; •Language Arts;
ISSUE NUMBER ——— •Reading Instruction; •Reading Interests;   PUBL. DATE
                 Student Attitudes; Surveys; Teaching Tech-
MAJOR AND MINOR ——— niques   PAGES
DESCRIPTORS   Results of a questionnaire indicated interest
(major descriptors are   in comic books or comic strips by both good
starred)   and poor readers at all educational levels. In-
             cludes suggestions for activities using comic
             books and strips in the classroom. (MKM) ——— ABSTRACTOR'S INITIALS
ANNOTATION ———

An Example of an Article Resume in *Current Index to Journals in Education*

Thesaurus of ERIC Descriptors

The *Thesaurus of ERIC Descriptors* is the key to the subject approach of the ERIC system whether the search is done manually or by computer. A controlled vocabulary of educational terms called "descriptors" is used to index and enter documents into the ERIC system. The thesaurus must be consulted first before searching the system by subject, otherwise the user may be searching under descriptors (subject headings) which do not presently exist or have been deleted as of a particular date. Broader Terms (BT), narrower terms (NT), related terms (RT), and cross references are designated under each descriptor if required, so the user will select the most appropriate descriptors for the search.

Complete instructions on how to use the ERIC tools effectively are found in the front of each publication. As mentioned earlier, the documents in *RIE* are reproduced on microfiche, if ERIC has been given permission to reproduce them. If not, the information included in the document resume will indicate where the copyrighted material may be obtained. Always check the library's catalog for unavailable titles. The librarian may have purchased the publications for the library's collection. The periodical articles cited in *CIJE* will not be on microfiche. The user must locate the journal in the library's collection or obtain a reprint of the article. Using the computer to search the ERIC database is an efficient method of retrieving the information. A computer search may be obtained through the library's access terminal or through an ERIC clearinghouse. Consult the librarian for additional information and assistance in using the ERIC system.

Periodical Indexing and Abstracting Sources

In most libraries there is a catalog or periodicals printout which lists the journal titles and holdings of the library. The periodical indexes and abstracting sources are used in locating specific articles in the current and retrospective periodical literature. Periodical and abstracting sources useful to the teacher are *Current Index to Journals in Education, Education Index, Social Sciences Citation Index, Language and Language Behavior Abstracts, Psychological Abstracts, State Education Journal Index, P.A.I.S. Bulletin,* and the *Reader's Guide to Periodical Literature.* Some overlap may occur in the periodical coverage, but other types of sources are occasionally included in addition to the periodical literature. The following is a list of periodicals useful to teachers in reviewing and using instructional materials:

AV Guide
Appraisal-Science Books for Young People
Arithmetic Teacher
Arts and Activities
Booklist
Bulletin of the Center for Children's Books

Classroom Computer News
Curriculum Review
Electronic Education
Electronic Learning
English Journal
EPIE Materials Report
Gifted Child Quarterly
History Teacher

Interracial Books for Children Bulletin

Journal of Geography

Journal of Computers in Science and Mathematics Teaching

Journal of Reading

Language Arts

Learning, the Magazine for Creative Teaching

Mathematics Teacher

Media and Methods

Reading Improvement

Reading Teacher

School Arts

School Library Media Quarterly

School Science and Mathematics

Science Activities

Science and Children

Science Books and Films

Science Teacher

Social Education

Social Studies

Theory into Practice

Thinking

Today's Education

Wilson Library Bulletin

The Second Volume of Classroom Ideas for Encouraging Thinking and Feeling. By Frank E. Williams. Buffalo, N.Y.: D.O.K. Publications, 1982.

Lists 342 classroom ideas by subject area and learning strategies to stimulate creative and imaginative thinking skills. This second volume can be used as an extension of the 387 ideas included in the 1970 edition. Useful with grades K-9.

Educational Programs That Work: A Resource of Exemplary Education Programs Developed by Local School Districts and Approved by the Joint Dissemination Review Panel. San Francisco: Far West Laboratory for Educational Research and Development, (annual).

A guide describing curriculum projects, services available, materials used, and grade level for each project. The companion volume *Materials Inventory: U.S. Office of Education Exemplary Products* contains the list of materials, equipment, and teaching aids used in the programs described in *Educational Programs That Work.*

Information America. New York: Neal-Schuman Publishers, 1983, (3/yr).

A guide to approximately 12,000 print and nonprint materials available from organizations, industry, government agencies and specialized publishers. Arranged under broad subject headings.

Programmed Learning and Individually-Paced Instruction: Bibliography. By Carl H. Hendershot. 5th ed. Bay City, Mich.: Hendershot Programmed Learning, 1973. Suppls. 1-6, 1982.

Lists over 3,500 learner-paced texts and other individualized units in many formats and arranged by 222 subject areas. Updated by supplements.

Short-Span Activities: Ideas for Utilizing Spare Minutes in the Classroom. By Lynne Miller and Carol Batten. New York: Citation Press, 1973.

Lists over 80 suggestions of games and activities including subject areas in language arts, social studies, math, art, and science.

Sourcebook of Elementary Curricula, Programs, and Projects from the ALERT Information System. Edited by Samuel N. Henrie. San Francisco: Far West Laboratory for Educational Research and Development, 1972.

> Lists 300 innovative programs and projects in 14 elementary curriculum areas.

Teaching Human Beings: 101 Subversive Activities for the Classroom. By Jeffrey Schrank. Boston: Beacon Press, 1972.

> Lists over 100 activities dealing with unusual subject areas including additional materials of books, films, simulations, and games.

Whole Learning Catalog. Edited by Bruce Raskin. Palo Alto, Ca.: Pitman Learning, 1976.

> A collection of activities, games, and instructional materials covering reading, language arts, math, social studies, science, arts and crafts, and creativity. Reviews and recommendations for learning materials; print and nonprint materials are included.

Print Materials

Print materials as the traditional mode of transmitting information include the widely used medium of books, paperbacks, pamphlets, magazines, newspapers, and other such types. Print materials are easy to use, widely available, easily transported, and relatively inexpensive compared to other mediums, making them the most heavily used source in the curriculum. Books cover the entire range of knowledge recorded quickly and in-depth. Paperbacks permit the user to obtain often inexpensive materials which would otherwise be unavailable. Pamphlets provide a short, concise coverage of a single topic and are usually available free or at minimal cost. They are not meant to be retained on a long-term basis or classified through a complex system. Magazines and newspapers provide current information on all subjects with accessibility through indexes for easy retrieval.

Books for Secondary School Libraries. Compiled by the Ad Hoc Library Committee of the National Association of Independent Schools. 6th ed. New York: Bowker, Co. 1981.

> A well-chosen annotated list of over 9,000 nonfiction titles and series including all subject areas. Useful to librarians, teachers, and others as a comprehensive bibliographic guide and selection aid.

Books in Print. New York: Bowker Co., (annual).

> A publication listing all inprint titles from more than 13,900 publishers or distributors in the U.S. Subject approach is provided through the companion volume *Subject Guide to Books in Print.*

Children's Books in Print. New York: Bowker Co., (annual).

> Provides an author, title, and illustrator index to over 40,000 children's fiction and nonfiction books in print for preschool to young adults. Subject approach is provided through the companion volume *Subject Guide to Children's Books in Print*.

Children's Catalog. 14th ed. New York: H. W. Wilson Co., 1981.

> A well selected annotated list of books for needs of students and the curriculum. Covers books for preschool through the sixth grade. Supplements issued between editions.

Children's Magazine Guide. Madison, Wisconsin: Pleasant T. Rowland, Publisher, (9/yr).

> A subject approach to articles found in children's magazines. Indexes about 45 magazines commonly found in elementary and junior high school media centers.

Elementary School Library Collection: A Guide to Books and Other Media. Phases 1-2-3. Edited by Lois Wirkel. 13th ed. Newark, New Jersey: Bro-Dart, 1982.

> A valuable tool of over 13,000 print and nonprint materials. Useful to teachers and librarians in selecting curriculum and library materials.

El-Hi Textbooks in Print. New York: Bowker Co., (annual).

> Lists more than 27,000 elementary, junior high, and high school textbooks and supplementary readers arranged under 21 curriculum categories.

Guide to Reference Books for School Media Centers. By Christine Wynar. 2nd ed. Littleton, Colorado: Libraries Unlimited, 1981.

> Evaluates and annotates nearly 2,000 titles for use in elementary and secondary media centers. Covers a wide range of subject areas and interests.

Junior High School Library Catalog. 4th ed. New York: H. W. Wilson Co., 1980.

> A well-chosen annotated list of basic books, fiction, and nonfiction, for support of the junior high school curriculum and students' interests. Covers grades 7-9. Supplements issued between editions. Companion volumes are the *Children's Catalog* and *Senior High School Library Catalog*.

Paperbound Books in Print. New York: Bowker Co., (annual).

> Lists all paperbound books published or distributed in the U.S. under approximately 240 subject headings.

Periodicals for School Media Programs. By Selma K. Richardson. 2nd ed. Chicago: American Library Association, 1978.

> An annotated list of over 600 periodicals, newspapers, and periodical indexes, selected to meet the needs of students K-12 for both curricula and personal interests.

Reference Books for Children. By Carolyn S. Peterson and Ann D. Fenton. Metuchen, New Jersey: Scarecrow Press, 1981.

> An annotated guide to over 900 reference books and selection aids. Titles are arranged under broad categories which are subdivided into specific headings.

Sources for indexing book reviews are *Book Review Digest, Book Review Index, Children's Book Review Index* and *Education Index-Book Reviews* section. Periodicals most often used by teachers and librarians for book reviews include *Booklist, Choice, SLJ/School Library Journal, Kirkus Reviews, Appraisal: Science Books for Young People, Horn Book Magazine, Children's Book Review Service, Wilson Library Bulletin, Interracial Books for Children Bulletin,* and *Bulletin of the Center for Children's Books.* Lists of best books are published by associations and organizations including American Association of School Librarians, Association for Childhood Education International, Children's Book Council (N.Y.), Library of Congress Children's Literature Center, American Library Association, National Council for the Social Studies, American Association for the Advancement of Science, National Science Teachers Association, and others.

Nonprint Materials

Nonprint materials include audio, visual, and graphic materials, simulations, games, television and radio programs, and microcomputer software. Some of the mediums are quite expensive, others are available at minimal cost. Nonprint materials can be effective if selected carefully and accompanied with additional appropriate learning activities. This list includes comprehensive sources for all nonprint materials as well as specific sources for audio or visual mediums only.

Audiovisual Market Place: A Multimedia Guide with Names and Numbers. New York: Bowker Co., (annual).

> Lists media producers, distributors, manufacturers, educational radio and tv stations, associations, reference materials, and other related materials and information including a classification index of more than 625 subject headings.

Audiovisual Materials. Washington, D.C.: Library of Congress.

> A comprehensive quarterly publication listing approximately 10,000 titles per year for films, filmstrips, video recordings, slides, transparencies, and kits produced in the U.S. and Canada. Covers all subjects.

Children's Media Market Place. Edited by Carol A. Emmens. 2nd ed. New York: Neal-Schuman Publishers, 1982.

A directory of sources for locating children's materials, including publishers, audiovisual producers and distributors, periodicals for children, juvenile book clubs, reviewers of children's media, tv and radio programs, awards, and other sources of information.

Core Media Collection for Elementary Schools. By Lucy G. Brown. New York: Bowker Co., 1978.

A qualitative selection guide to over 3,000 nonprint media titles recommended through reviews, evaluations, or as award winners. Entries are arranged by subject, title, and producer. Covers many subject areas.

Core Media Collection for Secondary Schools. By Lucy G. Brown. 2nd ed. New York: Bowker Co., 1979.

Lists 3,000 nonprint materials recommended through reviews, evaluations, or as award winners. Arranged by subject, title, and producer. Covers many subject areas.

Educational Film Locator of the Consortium of University Film Centers and R. R. Bowker. 2nd ed. New York: Bowker Co., 1980.

A selective annotated listing of about 40,000 educational film titles for sale or rental and often requested by users from the University Film Centers. Arranged by subject, title, and series with audience level (preschool-adult) and producer/distributor information included.

Educators Progress Service, Inc. Randolph, Wisconsin.

Guides providing annotated listings of free media materials. Updated annually. Titles include:

Educators Guide to Free Films
Educators Guide to Free Filmstrips
Educators Guide to Free Audio and Video Materials
(For a complete list of Educators Guides see under **Free and Inexpensive Materials.**

Films—Too Good for Words: A Directory of Nonnarrated 16mm Films. By Salvatore J. Parlato, Jr. New York: Bowker Co., 1973.

Lists nearly 1,000 nonnarrated films covering many subjects. Valuable for selecting films for hearing-impaired students or students of low language abilities.

Let's See It Again: Free Films for Elementary Schools. By J. A. Kislia. Dayton, Ohio: Pflaum/Standard Publishing Co., 1975.

Over 200 films arranged by title, subject, and source. Annotations include evaluation, contents, remarks by students, and grade level.

National Information Center for Educational Media (NICEM) Series. University of Southern California, University Park, Los Angeles.

An automated retrieval system containing information on nonprint educational media and materials. Indexes are updated every 2½ years. *Update of Nonbook Media* is issued between editions.

Single Media Indexes include:
Index to Educational Audio Tapes
Index to Educational Overhead Transparencies
Index to Educational Records
Index to 16mm Educational Films
Index to Educational Slides
Index to Educational Video Tapes
Index to 8mm Motion Cartridges
Index to Producers and Distributors
Index to 35mm Educational Filmstrips

Multimedia content area indexes include:
Index to Environmental Studies—Multimedia
Index to Health and Safety Education—Multimedia
Index to Nonprint Special Education Materials—Learner Volume
Index to Nonprint Special Education Materials—Professional Volume
Index to Psychology—Multimedia
Index to Vocational and Technical Education—Multimedia

NICEM also publishes and distributes indexes containing information on special education materials developed by the National Information Center for Special Education Materials (NICSEM). (See sources listed in the EXCEPTIONAL STUDENTS section.)

Schwann Record and Tape Guide. Boston: ABC Schwann Publications, Inc., (2/yr).

A selective guide to recorded music for all ages and subjects. Beginning in 1983, includes a separate section of children's records and tapes.

Superfilms: An International Guide to Award-Winning Educational Films. By Salvatore J. Parlato, Jr. Metuchen, New Jersey: Scarecrow, 1976.

Lists recommended, award-winning educational films covering many subjects and all grade levels.

Video Source Book. 4th ed. Syosset, New York: National Video Clearinghouse, 1982.

An annotated list of over 35,000 video programs covering a wide range of subjects.

Video Tape/Disc Guide to Home Entertainment. 3rd ed. New York: National Video Clearinghouse, 1982.

Over 4,000 listings of the most popular movies, sports, children's and entertainment programs. A subject, cast, disc and stereo index is included.

What to Do When the Lights Go On: A Comprehensive Guide to 16mm Films and Related Activities for Children. By Maureen Gaffney and Gerry B. Laybourne. Phoenix, Arizona: Oryx Press, 1981.

Approximately 340 film titles are used with 30 programs and activities and an additional 40 activities supported with films and other experiences. Updates *More Films Kids Like: A Catalog of Short Films for Children* and *Films Kids Like.*

Some of the periodicals which include media reviews are *Booklist, Childhood Education, Children's House, Curriculum Review, Film Library Quarterly, Instructional Innovator, Instructor and Teacher, Learning— Magazine for Creative Teaching, Landers Film Reviews, Language Arts, Media and Methods, Media Review, School Library Journal, School Library Media Quarterly, Science and Children, Science Books and Films, Sightlines,* and *Wilson Library Bulletin. Media Review Digest* indexes most media reviews.

Graphic Materials, Simulations, Games, and Television

Graphic materials include media such as art materials, posters, prints, photographs, maps, and globes. Libraries, museums, galleries, historical and government agencies are excellent sources for these kinds of materials. Simulations and games can be subject-oriented and effectively introduced into a learning activity to provide a means for improving motor, verbal, visual, thinking, and social skills. They can create interest, offer challenges, are easily adapted to one person or a group, and require an active rather than passive participation. Television as an educational medium has had its proponents and critics. Teachers must decide on its merits in the classroom and continue to explore its use as an instructional medium.

Active Learning: Games to Enhance Academic Abilities. By Bryant J. Cratty. Englewood Cliffs, New Jersey: Prentice Hall, 1971.
> Covers over 100 active learning games designed to improve coordination while teaching geometry, numbers, letters, language arts, etc.

AIT Catalog of Educational Materials. Bloomington, Ind.: Agency for Instructional Television., (annual).
> Lists educational videocassettes and videorecordings. A subject and grade index are included. The catalog of Great Plains National Instructional Television Library, Lincoln, Neb., should also be consulted as a source for instructional television series. Both are revised annually and are free.

Classroom Portfolio of Energizers, Puzzles, Quizzes, Games, and Brain Teasers. By Fred B. Chernow and Carol Chernow. West Nyack, New York: Parker Publishing Co., 1979.
> Over 200 classroom-tested activities provided to encourage and stimulate learning in language arts, math, social studies, science, consumer education, crafts, physical education, guidance, and career education.

251

Contemporary Games: A Directory and Bibliography Covering Games and Play Situations or Simulations Used for Instruction and Training by Schools, Colleges and Universities, Government, Business, and Management. Compiled by Jean Belch. Detroit: Gale Research Co., 1973-74. 2 volumes.

> A list of instructional games, both manual and computer operated, covering all subjects with emphasis on social sciences, education, languages, and math. Includes games for elementary to adult level.

Developmental Games and Rhythms for Children. By Albert M. Farina. Springfield, Illinois: C. C. Thomas, 1980.

> Contains approximately 400 games and rhythms with 300 additional variations. Active and passive games are grouped under each age from 4-11.

Guide to Simulations/Games for Education and Training. Edited by Robert E. Horn and Anne Cleaves. 4th ed. Beverly Hills, Ca.: Sage, 1980.

> Lists educational simulations and games for junior high through adult level. Covers all subject areas.

Handy Key to Your National Geographics: Subject and Picture Locator, 1915-1981. Compiled by Charles S. Underhill. 15th ed. East Aurora, New York: C. S. Underhill, 1982.

> A subject index of graphic materials and maps appearing in the *National Geographic* magazine.

Illustrated Treasury of Classroom Games and Activities. By Muriel Schoenbrun Karlin. West Nyack, New York: Parker Publishing Co., 1980.

> Over 100 classroom-tested games and activities covering reading, writing, spelling, grammar, math, social studies, science, health, and art.

Illustration Index. Edited by Marsha C. Appel. 4th ed. Metuchen, New Jersey: Scarecrow Press, 1980.

> Indexes approximately 12,500 illustrations in 8 periodicals: *American Heritage, Ebony, Holiday, National Geographic, National Wildlife, Natural History, Smithsonian,* and *Sports Illustrated.*

Learning from Pictures. By Catharine M. Williams. 2nd ed. Washington, D.C.: Association for Educational Communications and Technology, 1968.

> A classic which presents hundreds of ideas for locating and using pictures in all curriculum areas.

Picture Searching: Techniques and Tools. By Renata V. Shaw. 2nd ed. New York: Special Libraries Association, 1982.

> Lists sources of illustrations grouped in broad subject categories.

Picture Sources 4: Collections of Prints and Photographs in the United States and Canada. Edited by Ernest H. Robl. New York: Special Libraries Association, 1983.

> An index to 1,200 picture sources such as libraries, government agencies, museums, historical societies, and others.

Teachers Guide to Television. New York: National Association of Broadcasters., (semiannual).

> A publication providing information on commercial programs of educational value. The guide also includes lesson plans, activities, and reading lists.

The *Reader's Guide to Periodical Literature* indexes illustrations in popular periodicals. Government agencies such as the National Ocean Survey and the U.S. Geological Survey (for maps), the Smithsonian and its many galleries (for prints, etc.) are excellent sources for obtaining graphic materials. Publication lists are usually available free from each of these agencies.

Microcomputers

Microcomputers are gaining in accessibility and usefulness as an integral part of the educational setting. Only in the last few years have guides and resources become available to aid in the selection and purchase of microcomputer software. The tools necessary for review and evaluation are increasing as the demands of the users continue to grow. In this early stage of microcomputer development and usage as an instructional medium, organizations and associations are excellent sources of information and ideas for the computer using educator. Some major ones are International Council for Computers in Education, Association for Computers in Mathematics and Science Teaching, Association for Educational Communications and Technology, Minnesota Educational Computing Consortium, Michigan Association for Computer Users in Learning, and EPIE Institute. The national associations such as the National Education Association, National Council of Teachers of English, National Council for Teachers of Mathematics, National Council for the Social Studies and others are publishing professional publications covering all aspects of educational computing and its uses and products. A selected number of periodicals that will be helpful have been included in the list of periodicals useful to teachers for reviewing and using instructional materials. The *Microcomputer Index,* a specialized periodical indexing source, covers more than twenty-five computer magazines. ERIC's *CIJE* and *Education Index* also index articles about the instructional use of microcomputers.

Addison-Wesley Book of Apple Computer Software. Lawndale, Ca.: Book Co., 1983.

> A directory which describes and rates a large selection of Apple-compatible software including educational packages. Updates are issued quarterly.

Classroom Computer News Directory of Educational Computing Resources. Watertown, Mass.: Intentional Educations, Inc., (annual).

> Provides information on organizations, associations, resource centers, and clearinghouses. Also included are print and nonprint sources such as directories, periodicals, reviews, and databases.

Courseware Report Card. Compton, Ca.: Courseware Report Card, (5/yr).

> Issued in two editions, elementary and secondary. Includes over 100 software reviews covering Apple, Radio Shack, Atari, Commodore, and Texas Instruments educational programs. Descriptions and ratings are given for each.

EPIE Micro-Courseware PRO/FILE and Evaluation. New York: EPIE Institute, (annual with updates).

> An excellent source providing a 1-2 page comparative evaluation on each of the major software curriculum packages.

EPIE Micro-Hardware PRO/FILE and Evaluation. New York: EPIE Institute, (annual with updates).

> Provides a 4-page comparative evaluation on each of the major microcomputer systems currently available to schools.

Index to Computer-Based Learning. Edited by Anastasia Wang. Milwaukee: Instructional Media Laboratory, University of Wisconsin, 1981.

> Abstracts over 4,800 programs for elementary and secondary schools and colleges.

Instructor's 1982-83 Computer Directory for Schools. Duluth, Minn.: Instructor Publications, Inc., (annual).

> A guide to the selection of microcomputers and instructional software. Also includes books, resources, free materials, periodicals, and articles on the selection of computer materials.

Sources for Courses. Oak Park, Illinois: TALMIS, Inc., (annual).

> Lists over 900 programs for K-college level, indexed by title, subject, grade level, and publisher. Also includes information on reviews, format, price, running time, and related print and nonprint materials.

Swift's Directory of Educational Software, Apple II Edition. Austin, Texas: Sterling Swift Publishing Co., 1982.

> Contains descriptors of educational programs, commercial and noncommercial, for the apple microcomputer. Indexed by discipline and grade level.

Government Publications

Government publications can be obtained from local, state, federal, and international agencies and convey accurate and factual information on many topics. They are useful in the educational setting and can be effectively incorporated into learning activities. Most university and large public libraries are depositories for local, state, and federal documents, providing easy access to these documents.

Consumer Information Catalog: A Catalog of Selected Federal Publications of Consumer Interest. Pueblo, Colorado: Consumer Information Center.

Lists mostly free government publications available in many subject areas.

Government Reference Books 1980/81; A Biennial Guide to U.S. Government Publications. By Walter L. Newsome. 7th ed. Littleton, Colorado: Libraries Unlimited, 1982.

Lists approximately 2,000 reference publications issued during the two-year period covered. Includes agency, publication date, price, ordering information, and annotation.

Monthly Catalog of United States Government Publications. Washington, D.C.: Government Printing Office.

A monthly listing of government publications including books, pamphlets, maps, and periodicals in all subject areas.

Monthly Checklist of State Publications. Washington, D.C.: Library of Congress.

A monthly listing of state documents supplied by the individual states to the Library of Congress.

Posters, Charts, Picture Sets, and Decals. Washington, D.C.: Government Printing Office, 1982.

A *Subject Bibliography* issue listing the items and their cost.

Reference List of Audiovisual Materials Produced by the United States Government. Washington, D.C.: National Audiovisual Center, 1978. Supplement, 1980.

A catalog of over 6,000 audiovisual materials produced by approximately 175 agencies and available for sale or rent. Indexed by subject.

Selected U.S. Government Publications. Washington, D.C.: Government Printing Office.

A monthly listing of new and popular titles including ordering information and grade level.

State Government Reference Publications: An Annotated Bibliography. By David W. Parish. 2nd ed. Littleton, Colorado: Libraries Unlimited, 1981.

Lists over 1700 publications from the 50 states. Includes agency, publication date, price, and annotation.

Subject Bibliographies. Washington, D.C.: Government Printing Office.

Each issue usually covers a single topic and lists government documents and prices of each pertaining to the subject. Covers some 300 topics.

UNDOC: Current Index. United Nations Documents Index. New York: Dag Hammarskjold Library.

> A quarterly listing of United Nations publications received in the U.N. Library.

U.S. Government Publications for the School Media Center. By Alice J. Wittig. Littleton, Colorado: Libraries Unlimited, 1978.

> Includes approximately 350 government publications, maps, and pictorial materials covering 17 subject categories.

ERIC's *Resources in Education* and the *P.A.I.S. Bulletin* index some U.S., state, and international documents such as the UNESCO publications.

Free and Inexpensive Materials

Free and inexpensive materials are usually produced by government, industry, professional, and trade organizations and may or may not be originally intended for educational purposes. Many such items are slanted toward the producer's point of view and should be carefully selected and used with a balance of other materials. Recyclable and do-it-yourself materials can be included in this category.

Educators Progress Service, Inc. Randolph, Wisconsin.

> Guides provide annotated listings of all types of print and nonprint free materials including government publications, maps, and graphic materials. All grade levels and subject areas are represented. Updated annually.

> Titles include:
> > Educators Grade Guide to Free Teaching Aids
> > Educators Guide to Free Films
> > Educators Guide to Free Filmstrips
> > Educators Guide to Free Guidance Materials
> > Educators Guide to Free Health, Physical Education, and Recreation Materials
> > Educators Guide to Free Science Materials
> > Educators Guide to Free Social Studies Materials
> > Educators Guide to Free Audio and Video Materials
> > Educators Index of Free Materials
> > Elementary Teachers Guide to Free Curriculum Materials

Free and Inexpensive Learning Materials. Nashville, Tennessee: George Peabody College for Teachers, (biennial).

> Recommended listing of more than 3,000 instructional aids for all grade levels covering over 100 subject areas.

Index to Free Periodicals. Ann Arbor, Michigan: Pierian Press, (2/yr).

> An author, title, and subject index to approximately 50 free periodicals covering all subjects and grade levels.

Selected Free Materials for Classroom Teachers. By Ruth H. Aubrey. 6th ed. Belmont, Ca.: Pitman Learning, Inc., 1978.

> Recommended print and nonprint materials for the intermediate and secondary level covering approximately 50 curricular categories.

Vertical File Index. New York: H. W. Wilson Co., (11/yr).

> A subject and title index to selected pamphlets covering all grade levels and subjects.

Special Subjects

The sources included in the special subjects section are examples of the many publications available through national associations and organizations, government agencies, and regional programs. Publications catalogs of these organizations are available and can be consulted for a brief description, price, and ordering information. The ERIC *Resources in Education* indexes many of these publications and those which are not copyrighted are included in the microfiche collection. Reference sources such as guides to historical fiction, poetry, authors, and illustrators have been excluded. Christine Wynar's *Guide to Reference Books for School Media Centers*, Sheehy's *Guide to Reference Books*, and H. W. Wilson's *Children's Catalog, Junior High School Library Catalog*, and *Senior High School Library Catalog* can be used to identify these kinds of reference sources.

Language Arts/English

Adventuring with Books: A Booklist for Pre-K—6. Edited by Mary L. White. Urbana, Illinois: Committee on the Elementary School Booklist, National Council of Teachers of English, 1981.

Best Books for Children: Preschool Through the Middle Grades. Edited by John R. Gillespie and Christine B. Gilbert. 2nd ed. New York: Bowker Co., 1981.

> Annotates approximately 13,000 titles as recommended through booklists, reviews, sources, and committees. Arranged under 34 broad subject headings with grade level included for each title.

Best in Children's Books: The University of Chicago Guide to Children's Literature, 1973-1978. Edited by Zena Sutherland. Chicago: University of Chicago Press, 1980.

Reviews of books especially useful for teachers. Indexes for developmental values, curricula, subject, reading level, title, and genre are included.

Black Literature for High School Students. By Barbara D. Stanford and Karima Amin. Urbana, Illinois: National Council of Teachers of English, 1978.

A survey of black literature with supplementary bibliographies. Also includes units, activities, and games for classroom uses of black literature.

Black World in Literature for Children: A Bibliography of Print and Nonprint Materials. Edited by Joyce W. Mills. Atlanta: Atlanta University School of Library Service, 1975-1977. 3 vols.

An annotated list of print and nonprint materials about the black experience, black people, or with black characters in the U.S. and Africa. For ages 3-13.

Book Bait: Detailed Notes on Adult Books Popular with Young People. Compiled by Elinor Walker. 3rd ed. Chicago: American Library Association, 1979.

A selection of adult books for young people including a summary of each and ideas for presentation.

Bookfinder: A Guide to Children's Literature About the Needs and Problems of Youth Aged 2-15. By Sharon S. Dreyer. Circle Pines, Minn.: American Guidance Service, 1977-1981. 2 vols.

A well-annotated list of books that deal with many real life situations. Over 450 psychological, behavioral, and developmental topics of concern to children and young adolescents are used in categorizing the books.

Books for You: A Booklist for Senior High Students. Edited by Robert C. Small, Jr. 7th ed. Urbana, Illinois: National Council of Teachers of English, 1982.

An annotated list of nearly 1,400 pleasurable reading books for high school students. Arranged under 35 subject headings.

Classroom Practices in Teaching English Series. Urbana, Illinois: National Council of Teachers of English, (biennial).

Each is devoted to a single topic such as minorities, sexism, basics, etc.

Films and Filmstrips for Language Arts; An Annotated Bibliography. By Jill P. May. Urbana, Illinois: National Council of Teachers of English, 1981.

Reviews nearly 300 films and filmstrips for use with children ages 5-12. Titles were selected for usefulness in generating classroom activities.

Handbook for Story Tellers. By Caroline F. Bauer. Chicago: American Library Association, 1977.

Presents techniques and skills in telling a story and demonstrates ways to use media in presenting stories to the preschool to senior grade levels.

I Read, You Read, We Read; I See, You See, We See; I Hear, You Hear, We Hear; I Learn, You Learn, We Learn. By the Committee on Library Service to the Disadvantaged Child. Chicago: American Library Association, 1971.

> An annotated list of books, stories, poems, films, and recordings for the disadvantaged child, preschool to 14 years of age.

Ideas for Teachers from Teachers: Elementary Language Arts. Edited by Audrey Hodgins. Urbana, Illinois: National Council of Teachers of English, 1983.

> Over 100 activities and ideas submitted by teachers cover the teaching of reading and writing, using dictionaries, punctuation, grammar, observation, and evaluation.

Ideas for Teaching English in the Junior High and Middle Schools. Edited by Candy Carter and Zora Rashkis. Urbana, Illinois: National Council of Teachers of English, 1980.

> Includes nearly 200 successful activities for teaching English including language study, communication, reading and literature, writing, and listening and viewing.

International Reading Association. IRA Reading Aids Series.

> A series of monographs published by IRA to help teachers with reading in all subject areas. Some published titles include *Using Sports and Physical Education to Strengthen Reading Skills* (1980), *Improving Reading in Science* (1976), *Teaching Reading and Mathematics* (1976), and *Prereading Activities for Content Area Reading and Learning* (1982).

Introducing More Books: A Guide for the Middle Grades. By Diana L. Spirt. New York: Bowker Co., 1978.

> A list of 72 titles arranged under nine appropriate developmental goals. Includes a summary, thematic analysis, discussion materials, and related books. Useful with children ages nine to fourteen.

Inventing and Playing Games in the English Classroom: A Handbook for Teachers. Edited by Kenneth Davis and John Hollowell. Urbana, Ill.: National Council of Teachers of English, 1977.

> Presents the use of simulation games as a teaching method in the study of composition, language, and literature. Includes classroom-tested games and an annotated bibliography of commercially prepared games.

Listening Aids Through the Grades—232 Listening Activities. By David H. Russell and Elizabeth F. Russell. Revised and enlarged by Dorothy G. Henning. New York: Teachers College Press, 1979.

> Provides listening activities for kindergarten through intermediate grades which are literature-oriented and includes a multimedia approach. A listing of books and multimedia packages are also included.

A Multimedia Approach to Children's Literature; A Selective List of Films, Filmstrips, and Recordings Based on Children's Books. By Ellin Greene and Madalynne Schoenfeld. Chicago: American Library Association, 1977.

259

An annotated listing of selected media useful for introducing books to primary and intermediate levels.

Newbery and Caldecott Medalists and Honor Book Winners: Bibliographies and Resource Materials Through 1977. Compiled by Jim Roginski. Littleton, Colorado: Libraries Unlimited, 1982.

Lists publications and materials of 266 authors and illustrators who have been recipients of the Newbery, Caldecott, and Honor Book medals. Each author and/or illustrator entry includes awards, bibliography, nonprint media, exhibitions, collections, and background readings.

Prizewinning Books for Children: Themes and Stereotypes in U.S. Prizewinning Prose Fiction for Children. By Jaqueline S. Weiss. Lexington, Mass.: Lexington Books, 1983.

Contains over 700 prizewinning titles which are grouped under broad headings and then subdivided within each grouping, covering K-6 grade level. Excluded are nonfiction, alphabet and counting books, rhyming and wordless picture books, poetry and drama, and foreign publishers.

Reading Activities in Content Areas; An Ideabook for Middle and Secondary Schools. By Dorothy Piercey. 2nd ed. Boston: Allyn and Bacon, 1982.

Offers activities for use by upper elementary, junior and senior high, and postsecondary teachers. Provides guidelines for teacher behaviors and student activities. Each activity includes subject area, grade level, objectives, student and teacher preparation, and procedures.

Reading Aids for Every Class: 400 Activities for Instruction and Enrichment. By Ellen L. Thomas. Boston: Allyn and Bacon, 1980.

Lists activities and aids grouped under eight broad reading skills. Indexes include a reading achievement-level index and subject area index.

Reading and Language Arts: Products from NIE. San Francisco: Far West Laboratory for Educational Research and Development, 1977.

Lists 75 products in reading and language arts including a directory of resources for locating quality products and programs.

Shakespeare: Annotated Bibliographies and Media Guide for Teachers. By Andrew M. McLean. Urbana, Ill.: National Council of Teachers of English, 1980.

An annotated list of resources for the various approaches in teaching Shakespeare.

Storyteller's Sourcebook: A Subject, Title, and Motif Index to Folklore Collections for Children. By Margaret R. MacDonald. New York: Neal-Schuman, 1982.

Indexes 556 folktale collections and 389 picture books by motif, tale title, subject, ethnic, and geographic. Stith Thompson's motif index has been used with some adaptation.

Teacher's Directory of Reading Skill Aids and Materials. By Emerald Dechant. West Nyack, N.Y.: Parker Publishing Co., 1981.

A comprehensive sourcebook of commercially published multimedia instructional materials designed to aid in the development of reading skills. Each entry, organized under skill area, identifies skills, grade level, type of material (i.e. book, recording, kit, etc.), and level and type of interest.

Thematic Units in Teaching English and the Humanities. Edited by Sylvia Spann and May B. Culp. Urbana, Illinois: National Council of Teachers of English, 1975. Supplements 1977-1980.

Unit plans focus on involving students and their language skills. Includes an overview, objectives, lists of materials needed, lesson plans, activities, supplementary reading and teaching materials, and bibliographies.

What Can I Write About? 7000 Topics for High School Students. By David Powell. Urbana, Illinois: National Council of Teachers of English, 1981.

Arranged under twelve broad categories of the kinds of writing such as description, comparison, narrative, cause and effect, critical writing, etc., and then subdivided within each category. Preceding each category are notes giving the definition, how-to, and locating subjects for each category.

Whole Word Catalog 2. Edited by Ron Podgett and Bill Zabatsky. New York: Teachers and Writers Collaborative, 1977. A collection of assignments and activities for stimulating student writing. Includes supplementary materials.

Your Reading: A Booklist for Junior High Students. Edited by Jerry L. Walker. 5th ed. Urbana, Illinois: National Council of Teachers of English, 1975.

A list of more than 1,600 titles both fiction and nonfiction designed for use by students themselves. Over 40 subject headings are used.

Social Studies/Social Science

China: A Multimedia Guide. By Mary R. Sive. New York: Neal-Schuman, 1982.

Lists approximately 400 print and nonprint materials, government publications, maps, kits, and other materials. Includes an annotation, publisher/producer, date, price, and grade level.

Consumer Education Sourcebook. By Dorothy Lungmus. Boulder, Colorado: Social Science Education Consortium, Inc., 1980.

Contains descriptions and analyses of consumer education materials. Lists of organizations and periodicals are also included.

Criminal Justice Audiovisual Materials Directory. By the Law Enforcement Assistance Administration, Dept. of Justice. 3rd ed. Washington, D.C.: Supt. of Documents, 1978.

Lists audiovisual materials available from commercial, academic, and government sources covering topics such as courts, prisons, police, etc. Useful for the secondary level.

Data Book of Social Studies Materials and Resources. Edited by Judith E. Hedstrom. Boulder, Colorado: Social Science Education Consortium, Inc., and ERIC Clearinghouse for Social Studies/Social Science Education, (annual).

The original three-volume set *Social Studies Curriculum Materials Databook* was published 1971-1978. Now annually produced, this source contains descriptions and analyses of print and nonprint social studies resources for K-12. Indexed by grade level, subject area, title, and publisher.

Directory of Law-Related Curriculum Materials. Chicago: American Bar Association, 1978.

A descriptive listing of subjects, activities, and materials for over 400 state and national projects in law-related education with grades K-12. Additional publications to supplement the directory are *Bibliography of Law-Related Curriculum Materials* (1976), *Gaming: An Annotated Catalogue of Law-Related Games and Simulations* (1975), and *Media: An Annotated Catalogue of Law-Related Audio-Visual Materials* (1975).

Drugs: A Multimedia Sourcebook for Children and Young Adults. By Sharon A. Charles and Sari Feldman. New York: Neal-Schuman Publishers, 1980.

Describes 424 print and nonprint materials for use with grades 6-12. Includes publisher/producer, type of media, date, price, and grade level.

Economics Education; A Guide to Information Sources. By Catherine A. Hughes. Detroit: Gale Research Co., 1977.

Lists books, pamphlets, charts, tapes, games, transparencies, films, filmstrips, pictures, and kits for preschool through high school. Each annotated entry includes grade level.

Educators Guide to Free Social Studies Materials. Randolph, Wisconsin: Educators Progress Service, (annual).

A listing of free print and nonprint materials available for use in the elementary and secondary levels.

Ethnic Film and Filmstrip Guide for Libraries and Media Center; A Selective Filmography. By Lubomyr R. Wynar and Lois Buttlar. Littleton, Colorado: Libraries Unlimited, 1980.

Lists nearly 1,400 titles representing 46 ethnic groups. Description, type of media, producer, date, price, and grade level are included. Supplements *Building Ethnic Collections* (1977).

Ethnic Studies Sampler: The Best of the Title IX Project Materials. Edited by Frances Haley. Boulder, Colorado: Social Science Education Consortium, Inc., 1981.

Includes selected project materials and descriptions of additional resources produced by the Title IX Ethnic Heritage Studies projects funded between 1974 and 1979. Arranged under classroom activities, assessment and design materials, and teacher training materials. Indexed by grade level, project, and ethnic focus. Projects originally published in *Ethnic Heritage Studies Program Catalog: 1974-1979* and *1978-1980 Supplement.*

The Future: A Guide to Information Sources. Edited by E. Cornish. Washington, D.C.: World Future Society, 1977.

A guide to individuals, organizations, educational programs, print and nonprint materials, games, and simulations.

Global Issues in the Intermediate Classroom, Grades 5-8. By Jacquelyn Johnson and John Beneger. Boulder, Colorado: Social Science Education Consortium, Inc., 1981.

Contains 14 lesson plans and 34 student handouts. Also provides a bibliography of related sources in ERIC and a directory of organizations. A companion volume for high school is *Global Issues; Activities and Resources for the High School Teacher* (1979).

Guidebook for Teaching United States History—Earliest Times to the Civil War. By Tedd Levy and Donna C. Krasnow. Boston: Allyn and Bacon, 1979.

Provides a variety of ideas, resources, and activities for developing history and social science skills. The companion volume is *A Guide for Teaching United States History—Mid Nineteenth Century to the Present.*

Index to Maps of the American Revolution in Books and Periodicals. Westport, Conn.: Greenwood Press, 1968. Supplements 1971-76.

Covers 1,000 sources in locating maps useful in the study of American history.

Law in the Classroom; Activities and Resources. By Mary J. Turner. Boulder, Colorado: Social Science Education Consortium, Inc., 1979.

A handbook containing lesson plans, guidelines, recommended media kits, filmstrips and games, and reproducible handouts. For use with secondary level students.

National Council for the Social Studies: How-To-Do-It Series. Washington, D.C.: National Council for the Social Studies, (irregular).

Guides designed for elementary and secondary level studies include activities, supplementary reading resources, and print and nonprint materials for use in the social studies classroom. Recent titles include *Using Questions in Social Studies* (1977), *Architecture as a Primary Source for Social Studies* (1978), *Oral History in the Classroom* (1979), *Using Popular Culture in the Social Studies* (1979), *Computers in the Social Studies Classroom* (1981), and *Popular Music in the Social Studies Classroom: Audio Resources for Teachers* (1981).

263

The Newspaper; An Alternative Textbook. By J. Rodney Short and Bev Dickerson. Belmont, Ca.: Pitman Learning, Inc., 1980.

> Includes activities designed to develop reading, writing, and computational and other skills in content areas. Useful for grades 4-12.

Notable Children's Trade Books in the Field of Social Studies. By the Joint Committee of the Children's Book Council and the National Council for the Social Studies. New York: Children's Book Council.

> An annual listing of recommended books which also appear in *Social Education.*

Open Minds to Equality; A Sourcebook of Learning Activities to Promote Race, Sex, Class, and Age Equity. By Nancy Schniedewind and Ellen Davidson. Englewood Cliffs, N.J.: Prentice Hall, 1983.

> Provides learning activities to help elementary and middle school students understand equality among themselves and society and develop strategies for change.

Reading Ladders for Human Relations. Edited by Eileen Tway. 6th ed. Washington, D.C.: American Council on Education, 1981.

> An annotated reading list for preschool through high school emphasizing the understanding of people, their values, and their ways of living.

Survival Themes in Fiction for Children and Young People. By Binnie T. Wilkin. Metuchen, New Jersey: Scarecrow Press, 1978.

> A selected annotated list of 261 books covering individual and societal issues such as friendship, aloneness, and feelings encountered by children and young people.

Teaching Local History: Trends, Tips and Resources. By Fay D. Metcalf and Matthew T. Downey. Boulder, Colorado: Social Science Education Consortium, Inc., 1977.

> Presents suggestions and activities for local history using the community, family, architecture, folklore, etc.

Teaching of World History. By Gerald Leinwand. Washington, D.C.: National Council for the Social Studies, 1978.

> Provides ideas for the study of world history including suggestions for improving student skills in reading, writing, and discussing. Includes lesson plans, activities, and a directory of organizations as sources of information.

World History in Juvenile Books: A Geographical and Chronological Guide. By Seymour Metzner. New York: H. W. Wilson Co., 1973.

> A geographical and chronological listing of more than 2,700 trade books, fiction, and nonfiction for elementary and junior high students.

Yellow Pages of Learning Resources: Resources Directory Area Code 800. Edited by Richard S. Wurman. Cambridge, Mass.: MIT Press, 1972.

> A unique source of methods using the city as a learning resource. Useful in the elementary social studies area.

Mathematics

Activities for Junior High School and Middle School Mathematics; Readings from the Arithmetic Teacher and the Mathematics Teachers. Edited by Kenneth E. Easterday and others. Reston, Va.: National Council of Teachers of Mathematics, 1981.

>   Selected activities from articles in the two periodicals. Arranged under 10 math categories.

Activities for the Maintenance of Computational Skills and the Discovery of Patterns. By Bonnie H. Litwiller and David R. Duncan. Reston, Va.: National Council of Teachers of Mathematics, 1980.

>   Presents many non-routine math activities for the commonly used addition, multiplication, and subtraction tables and the Hundred Square. Useful with middle and junior high students.

Activities Handbook for Teaching with the Hand-Held Calculator. By Gary G. Bitter and Jerald Mikesell. Boston: Allyn and Bacon, 1980.

>   Provides activities for individual or group participants using the calculator in the curriculum. Arranged by math topics. Useful with all ages from elementary and up.

Films in the Mathematics Classroom. By Barbara J. Bestgen and Robert E. Reys. Reston, Va.: National Council of Teachers of Mathematics, 1982.

>   Lists 239 math films for elementary and secondary level. Each entry contains description and reviews, grade level, length, producer/distributor, and date. Also rates each on a scale 0-4.

400 Group Games and Activities for Teaching Math. By Edward F. DeRoche and Erika G. Bogenschild. West Nyack, New Jersey: Parker Publishing Co., 1977.

>   Provides group activities and games for learning math and using "the real world" sources such as telephone books, catalogs, the yellow pages, newspapers, and money. Useful at elementary and junior high level.

Games and Puzzles for Elementary and Middle School Math; Readings from the Arithmetic Teacher. By Seaton E. Smith, Jr. Reston, Va.: National Council of Teachers of Mathematics, 1975.

>   A collection of articles presenting games, puzzles, board games, manipulative puzzles, and other activities developed by teachers and students.

High School Mathematics Library. By William L. Schaaf. 7th ed. Reston, Va.: National Council of Teachers of Mathematics, 1982.

>   An annotated guide for teachers, students, and librarians to meet students' interests in mathematics and aid in building a good math collection. Reflects new trends in areas such as computers, data processing, and recreational mathematics.

Ideas from the Arithmetic Teacher: Grades 1-4 Primary. Compiled by George Immerzeel and Marvin L. Thomas. Reston, Va.: National Council of Teachers of Mathematics, 1982.

265

A collection of the "Ideas" sections of *Arithmetic Teacher* and arranged by math topic. Companion titles are *Ideas from the Arithmetic Teacher: Grades 4-6 Intermediate* (1979), and *Ideas from the Arithmetic Teacher: Grades 6-8 Middle School* (1982).

Instructional Aids in Mathematics. Reston, Va.: National Council of Teachers of Mathematics, 1973.

An illustrated guide to instructional aids in mathematics including activities and ideas for their construction. Issued as the 34th *NCTM Yearbook*.

Interactions of Science and Mathematics: A Set of Activities. By Peggy House. Columbus, Ohio, ERIC Clearinghouse for Science, Mathematics, and Environmental Education, 1980.

Activities designed for developing math concepts and principles as related to the physical world. Useful with students in the junior and senior high level.

Math Activities for Child Involvement. By C. W. Schminke and Enoch Dumas. 3rd ed. Boston: Allyn and Bacon, 1981.

A book of ideas for math activities, projects, games, puzzles, charts, and displays in the elementary math classroom.

Mathematical History: Activities, Puzzles, Stories, and Games. By Merle Mitchell. Reston, Va.: National Council of Teachers of Mathematics, 1978.

Provides materials and activities useful in the teaching of history of mathematics in grade 4-6.

Mathematics and Humor. Edited by Aggie Vinik. Reston, Va.: National Council of Teachers of Mathematics, 1978.

A collection of stories, jokes, riddles, verses, cartoons, etc. using math. Useful in stimulating students' creative writing or for bulletin board ideas.

Mathematics and Science: An Adventure in Postage Stamps. By William L. Schaaf. Reston, Va.: National Council of Teachers of Mathematics, 1978.

Presents a background on the influence of math on technology and thus on civilization as seen through postage stamps. A set of 8 full-color posters, each portraying international stamps representing a particular use of mathematics is also available.

Mathematics Library: Elementary and Junior High School. By Margariete M. Wheeler and Clarence E. Hardgrove. 4th ed. Reston, Va.: National Council of Teachers of Mathematics, 1978.

An annotated guide for teachers and librarians selecting sources of recreational and informational reading in mathematics. Grade level included with each entry.

Mathematics Projects Handbook. By Adrien L. Hess. 2nd ed. Reston, Va.: National Council of Teachers of Mathematics, 1982.

A guide for teachers and students in selecting and developing math projects from a simple demonstration to an exhibit at a fair. Also includes an annotated bibliography and publishers information.

Mathematics Through Paper Folding. By Alton R. Olson. Reston, Va.: National Council of Teachers of Mathematics, 1975.

Provides 72 exercises in paper folding for junior and high school students.

Mathmatters! Developing Computational Skills with Developmental Activity Sequences. By Randall J. Souviney. Santa Monica, Calif.: Goodyear Publishing Co., 1978.

A collection of activities and skills for the elementary math classroom.

Minicalculators in the Classroom. By Joseph R. Caravella. Washington, D.C.: National Education Association, 1977.

Discusses use of the minicalculator as an instructional aid and includes activities for classroom use.

Multicultural Mathematics Materials. By Marina C. Krause. Reston, Va.: National Council of Teachers of Mathematics, 1983.

Contains games and activities from around the world. Introduces children in grades 1-9 to the ethnic heritage of others.

Project-A-Puzzle. By Richard D. Porter. 2nd ed. Reston, Va.: National Council of Teachers of Mathematics, 1978.

A set of transparency masters of math puzzles for the development of logical and perceptual skills. The puzzles include patterns, magic squares, and counting problems. Follow-up suggestions are provided for each.

Sourcebook for Applications of School Mathematics. By the Joint Committee of the Mathematical Association of America and the National Council of Teachers of Mathematics. Reston, Va.: National Council of Teachers of Mathematics, 1980.

Provides a collection of realistic problems for use in the secondary math classroom. Includes answers and an annotated bibliography.

Teaching Mathematics: A Sourcebook of Aids, Activities, and Strategies. By Max A. Sobel and Evan M. Maletsky. Englewood Cliffs, New Jersey: Prentice Hall, 1975.

A series of ideas suitable for many grade levels. Provides motivational ideas, recreational activities, laboratory experiments, classroom aids and models, and audiovisual facilities and resources.

Science

AAAS Science Book List for Children: A Selected and Annotated List of Science and Mathematics Books for Children in Elementary Schools and for Children's Collections in Public Libraries. 3rd ed. Washington, D.C.: American Association for the Advancement of Science, 1972. Supplement, 1978.

An annotated list of recommended books in the field of pure and applied science including math for K-8 and biographies. AAAS also publishes *AAAS Science Book List* (for young adults and adults), *Films in the Sciences: Reviews and Recommendations,* and *Science Books and Films,* a review journal which updates the lists.

Directory of Audio-Visual Sources: History of Science, Medicine and Technology. By Bruce Eastwood. New York: Science History Publications, 1979.

A selective annotated list of audio-visual materials covering 26 subject areas in the history of science, medicine, and technology.

Educators Guide to Free Science Materials. Randolph, Wisconsin: Educators Progress Service, (annual).

A list of free print and nonprint materials in science, energy, and environmental education for all grade levels.

Energy: A Multimedia Guide for Children and Young Adults. By Judith H. Higgins. New York: Neal-Schuman, 1979.

An annotated guide to multimedia energy materials, curriculum materials, selection aids, and information sources.

Energy Environment Source Book. Washington, D.C.: National Science Teachers Association, 1980. 2 vols.

Lists print and nonprint materials, curriculum aids, sources of information and government publications.

Environmental Education: A Guide to Information Sources. By William B. Stapp and Mary D. Liston. Detroit: Gale Research Co., 1975.

A guide to sources including reference materials, lists of magazines, newsletters, associations, organizations, and government agencies.

Films in the Sciences: Reviews and Recommendations. Edited by Michele M. Newman and Madelyn A. McRae. Washington, D.C.: American Association for the Advancement of Science, 1980.

Provides summaries and evaluations for nearly 1,000 science films produced between 1975-1980.

Games for the Science Classroom: An Annotated Bibliography. By Paul B. Hounshell and Ira R. Trollinger. Washington, D.C.: National Science Teachers Association, 1977.

Lists over 100 science and science-related games in the areas of biological, physical, earth/space, and general science.

Index to Environmental Studies—Multimedia (NICEM). Los Angeles: National Information Center for Educational Materials, (updated every 2½ yrs).

A bibliographic guide to nearly 29,000 commercially-produced nonprint materials in the area of environmental studies. Represents eight different media and is intended for preschool through adult-professional levels.

Index to Illustrations of the Natural World: Where to Find Pictures of the Living Things of North America. Hamden, Conn.: Shoe String Press, 1980.

Indexes over 6,000 illustrations in 178 books published since 1960.

Index to Illustrations of Living Things Outside of North America: Where to Find Pictures of Flora and Fauna. By Lucile R. Munz and Nedra Slauson. Hamden, Conn.: Shoe String Press, 1981.

Indexes more than 9,000 plant and animal illustrations in 206 books published since 1963.

Outstanding Science Trade Books for Children. By the National Science Teachers Association and Children's Book Council. New York: Children's Book Council, (annual).

An annual selection guide of nearly 80 outstanding children's science trade books. Appears also in the periodical *Science and Children.*

Reading in the Science Classroom. By Judith Bechtel and Bettie Franzblau. Washington, D.C.: National Education Association, 1980.

Provides techniques, classroom activities, and supplementary print sources for teaching reading in the science classroom.

Recyclopedia: Games, Science Equipment, and Crafts from Recycled Materials. By Robin Simons. Boston: Houghton Mifflin Co., 1976.

Includes directions for making games, musical instruments, science equipment, and other class projects from inexpensive materials. Most ideas originated at the Boston Children's Museum.

Science and Society: A Bibliography. By Joseph M. Dasback. 6th ed. Washington, D.C.: American Association for the Advancement of Science, 1976.

A resource of ideas for use in minicourses and independent study, focusing on relationships between man, the environment, science, and technology. Print and nonprint materials are included.

Sciences: A Select List of U.S. Government-Produced Audiovisual Materials. Washington, D.C.: National Audiovisual Center, 1978.

Lists over 600 government-produced nonprint materials, mostly films, in twelve subject areas such as aerospace, biology, energy, environment, oceanography, and weather. Useful with secondary level students.

Sourcebook: Learning by Design; the Environmental Education Program of the American Institute of Architects. Washington, D.C.: American Institute of Architects, 1981.

A catalog of teaching resources related to both the built and natural environment including model programs, resources of teaching aids and activities, annotated bibliography, and listing of people and organizations. Resources of teaching aids and activities are indexed by grade level, subject areas (art, science, social studies, etc.), resource type (teacher guide, student resource), setting for use (classroom, studio, field trip, etc.), and learning area (communities, structures, design, natural laws).

Water-Related Teaching Activities. By Herbert L. Coon and Charles L. Price. Columbus, Ohio: ERIC Information Analysis Center for Science, Mathematics, and Environmental Education, 1977.

Activities for use in science, social science, mathematics, art, language

269

arts, and music. Also includes a list of films, filmstrips, and water-testing equipment.

Exceptional Students

Books for the Gifted Child. By Barbara H. Baskin and Karen H. Harris. New York: Bowker Co., 1980.

> Provides a survey of gifted children and their special capabilities. Included is an annotated guide to the selection of "intellectually demanding" books for preschool through 12 years of age.

Catalog of Educational Captioned Films for the Deaf. Silver Springs, Maryland: Association for Education of the Deaf, 1980.

> Lists approximately 1,200 captioned titles including description, subject topics, grade level, producer, and date. A variety of subjects is included for all grade levels.

Catalog of Instructional Materials for the Handicapped Learner. Bloomington: Ind.: Handicapped Learner Materials Distribution Center, Audio-Visual Center, Indiana University, 1979. Supplements.

> Lists over 450 titles including films, audio and video recordings, kits, manipulative materials, transparencies, and pictorial materials. Subject index included.

Easy Reading: Book Series and Periodicals for Less Able Readers. By Michael F. Graves. Newark, Del.: International Reading Association, 1979.

> An annotated guide to books in series and periodicals for the intermediate and secondary students who read below their grade level. Supplementary materials, evaluations, and ordering information are included.

Exploring Books with Gifted Children. By Nancy Polette and Majorie Hamlin. Littleton, Colorado: Libraries Unlimited, 1980.

> A guide providing strategies and techniques to stimulate creative thinking and interest in reading. Recommended titles, units of study, and activities included.

For Younger Readers: Braille and Talking Books: A Catalog of Braille, Disc, and Cassette Books Announced in Braille Book Review and Talking Book Topics. Washington, D.C.: Library of Congress, National Library Service for the Blind and Physically Handicapped, 1978-79.

> An annotated list of fiction and nonfiction books for very young readers. Available through the free loan program of the Library of Congress.

Gateways to Readable Books: An Annotated Graded List of Books in Many Fields for Adolescents Who Are Reluctant to Read or Find Reading Difficult. By Dorothy E. Withrow. New York: H. W. Wilson Co., 1975.

> An annotated list of over 1,000 titles for retarded and reluctant adoles-

cents covering varied subject areas and arranged from preschool to 8th grade level.

Good Reading for Poor Readers. By George D. Spache. Champaign, Ill.: Gerrard, 1978.
Lists titles for remedial reading including materials, games, and visual aids.

Good Reading for the Disadvantaged Reader: Multi-ethnic Resources. By George D. Spache. Champaign, Ill.: Gerrard, 1975.
Lists ethnic reading materials graded for readability. Includes chapter on audiovisual materials.

Handbook of Instructional Resources and References for Teaching the Gifted, Second Edition. By Frances Karnes and Emily Collins. Boston: Allyn and Bacon, 1984.
Lists and evaluates commercially-produced materials appropriate for gifted elementary and junior high students. Includes an annotated bibliography of professional reading on teaching the gifted.

High-Interest Books for Teens: A Guide to Book Reviews and Biographical Sources. Edited by Adele Sarkissian. Detroit: Gale Research Co., 1981.
Lists 2,000 high interest titles for the average or slow junior and senior high reader. Each entry includes author's brief biographical sketch and citations to book reviews.

High Interest—Easy Reading: For Junior and Senior High Students. Edited by Marian White. 3rd ed. Urbana, Ill.: National Council of Teachers of English, 1979.
A list of more than 400 quality titles that deal with topics of interest to the adolescent. Intended for use by reluctant readers.

High/Low Consensus. By Helen E. Williams. Williamsport, Pa.: Bro-Dart Publishing Co., 1980.
An annotated list of 1,100 high interest/low reading level books for junior and senior high students. Each entry includes reading level, readability formula, interest level, recommended source, and subject topics.

High/Low Handbook: Books, Materials, and Services for the Teenage Problem Reader. Edited by Ellen V. Libretto. New York: Bowker Co., 1981.
Lists 275 titles recommended for the problem reader. Each annotated entry includes reading and interest level, price, fiction or nonfiction, and paper availability.

Large Type Books in Print. New York: Bowker Co., (biennial).
A guide to over 4,000 titles in large type supplied by more than 65 publishers. Includes fiction, nonfiction, and textbooks.

Learning Activities and Teaching Ideas for the Special Child in the Regular Classroom. By Peggy Glazzard. Englewood Cliffs, N.J.: Prentice Hall, 1982.
Activities and ideas for students with behavioral or academic problems.

Each entry contains subject topics, grade level, description, objectives, materials, procedure, and additional suggestions.

Mainstreaming in the Social Studies. Edited by John G. Herlihy and Myra R. Herlihy. Washington, D.C.: National Council for the Social Studies, 1980.
Explores various aspects of mainstreaming handicapped youngsters into regular K-12 social studies classrooms. Includes suggestions for individualized instruction, activities, and using the community organizations.

Mainstreaming Science and Mathematics: Special Ideas and Activities for the Whole Class. By Charles R. Coble. Santa Monica, Ca.: Goodyear Publishing Co., 1977.
A collection of ideas and activities for use with all elementary and junior high students including the exceptional student.

Multi-Sensory Educational Aids from Scrap. By Kendrick Coy. Springfield, Ill.: Charles C. Thomas, 1980.
Provides over 250 illustrations and patterns for the construction of 70 educational aids useful to children with various handicapping conditions.

National Information Center for Special Education Materials (NICSEM).
NICSEM offers detailed information in a variety of formats on media and materials resources that are usable with the handicapped. The publications are produced by NICSEM and published by National Information Center for Educational Materials (NICEM). The publications are updated every 2½ years. Titles include:

NICEM Index to Nonprint Special Education Materials—Multimedia (Professional vol.)

NICEM Index to Nonprint Special Education Materials—Multimedia (Learner vol.)

NICSEM Master Index to Special Education Materials

NICSEM Mini-Index to Special Education Materials: Family Life and Sex Education

NICSEM Mini-Index to Special Education Materials: Functional Communication Skills

NICSEM Mini-Index to Special Education Materials: High Interest, Controlled Vocabulary Supplementary Reading Materials for Adolescents and Young Adults

NICSEM Mini-Index to Special Education Materials: Independent Living Skills for Moderately and Severely Handicapped Students

NICSEM Mini-Index to Special Education: Personal and Social Development for Moderately and Severely Handicapped Students

NICSEM Source Directory

NICSEM Special Education Thesaurus

Special Education Index to Assessment Materials

Special Education Index to In-Service Training Materials

Special Education Index to Learner Materials
Special Education Index to Parent Materials

Perceptual Training Activities Handbook: 250 Games and Exercises for Helping Children Develop Sensory Skills. By Betty Van Witsen. 2nd ed. New York: Teachers College Press, 1979.

Activities for the practice of sensory skills—visual, auditory, tactile, olfactory, gustatory, and kinesthetic, with children having learning and other disabilities.

Talking Books Adult: A Catalog of Disc Books Announced in "Talking Books Topics." Washington, D.C.: Library of Congress, National Library Service for the Blind and Physically Handicapped, (biennial).

An annotated list of fiction and nonfiction disc books covering 44 subject areas for young adults and adults. Available through the free loan program from the Library of Congress.

Teaching Aids for Blind and Visually Limited Children. By Barbara Dorward and Natalie Barraga. New York: American Foundation for the Blind, 1968.

Thirty-two toys and aids designed to develop physical and mental capabilities of blind children. Includes instructions on how to construct many of the teaching aids with the help of the industrial arts students.

224 Remedial Ideas. By W. C. Nesbit. Toronto: Methuen Publications, 1979.

Presents a brief description of specific types of learning problems. Includes 224 noncommercial remedial ideas covering many subject areas for use with students.

CHAPTER 16

Exemplary Units of Instruction

Content instruction and literacy development
can be organized concurrently.

This chapter is composed of four units of study prepared by four teachers for use in their classes. We have chosen these units to exemplify many of the organizational and instructional practices we have argued for in earlier chapters. Space limitations prohibit inclusion of more than four units, so we have chosen one each for English, math, science, and social studies. But even within these four basic content areas there is a necessary restriction to one rather narrow topic. Examine the units, then, for their form. Each contains somewhat different ideas of how to organize for instruction. No matter what the topic or content area of the unit you're interested in developing, we think you'll find good ideas in each of the ones we have included.

A Unit of Study in English—Macbeth: Ascent vs. Descent*

Introduction

Sophomore high school students of very general, average reading and writing ability will study William Shakespeare's tragedy, *Macbeth,* for approxi-

*Prepared by Ms. Julie Stockwell and reproduced here with her permission.

mately three weeks. The students will first complete a close reading of the text so that they can later comprehend the action in Polanski's movie. However, viewing the movie (preferably Polanski's version because of its proven attention-holding capacity when shown to high school students) is vital as a complement to the reading. The movie gives life to an otherwise bare text, as it will inevitably appear to high school students.

Conceptual Objectives

1. Shakespeare is one of the greatest writers of western civilization, and his play *Macbeth* is one of his four major tragedies.
2. A paradox is a phrase or sentence in which two seemingly contradictory statements are combined to form a true statement.
3. Macbeth changes from a man who is persuaded that violence is a necessary, if abhorred, means to an end, to a man who believes violence is the only means to keep that end.
4. Tragedy involves the descent of a great man to defeat or death.
5. Because Shakespeare wrote few stage directions, a director has great freedom in interpreting the plays for production.

Performance Objectives

1. The student will use the terms tragedy and paradox in their speech and writing correctly.
2. The student will write sentences for the vocabulary words taken from the play, demonstrating their meaning within the context of the sentence.
3. The students will demonstrate their comprehension of the play's plot structure in writing assignments.
4. The students will actively watch the movie "Macbeth," questioning and commenting on what they see, comparing it to what they have read.

Materials Key for *Macbeth*

MATERIALS/OBJECTIVES	CONCEPTUAL						PERFORMANCE			
	1	2	3	4	5		1	2	3	4
1. "The Monkey's Paw"		X		X			X			
2. *Shakespeare's World*	X		X		X			X		
3. *Macbeth,* Act I	X	X	X	X	X		X	X	X	X
4. *Macbeth,* Act II	X		X	X	X		X	X	X	X
5. *Macbeth,* Act III	X		X	X	X		X	X	X	X
6. *Macbeth,* Act IV	X		X	X	X		X	X	X	X
7. *Macbeth,* Act V	X		X	X	X		X	X	X	X
8. *Cliff's Notes*	X	X	X	X					X	
9. *Monarch Notes*	X	X	X	X					X	
10. *Abridged Shakespeare*	X	X	X	X	X		X	X	X	
11. Polanski's "Macbeth"				X	X					X

Activities Key for *Macbeth*

ACTIVITIES/OBJECTIVES	CONCEPTUAL						PERFORMANCE			
	1	2	3	4	5		1	2	3	4
1. Attitude scale on power, motivation			X	X					X	
2. Lesson on motivation using "The Monkey's Paw"		X		X			X			
3. Key literary activities (introd. & word puzzles)	X	X		X	X		X	X	X	X

276

ACTIVITIES/OBJECTIVES	CONCEPTUAL						PERFORMANCE			
	1	2	3	4	5		1	2	3	4
4. Lecture on Shakespeare	X				X					X
5. CRL, Act One	X		X	X	X		X	X	X	
6. Combination guide, Act I			X	X	X				X	
7. Preteach vocab., Act II				X	X				X	
8. How to study Shakespeare, lecture on supp. materials	X	X	X	X	X		X	X	X	X
9. CRL, Act Two	X		X	X	X		X	X	X	
10. 3-level guide, Act II			X	X					X	
11. CRL, Act Three	X	X	X	X			X		X	
12. Writing activity Act III		X	X	X			X	X	X	
13. Vocab. puzzles, Acts I–III		X	X	X			X	X	X	
14. Combination guide, Act IV		X	X	X			X	X	X	
15. CRL, Act Five	X	X	X	X	X		X	X	X	
16. Small group discussions on theme & personal interpretation		X	X	X			X	X	X	
17. Cinquains	X	X	X	X	X		X	X	X	
18. Post-graphic organizers	X	X	X	X	X		X	X	X	
19. View film	X	X	X	X	X		X			X
20. Construct guide for other students to complete after third day of film	X	X	X	X	X		X		X	X
21. Comparison discussion after seeing film	X	X	X	X	X		X		X	X
22. Attitude, post test			X	X					X	
23. Review discussion & their design of test items for possible inclusion on test	X	X	X	X	X		X		X	

277

Activity Schedule for *Macbeth*

	DAY ONE	DAY TWO	DAY THREE	DAY FOUR	DAY FIVE
WEEK ONE	**Lesson on motivation using "The Monkey's Paw"	a. Preteach key literary vocabulary b. Give backgd. info. on Shakespeare c. Using Content Reading Lesson (CRL), begin Act I	Finish Act I with CRL. Do study guide indiv. When finished, discuss responses with whole class. Clarify who is who of the characters.	Preteach new vocab. for Act II & discuss key concepts for Act II. Show supplementary materials & suggest ways they might use them. Begin CRL of Act II	Complete CRL of Act II. Distribute 3-level guide (**) Complete & discuss guide (for format of discussions, see directions on guide).
WEEK TWO	CRL, Act III, Scene 1 (**) Continue CRL for rest of Act III	Finish Act III with CRL. Give assign. to be started in class: Write a paragraph of 7–10 sentences on *one* of: a. Macbeth deserves to succeed b. Macbeth deserves to fail. c. All fault rests with Lady Macbeth. Also design two vocab. puzzles with words from Acts I, II, & III	Students read Act IV on own and complete study guide. Teacher meets with students on papers. Any students who finish get in groups & discuss responses to guide & work on puzzles together.	Go over guides. Begin Act V with CRL. Assign to finish play at home.	Discuss Act V. Discuss tragedy and paradox. What does the play say to each of them? Disc. in small groups. Write a group cinquain about the main theme of the play. Share cinquains.

**Starred activities are included in this text on pages following the schedule.

278

	DAY ONE	DAY TWO	DAY THREE	DAY FOUR	DAY FIVE
WEEK THREE	Construct a post-organizer with the class for the play.	View Polanski's version of *Macbeth*			Discuss views of play after seeing movie as compared to before seeing film. Prepare for test. Review. (Test on Day One of Week Four)

A PREREADING ANTICIPATION LESSON PLAN FOR A UNIT ON MACBETH (WEEK ONE, DAY ONE)

Conceptual Objectives

1. People's motivations influence their behavior and attitudes about their behavior.
2. Once a person believes something is possible, he or she will often work to make that possibility a reality.

Behavioral Objectives

1. Each student will list his or her motivations for doing certain activities.
2. Each student will write a brief narrative story illustration, with the use of prophecy as motivation.

Lesson Plan

1. Every day the students write anything they want for 5–8 minutes on a word the teacher assigns them for their journal topic. Today the topic is "MOTIVATION."
2. Ask the students questions. Ask them to write each of their responses down instead of responding orally.
   Why do you come to school? Why do you play football, tennis, or any other sport?
   Why do you read books, magazines, papers?
   Why do you go to concerts?

279

Why do people perform concerts?
Why do teachers teach?
Why did Reagan run for president?

3. Collect the responses. Select some of them and discuss them with the class.

4. Develop a hypothetical situation. Suppose a stranger or some outer space person told you that you would be $1,000.00 richer in four weeks. Would you believe him? Would you wait for it, or would you do something to make it happen?

5. Read "The Monkey's Paw" by W. Jacobs. Discuss the story and be sure to discuss these questions:
   A. Do you believe the monkey's paw is magic? If not, how was the first wish granted?
   B. What is the third wish? Are the second and third wishes truly granted?
   C. What is the meaning of the sergeant major's statement, "He wanted to show that fate ruled people's lives, and that those who interfered with it did so to their sorrow."

6. Connect these conclusions with Macbeth. He was a man who took prophecies by witches seriously and used those predictions as a motivation for making them happen. The students should watch Macbeth's motivations as he acts in the story.

7. Tell students they are now to write a brief narrative story like "The Monkey's Paw" where a prophecy of some kind, be it a witch, a fortune teller, or an astrologer who tells it, influences the motivations and actions of a person. The stories will be due at the beginning of the next period, at which the class will begin *Macbeth* with a filmstrip.

This activity will *mobilize* prior knowledge of motivation, a key factor in understanding Macbeth's actions in Shakespeare's tragedy. The students will study their own motivations and those they've gleaned from reading, T.V. ("Bewitched," three wishes granted in cartoons, "Fantasy Island," etc.), and other sources so that they will have a much more complete understanding of the concept, "motivation," than they would if they started reading *Macbeth* without this preparation. Thus the activity is one for prereading anticipation because it unifies scattered raw knowledge that the students have and concentrates it on one key topic in a play we will study.

THREE LEVEL STUDY GUIDE (WEEK ONE, DAY 5)

Macbeth, Act II

Directions   Complete this study guide on your own, first. You may refer to the text if necessary.

Upon completion, you will be assigned to a group of four to compare your responses.

Finally, group responses will be shared and discussed among the whole class for reactions.

Level One: Answer each of the following questions.

1. What instrument of danger did Macbeth "see"?
2. What did Macbeth do with the daggers?
3. What did Lady Macbeth do with the daggers?
4. Why didn't Lady Macbeth kill Duncan?
5. Who discovered Duncan's body?
6. What happened to the guards?
7. What did Malcolm and Donalbain decide to do after the murder?
8. Where will Macduff go instead of going to Scone where Macbeth will be crowned?

Level Two: Explain why you agree or disagree with each of the following statements:

1. Macbeth's bravery and ambition enable him to visualize the weapon he will use to murder Duncan.
2. Macbeth killed Duncan because his wife forced him to this dastardly deed.
3. Macbeth killed the guards to avenge their obvious murder of Duncan.
4. In gratitude for his revenge on the guards, Malcolm gave the kingship to Macbeth.
5. Macduff misses Macbeth's coronation because he is ill.

Level Three: Think carefully about the following questions. Then write out a response to each.

1. If a teacher ever told you that you could get a grade higher than you could, did or would you work to get that higher grade?
2. Did you ever learn a new word or learn about a new car, and then suddenly see that new word or new car all over the place?
3. Do you ever avoid people even though you aren't quite sure what you don't like about them?
4. Did you ever do something a little less than honest to get something you decided you couldn't live without? (Do not write your response to this question IF to do so will make you feel uncomfortable.)

A CONTENT READING LESSON FOR *MACBETH*

Act III, Scene 1

Planned outline of questions and probes

A. Prereading
   1. In the last scene we read that Duncan's murdered body had been discovered and Macbeth went to Scone to be crowned king. Let's review
   some things.
   (Put items on board. Ask students to jot down answers on a sheet of
   paper to allow them to think before talking. Put their responses on
   the board for reference. Refer to text if necessary to clarify or resolve
   disagreements.)
      a. How was Duncan murdered?
      b. What characters in the play know how Duncan was murdered?
      How do they know?
      c. Why did Macbeth want to become king?
      d. Whom might Macbeth need to fear?
      e. Which of the witches' predictions have come true?
      f. What do you expect will happen next? Why do you think so?
      g. How do you *want* things to turn out? Why?
B. Read Banquo's speech, then stop.
C. Reflection and prereading questions:
   1. What has Banquo said?
   2. Whom is he talking to?
   3. What is Banquo's big worry and why is he worried?
   4. Any changes in our answers to question 1b?
   5. What will Banquo do about his worries?
   6. What do you expect will happen next? What are the possibilities?
D. Read to the end of line 40.
E. Reflection and prereading questions:
   1. Who is Macbeth's "Chief guest"?
   2. Who is the "our" and "we" Macbeth refers to?
   3. What are Banquo's plans for the afternoon? How does Macbeth react
   to them? To Banquo himself?
   4. Who are the "bloody cousins" Macbeth speaks of? Why does he talk
   about them?
F. Now read to line 73 and stop.
G. Reflecting and prereading questions:
   1. Paraphrase, "To be thus is nothing, but to be safely thus . . . ."
   2. Do you wish to make any changes or elaborations about Banquo's
   plans?
   3. What two reasons does Macbeth say he has to fear Banquo? Are both
   of these reasons valid, given what you know?

4. Summarize Macbeth's behavior and attitudes toward Banquo. Where before have we seen such a dichotomy between these two indicators? (Lady Macbeth toward Duncan, Act I.)

5. Name some people you know who would insist on telling the truth, even in the face of great danger for their lives. Macbeth believes that Banquo has this same quality. He calls it "dauntless temper," a form of courage, bravery. (Write all terms on board.)

6. What do trees look like in the winter? (List responses.) Another word like these is barren, or empty, fruitless. The word was also used to describe women who never bore children. Lady Macbeth was such a lady—she never had any children.
   a. Name several "barren" women.
   b. Why do you think Macbeth calls his scepter a barren one?
   c. Why is it important for a king to have children? What happens if he doesn't?

7. Whose sons are to be kings even though the father isn't?
   a. Can you name any examples of such an occurrence in history? Such examples are kings and queens who do not follow the normal family line of rulers; they are outsiders who are brought in to rule. An outside ruler who does not follow the family line, like Queen Anne (or another student example), is called an *unlineal* ruler; that is, a ruler who does not follow the line.
   b. Who, then, in *Macbeth* may become unlineal rulers? Why? How do you know?
   c. Who is the "unlineal hand" that Macbeth refers to? How do you know? How does Macbeth feel about this "unlineal hand"?

8. Why do you think Macbeth is going to do about his feelings? Now go on in the reading.

H. Read now to line 92.
I. Reflection and prereading questions:
   1. Who is Macbeth talking to? What is he telling them?
   2. Given what we know about Banquo, do you believe Macbeth's story? What is another plausible explanation for the past treatment of these men?
   3. What do you think is going to happen next? Why?
J. Now read to the end of the scene.
K. Reflection questions:
   1. What is Macbeth plotting with these men? Does this plot alter any of your answers to I,3? Does this plot alter your feelings toward Macbeth? How?
   2. Let's review quickly. Why is Macbeth plotting this latest murder? Recalling what Banquo said in his soliloquy, is Macbeth correct in his fears about Banquo? Why not?
   3. Reread lines 105–108. Why is Macbeth's "health" "perfect" once Banquo is dead? (Remember line 48.)

      4. Why are these murderers so eager to kill Banquo? How has Macbeth convinced them?

      5. Why can't Macbeth order men to openly kill Banquo? If Reagan wanted to get rid of a Senator who was bothering him, could he just fire him? Why not? (Apart from legal and constitutional reasons.)

      6. Do you think then, that Macbeth can make certain prophecies come true and prevent others from coming true? Keep your answers to this question in mind. What do you think will happen in the rest of this act? Why?

L. Overall reflection question:

      1. Recalling that a tragedy is the story of how a great, powerful man changes and declines to his defeat and/or death, how has Macbeth changed since we first met him? Since Duncan's murder?

M. Extension (discuss orally):

      1. How can we find out more about medieval banquet ceremonies? I need two people to research them for us for tomorrow.

      2. Right now I want you to make up some word games or puzzles for the underlined words on the board. They can be scrambles, crossword puzzles, search-a-word, anything like that. Tomorrow we'll exchange these after Sue and Joe make their presentations, and work each other's out.

      3. Tomorrow, after we've worked the games, we'll have a brief free association game with each of the main words we've learned today. I'll want you to hand those lists in along with your games so I can check on how well you're understanding the words. Then we'll go onto the next scenes.

A Unit of Study in Math—Plane Geometry: Circles*

Introduction

The unit outlined in the next few pages deals with circles. The unit will be concerned with principles related to circles, lines, and segments. This unit will take approximately fifteen days.

   The students will be expanding their present knowledge of circles. This will enable them to understand and appreciate this geometric figure which appears so frequently in our natural as well as our fabricated environment. Also it will enhance the course by using the circle in conjunction with other geometric figures. Since circles play an important role in everyday life and since it's such a basic yet important geometric figure, it is necessary to present, in some depth, the different concepts related to circles in a high school geometry course.

Conceptual Objectives

1. Circles can share the same common tangent line(s) and circles can be tangent to each other.
2. A variety of angles can be formed within a circle with chords, radii, tangents, and secants.
3. Diameters can intersect with tangents and chords, and diameters that are perpendicular to chords bisect the chords and their arcs.
4. When working in the same circle or congruent circles:
   a. Congruent arcs have congruent central angles and congruent chords.
   b. Congruent chords are equidistant from the center.
5. Certain specific segment products and geometric proportions are created when chords intersect, secants intersect, and a secant and tangent intersect.
6. Theorems related to circles can be extended and applied to geometric constructions.

Performance Objectives

Students will be able to:

1. Recognize circles and the lines and segments related to circles (i.e., radius, chord, diameter, tangent, secant).
2. State and apply theorems relating to tangents of circles.

*Prepared by Ms. Noreen Wang and reproduced here with her permission

3. Recognize the difference between tangent circles and lines tangent to circles.
4. State and apply theorems relating to chords of a circle.
5. Recognize inscribed and circumscribed circles and polygons.
6. Define arcs (major and minor) and central angles of a circle.
7. State and apply theorems concerning chords and arcs of a circle.
8. Recognize inscribed angles and the arcs they intercept.
9. State and apply theorems concerning the measures of inscribed angles.
10. State and apply theorems relating to the measures of the angles formed by secants and tangents, a tangent and a chord, and two chords.
11. State and apply theorems relating to the lengths of chords, secant segments, and tangent segments.
12. Construct with compass and straightedge the constructions related to the circle.

Materials Key

SOURCE

	CONCEPTUAL OBJECTIVES					
	1	2	3	4	5	6
1. *Modern School Mathematics—Geometry* by Jurgensen, Donnelly and Dolciani a. Pg. 359–364	x		x			
b. Pg. 364–369		x		x		
c. Pg. 369–376			x	x		
d. Pg. 376–384		x				
e. Pg. 384–388		x				
f. Pg. 388–393					x	
g. Pg. 393–404	x	x	x	x	x	
2. *Plane Geometry* by Welchons, Krickenberger and Pearson a. Pg. 295			x			
b. Pg. 296, 335, 338			x			x
c. Pg. 416		x				x
d. Pg. 318–319	x	x	x	x	x	x
e. Pg. 334–335	x	x	x	x	x	x
f. Pg. 305, 309		x	x	x	x	
3. *Tenth Year Mathematics*—Amsco Review Pg. 132–168	x	x	x	x	x	x
4. Geometry by Moise and Downs		x	x	x	x	

Activity Key

(Numbers in parentheses correspond to appropriate readings specified in materials key)

ACTIVITY	CONCEPTAL OBJECTIVES					
	1	2	3	4	5	6
A. Demonstrations and Discussions						
1. Construction #1 (2b, 3)			x			x
2. Construction #2 (2b, 3)			x			x
3. Conceptual Analysis on Inscribed Angles (1d, 3)		x				
4. Construction #3 (2b, 3)		x				x
5. Angles Formed by Tangents and Secants (1e, 3)		x				
6. Construction #4 (2c, 3)			x			x
7. Structured Overview (1, 2, 3)	x	x	x	x	x	x
B. Supplementary Activities						
1. Attitude Scale	x	x	x	x	x	x
2. Introduction to Circles (1a, 3)	x					
3. Crossword Puzzle on Circles (1abcd)	x	x		x		
4. Word Hunt on Circles (1abcd)	x	x		x		
5. Construction Homework #1 (2b, 3)			x			x
6. Construction Homework #2 (2b, 3)		x				x
7. Pattern Study Guide		x	x	x	x	
8. Proofs on Circles (1bcd, 3)		x	x	x		
9. Proof Quiz on Circles (1bc, 3)		x		x		
10. Measures of Angles and Arcs in Circles (1bcde, 3)		x				
11. Construction Homework #3 (2c, 3)			x			x
12. Review (1, 2, 3)		x	x	x	x	x
13. Unit Test (1, 2, 3)	x	x	x	x	x	x
14. Extra for Experts (1, 2, 4)	x	x	x	x	x	x

ACTIVITY	CONCEPTAL OBJECTIVES					
	1	2	3	4	5	6
C. Lessons						
1. Lesson of Vocabulary Instruction (1a)	x					
2. Content Reading Lesson I (1b)		x		x		
3. Content Reading Lesson II (1c)			x	x		
4. Prereading Anticipation and Circles (1f)			x		x	
5. Review II Lesson Plan (1, 2, 3)	x	x	x	x	x	x

A CROSSWORD PUZZLE ON CIRCLES

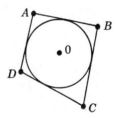

Figure A

ACROSS

1. In Figure A, quadrilateral *ABCD* is _____ about circle O.
3. A line that touches a circle.
5. In Figure A, circle O is _____ in quadrilateral *ABCD*.
8. A line segment from the center to a point on the circle.
9. Part of a circle.
10. An arc greater than 180 and less than 360⁰.
12. The set of points equidistant from a given point.
14. Circles having the same center.

DOWN

1. An angle equal in measure to its intercepted arc.
2. Circles having the same radii are _____.
4. An arc less than 180⁰.
5. An arc of a circle that is cut off by an angle.
6. An arc having a measure of 180⁰.
7. A line intersecting a circle in two points.
11. A chord through the center of a circle.
13. A segment joining two points of a circle.

A CONTENT READING LESSON

Text: *Modern School Mathematics — Geometry* by Jurgensen, Donnelly, and Dolciani, pp. 370–371

Lesson Plan:

A. Prereading questions
   1. What are congruent arcs again and what have we learned about them? (*discuss orally*)
   2. Does this happen with all circles? Right, they have to be in the same or congruent circles. What are congruent circles? (*discuss orally*)
   3. What was the converse of that theorem?
   4. All right, so congruent arcs are congruent central angles and congruent central angles have congruent areas provided we are working in the same or congruent circles. What else might be congruent if the arcs are congruent? (*discuss and demonstrate*)
B. Open your texts to page 370 and read theorem 10–7 in the middle of the page.
C. Reflection and Prereading Questions
   1. Were you right in your new assumption about congruent arcs? (*discuss orally*)
   2. Let's prove the new theorem.
      Theorem: In the same circle or congruent circles congruent arcs have congruent chords.
      Let's work in the same circle. What is the given? What has to be proved? We know that in the same circle or congruent circles congruent arcs have congruent central angles. Could that help here? Now what method are you going to use to get the chords congruent? Right congruent triangles. Let's write it up. (*work out on board*)
   3. Now we know that in the same circle or congruent circles congruent arcs have congruent central angles. What could happen if we had congruent chords? This is called the what of our new theorem? (*discuss orally*)
D. Open your text to page 370 and read theorem 10–6 and its proof.
E. Reflection and Prereading Questions
   1. Were you right about your assumption of congruent chords? (*discuss orally*)
   2. What did you notice about the proof of theorem 10–6? Right, it's almost the same as the proof we just did. Why is that? (*discuss orally*)
   3. Let's follow the proof in the text and fill in the missing statements. Now we're given $\overline{AB} \cong \overline{CD}$. Notice they have drawn in radii $\overline{OA}$, $\overline{OB}$, $\overline{OC}$, and $\overline{OD}$. Why can this be done? And so this leads to step two and what is the reason for step two? Reason for 3, 4, 5, and 6? (*follow text and discuss orally*)

4. What should the bisector of an arc do? Where the arc has been divided into congruent parts is called the what of the arc? (*demonstrate and discuss*)

5. What do you think the center of an arc is? (*demonstrate and list*)

F. Open your text and read to the bottom of page 370.

G. Reflection and Prereading Questions

1. So you were right about the bisector of an arc and its midpoint. Were you right about the center of an arc? So the center of an arc is not its midpoint. (*discuss and demonstrate*)

2. In circle O what is the center of $\overset{\frown}{AB}$? $\overset{\frown}{BC}$? $\overset{\frown}{CD}$? $\overset{\frown}{ABC}$? So they all have the same center — pt. O. (*demonstrate*)

3. Suppose a diameter of a circle intersects a chord. Could it ever bisect it? What chord would it always bisect? Right, another diameter. What might be a prerequisite to bisect a chord that's not a diameter? (*discuss and demonstrate*)

H. Open your text to page 371 and read the whole page.

I. Reflection and Prereading Questions

1. Was your assumption correct? (*discuss*)

2. You found out that if a diameter is perpendicular to a chord then it bisects the chord. What else does it bisect? Can you name the arcs being bisected? Right, major and minor arcs CD. (*demonstrate and discuss*)

3. In this theorem what is given? What is it we have to prove? What ways have we learned to prove arcs congruent? Which way might help us to prove the theorem? So, what are we going to use to get congruent segments and congruent arcs? Right, use congruent triangles. Let's write it up. (*work out on board*)

4. Will the converse of this theorem be true? Why not? Right, a diameter always bisects another diameter and it may or may not be perpendicular to it. (*discuss and demonstrate*)

J. Overall Reflection

1. Given:
$\overline{AC} \cong \overline{BD}$
Prove:
$\overset{\frown}{AB} \cong \overset{\frown}{CD}$

2. $CD = IO$, $CD \perp AB$,
$OE = 3$
Find $\overline{AB}$

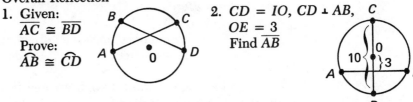

3. If a chord 12 inches long is 5 inches from the center of a circle, find the radius of the circle.

K. Extensions
   1. We learned today that in the same circle or congruent circles congruent arcs have congruent chords and its converse. What else might be congruent if chords are congruent?
   2. We also learned today that if a diameter is perpendicular to a chord it bisects the chord and its arc and that its converse is not true. Suppose we change the hypothesis of the converse to include a line that is the perpendicular bisector of a chord. What might be the conclusion?
   3. We discussed the bisector of an arc. How might you construct the bisector of an arc? Try to do this construction at home tonight and we'll discuss it in class tomorrow.
   4. Homework: Page 368 #3, pg. 369 #14, pg. 373 #1-4.

A PREREADING ANTICIPATION LESSON PLAN

Passage To Be Read

Homework: *Modern School Mathematics—Geometry* by Jurgensen, Donnelly and Dolciani
pages: 382 #9, 15, 16
383 #17, 24, 25, 28

Key Concepts

1. When a polygon is inscribed in a circle its angles become inscribed angles in the circle.
   a. Opposite angles of a quadrilateral are supplementary.
2. Inscribed angles are congruent or right angles depending on the nature of the arcs they intercept.

Key Concept Words

1. inscribed angles	3. intercepted arc
2. semicircle	4. congruent arcs

The key concept words have been previously introduced. Inscribed angles the day before and the others earlier in the chapter. I didn't want to use the new vocabulary words of the chapter because I felt I exhausted them for this chapter and I wanted to remain working in this chapter. In geometry there are more concepts using vocabulary than actual vocabulary, so I wanted to do a conceptual analysis. From this activity I'd hope to see some logical deductions connecting old and new concepts. (See discussion of conceptual analysis in Chapter 7, *Vocabulary Diagnosis*.)

This activity precedes the theorem—"An inscribed angle is equal to one half the measure of its intercepted arc." Therefore the whole activity deals with properties of inscribed angles expressed in the three corollaries preceeding the theorem.

The students will be grouped in threes. Bright students together, average and slow students integrated.

Projected Analysis

Part I: The students should discover that the angles are inscribed and the sides are chords. This should set the tone for the rest of the activity since it deals with only inscribed angles.

Part II: With accurate measurements the opposite angles will be supplementary. I think most students will see this.

Part III: The students will probably conclude angles C, D, and E are right angles since each measures 90°. And therefore angles C, D, and E are also congruent. Some will see that these angles intercept a semicircle. The bright students will see the concept—an inscribed angle that intercepts a semicircle is a right angle.

Part IV: Students will have little difficulty concluding that the inscribed angles of the congruent arcs are congruent. (See "Inscribed Angles Worksheet.")

INSCRIBED ANGLES WORKSHEET

Directions Answer each question by working together in your groups. Resolve disagreements. Clear up questions. Any confusions or unresolved disagreements can eventually be presented during sharing time. You will, of course, be expected to explain what caused the confusion or disagreement and what the group has done to solve it.

  I. The following polygons are inscribed in circles. In relation to the circle, how could you categorize their angles? Their sides?

II. All of the quadrilaterals are inscribed in the circles. Using your protractor, measure all of the angles of each quadrilateral. What should their sum be?
Examine the measures you have within each quadrilateral. Can you arrive at a new conclusion?

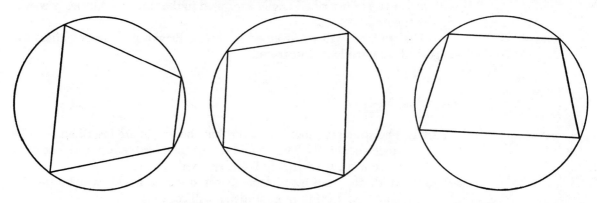

III. $\overline{AB}$ is a *diameter* of circle O. Using your protractor, measure angles C, D, and E. What can you conclude?

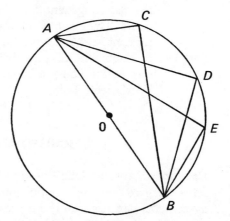

IV. Below are circles each having a pair of congruent arcs. What could be a general conclusion that could apply to all of the circles? (Hint: Examine the angles.)

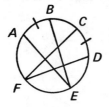
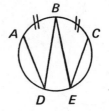
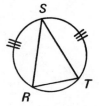

When the students have completed the activity we'll discuss their results in class. After parts I and II, I'll introduce the corollary: "If a quadrilateral is inscribed in a circle, opposite angles are supplementary," with an informal proof. After part III I'll introduce the next corollary: "an angle inscribed in a semi-circle is a right angle," with an informal proof. Part III should also introduce the concept: "inscribed angles intercepting the same are congruent." This will lead right into the corollary depicted in part IV: "inscribed angles intercepting the same or congruent arcs are congruent." Again having an informal proof.

Examples to follow:

1. Quadrilateral ABCD is inscribed in circle O. If angle A has 95°, find angle C.
2. Find x and y:

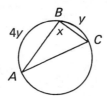

3. Prove: △ABE ~ △ECD

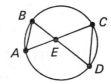

PATTERN STUDY GUIDE
HOW TO PROVE A PROOF WRITTEN AS A SENTENCE
(STEPS 7–9 ARE USED FOR ALL PROOFS)

1. Read carefully, being certain that you understand the problem.
2. Determine the hypothesis (given) and conclusion (prove). If it's not in "if-then" form find the verb. If you want, put the sentence into "if-then" form.
3. Draw a picture which illustrates the hypothesis.
4. Letter the picture and mark the parts that are congruent, parallel, perpendicular, etc.
5. From the hypothesis write what is given in terms of the picture.
6. From the conclusion write what there is to prove in terms of the picture.
7. Plan the proof. Select the definitions, theorems, etc., that apply.
8. Write the proof, giving a reason for each statement.

9. When you are finished, can you answer the following question with a yes?: Is your last statement the same as what is stated to be proved?

Example

1. Problem: Prove: An angle formed by two tangents is supplementary to the angle between the radii drawn to the points of contact.
2. If two tangents are drawn to a circle and meet radii at the points of contact

(hypothesis—given)

then the angle formed by the tangents is supplementary to the angle formed by the radii.

(conclusion—prove)

3. and 4.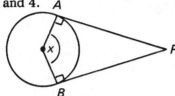

5. Given: $\overline{PA}$, $\overline{PB}$ tangents to circle O
$\overline{OA}$, $\overline{OB}$ radii

6. Prove: ⟨P supp ⟨x

7. and 8.

Statements	Reasons
1. $\overline{PA}$, $\overline{PB}$ tangents to ⊙O $\overline{OA}$, $\overline{OB}$ radii	1. Given
2. $\overline{OA} \perp \overline{AP}$, $\overline{OB} \perp \overline{BP}$	2. A tangent drawn to a circle is perpendicular to the radius at the point of contact.
3. ⟨OAP, ⟨OBP right angles	3. Perpendiculars form right angles.
4. ⟨OAP + ⟨OBP + ⟨X + ⟨P = 350°	4. The sum of the angles of a quad. is 360°.
5. ⟨OAP, ⟨OBP = 90°	5. Right angles measure 90°.
6. ⟨OAP + ⟨OBP = 180°	6. Addition property of equality.
7. ⟨x + ⟨P = 180°	7. Subtraction property of equality.
8. ⟨x supp. ⟨P	8. If the sum of two angles is 180°, they are supplementary.

PROOFS ON CIRCLES

(Practice exercises to follow pattern guide activity)

Directions Complete as many of the following proofs as you can during class time. When necessary *use the pattern study guide* for proofs written in sentences.

296

1. Given: $\overline{AB}$, $\overline{CD}$ diameters
   Prove: $\overline{BD} \cong \overline{CA}$

2. Given: $\odot 0$, $m\widehat{YZ} =$
   $m\widehat{ZW}$
   $m\widehat{XY} = k$
   $m\widehat{WV} = k$
   Prove: $m\langle XOZ = m\langle ZOV$

3. Given: $\overline{PT} \perp \overline{XY}$
   Prove: $\langle TXZ \cong \langle TYZ$

4. Given: $\overline{AB} \| \overline{CD}$
   Prove: $\widehat{AC} \cong \widehat{BD}$

5. Given: $\overline{DP}$, $\overline{EP}$ tangent to $\odot X$
   Prove: $\triangle DPE$ is isosceles

6. Given: $\overline{JN}$ diameter
   $\overline{OM} \| \overline{JK}$
   Prove: $\overline{KM} \cong \overline{MN}$

7. Prove: Tangents to a circle at the endpoints of a diameter are parallel.
8. Prove: A radius that bisects an arc bisects the chord of the arc.
9. Prove: If a tangent and a secant are parallel, they cut off congruent arcs on a circle.
10. Prove: An inscribed angle that intercepts a minor arc is an acute angle.
11. Given: $\triangle XYZ$ is inscribed in $\odot O$, $m\langle X = 30°$, $m\langle Y = 40°$.
    Prove: Points Z and O lie on opposite sides of $\overline{XY}$.

A Unit of Study in Science

CELLS: STRUCTURE AND FUNCTION*

Introduction

Because of my particular approach to the content of this unit, I feel it is necessary to give you the background needed to see this unit as I do. I am very much a proponent of a thinking education. I feel that all conceptualizations and generalizations should be a result of each individual student's thinking. It is not my intent to rationalize situations for students and have them memorize my opinions or generalizations. Thus, most of my instruction is based on individual thought-promoting activities.

All of my activities require a reflective reaction to the activity the student has completed. As part of the log sheet, the student is asked to describe the significance of that particular activity in terms of the conceptual objectives that the activity deals with. To insure that students will come to the "right conclusions," I have implemented the extensive use of small group discussions. These group activities are basically an opportunity to react to the material presented in the activity. (A discussion of small group discussion is included in the section describing activity types.) It is through these types of discussion activities (REAP, structured overview, post-graphic organizers, and cinquains) that the student is encouraged to think. Each of my activities is designed with this in mind.

I have developed specialized activities like vocabulary exercises and study guides where I think I can foresee problems in student comprehension. These activities I have designed are made to fill such a bill. As necessity dictates I will make others available as the unit progresses.

The first three books listed on the materials key are the three options for textual material I have found for use with this unit. The SMOG readability evaluations are included with each listing. Determination of the group readability levels will be evaluated by a CLOZE test. Individual readability will be coordinated with informal teacher evaluation. Through these means I hope to be able to choose the right text for each student to use.

Conceptual Objectives

1. The cell is the basic unit of life as we know it.
2. The cell is made up of organelles, each of which has a specific function within each cell. (Also cell components.)
3. Cells function on a molecular level.

*Prepared by Mr. Mark Emshwiller and reproduced here with his permission.

4. The specialization and diversity of cell types is in response to the function that the cell serves.

5. In multicellular organisms, groups of cells differentiate to function together for a specific purpose.

Weekly Schedule

Week One

Monday Attitude scale; Contracts; Introduction to activities; Discussion.

Tuesday Microscope reading; Microscope film; Demonstration of use; Student microscope work on classroom objects.

Wednesday Reading on cell theory; Contracts due; Small group discussion of reading; Group structured overview construction.

Thursday Reading on cell structure and function; Study guide; Small group discussion.

Friday Reflective-reaction activity on cell structure and function, includes microscope work.

Week Two

Monday Activity work day on cell functions.

Tuesday Reading on biological chemistry; Study guide; Small group discussions.

Wednesday Pre-reading anticipation activity on cellular processes.

Thursday Reading on cellular processes; Small group discussions; Reading on cells and environment.

Friday Small group discussions; Reading on DNA; Content reading lesson on DNA; Whole class discussion on DNA.

Week Three

Monday Activity day.

Tuesday Field trip—Collections.

Wednesday Microscope work, observing those specimens collected on the field trip.

Thursday Reading on specialization; Small group discussion; Group structured overview construction.

Friday Activity work day.

Week Four

Monday Unit Exam.

Materials and Readings Key

Books

	CONCEPTS				
	1	2	3	4	5
1. Oram, Hummer, Smoot. *Biology: Living Systems.* C. E. Merrill Publishing Co., 1976 (11th)	X	X	X	X	X
2. BSCS Green Version. *High School Biology.* Rand McNally and Company, 1968. (12th)	X	X	X	X	X
3. McElroy, Swanson, Buffaloe, Galston, Macey. *Foundations of Biology.* Prentice Hall Inc., 1968. (11th)	X	X	X	X	X
4. Boggs, Koob. *The Nature of Life,* Addison-Wesley Publishing Co., 1972.		X	X		
5. Butler. *Inside the Living Cell.* Basic Books, 1959.		X	X		
6. Swanson. *The Cell.* Prentice Hall Inc., 1964.	X	X	X		
7. Hawker. *An Introduction to the Biology of Microorganisms.* St. Martins, 1961.					X
8. Hooke. *Micrographia, or Some Physiological Descriptions of Minute Bodies.* Dover, 1665.	X				
9. Leeuwenhoek. *Little Animals.* Dover, 1932, 1960.	X				
10. Richards. *The Complementarity of Structure and Function.* Heath, 1963.				X	X

Magazines

	CONCEPTS				
	1	2	3	4	5
1. *Scientific American,* ''The Mitochondrion.'' (Jan. 1964).		X			
2. *S. A.,* ''Cilia.'' (Feb. 1961).		X			
3. *S. A.,* ''The Membrane of the Living Cell.'' (Apr. 1962).		X	X		X

	CONCEPTS				
	1	2	3	4	5
4. *S. A.,* "Heart Cells in Vitro." (May 1965).					X
5. *S. A.,* "Genetic Code." (Oct. 1962).		X			

Films

	1	2	3	4	5
1. *The Cell: Structural Unit of Life,* Coronet.	X				
2. *Cells and Their Functions,* Contemporary.				X	X
3. *The Microscope,* McGraw-Hill.					
4. *Life in a Drop of Water,* Coronet.					X
5. *The Stuff of Life,* Indiana University.		X	X		

Teacher Made Materials

	1	2	3	4	5
1. Attitude Scale					
2. Study Guide—Cell Structure and Function		X		X	
3. Reflective-Reaction: Cell Structure and Function		X		X	
4. Vocabulary crossword puzzle: Organelles		X			
5. Vocabulary word-meaning exercise		X		X	
6. Pre-Reading Anticipation: Cellular Processes		X	X		
7. Study Guide: Biological Chemistry			X		
8. Content Reading Lesson: DNA		X	X		
9. Associated Lab Materials	X	X	X	X	X
10. Unit Exam	X	X	X	X	X
11. CLOZE test					

Activity Key

	CONCEPTS				
	1	2	3	4	5
1. *Biology: Living Systems* Readings					
*a. The Cell Theory, pg. 60–63	X				
*b. Inside the Living Cell, pg. 63–71		X			
*c. The Cell and Its Environment, pg. 71–79			X	X	
*d. Levels of Organization, pg. 79–81				X	X
*e. Biological Chemistry, pg. 52–57			X		
*f. Reproduction: Chemical Aspects, pg. 181–186			X		
2. *High School Biology* Readings					
a. Cell Theory, pg. 373–381	X				
b. Cell Structure, pg. 381–386		X			
c. Some Cell Physiology, pg. 386–393			X	X	
d. Differentiation, pg. 400–404				X	X
e. Syntheses, pg. 421–426			X		
3. *Foundations of Biology* Readings					
a. The Microscope, pg. 137–141	X				
b. The Cell Theory, pg. 134–137	X				
c. Organelles, pg. 141–150		X			
d. Nucleus: Control Center, pg. 178–181		X	X		
e. Biological Compounds, pg. 204–217			X		
f. Metabolic Properties, pg. 220–228			X	X	X
4. Attitude Scale					
5. Study Guide: Cell Structure and Function		X		X	
6. Reflective Reaction: Cell Structure and Function		X		X	

	CONCEPTS				
	1	2	3	4	5
7. Pre-Reading Anticipation: Cellular Processes		X	X		
8. Study Guide: Biological Chemistry			X		
9. Vocabulary crossword puzzle		X			
10. Vocabulary word meaning exercise		X		X	
11. Content Reading Lesson: DNA		X	X		
12. Develop materials for a classroom bulletin board	X	X	X	X	X
13. Build a molecular model of cellular compounds (proteins, sugars, nucleic acids, etc.)			X		
14. Field Trip: Collecting and observing cell types		X		X	X
15. Construct a model of a cell		X			
16. Construct a vocabulary exercise	X	X	X	X	X
17. Construct a structured overview on one of the extra biological readings	X	X	X	X	X
18. Write a Research Paper					
a. Protein synthesis		X	X	X	
b. DNA replication		X	X		
c. Energy production		X	X		
d. Tissue specialization				X	X
e. Histology					X
f. Or topic approved by instructor	X	X	X	X	
19. View a film		X	X	X	X
20. Observe electron micrographs of organelles		X			
21. Lab: Do selective staining for identification of particular organelles		X			
22. Lab: Collect tissue samples and make permanent slides				X	X

	CONCEPTS				
	1	2	3	4	5
23. Lab: Fix and mount a chick embryo for observation				X	X
24. Lab: Test for sugars, proteins, etc., in plant leaves			X		
25. Lab: Chromatography experiment on pigments in plant leaves		X	X		
26. Lab: Catalysis enzyme activity			X		
27. Lab: Histology study on dissected frog		X		X	X
28. Make a model of DNA			X		
29. Develop a classification key for cells according to features of their tissues or cellular components		X		X	X
30. Read a science article and write a short summary	X	X	X	X	X
31. Read Hooke's original observations of cells	X				
32. Read Leeuwenhoek's descriptions of microorganisms	X				
33. Do a comparative study of the differences in plant and animal cells		X		X	X
34. Do a comparative study of unicellular and multicellular organisms.	X	X			X
35. Take a trip to the university and observe the preparation of cells for use with electron microscopes		X		X	
36. Set up a debate team, discussing the issue of whether or not mitochondria and chloroplasts evolved from bacteria		X		X	
37. Make a chart associating cell function with general shape				X	X
38. Classroom discussion: Cell Theory	X				

	CONCEPTS				
	1	2	3	4	5
39. Group construction of structured overview: Cell Theory	X				
40. Group discussion: Cell Structure and Function		X			
41. Group discussion: Biological Chemistry			X		
42. Group discussion: Cellular Processes			X		
43. Group discussion: Cells and Their Environment				X	X
44. Classroom discussion: DNA			X		
45. Microscope observation on classroom objects					
46. Microscope observation of specimens collected on field trip				X	X
47. Group discussion: Specialization				X	
48. Group construction of structured overview: Specialization				X	
49. Read and collect magazine and newspaper articles on cells and tissues	X	X	X	X	X
50. Prepare a classroom demonstration on one of the major concepts	X	X	X	X	X
51. Investigate the causes of aging in cells. What causes cells to die?			X		
52. Investigate the actual causes of differentiation			X		X
53. Calculate the exact sizes of different cells with a micrometer attachment for your microscope					
54. Test for carbohydrates in seeds. What does this indicate?			X		
55. CLOZE test					

Description of Activities

Small Group Discussions

All of my small group activities are designed as a synthesizing and thought processing experience. They are intended to stimulate reflection and reaction to those ideas and concepts just discovered in the reading selection. These activities are intended to be directed by students, with teacher intervention as needed (for answering specific questions only, not for synthesizing material for groups of students).

The basic format of such small group work develops a self-awareness of process oriented thinking through reflective-reaction activities. I will hand out reproductions of sample procedures for students to follow. As the students come to grips with these strategies, written instructions and forms will become unnecessary.

Small group work promotes discussion, interaction, the formulation of opinions, and thinking, all of which are at the very heart of what I'm trying to do. The primary purpose of small group activities is to get the students to reach their own conclusions about concepts they have explored. I do not want my students to memorize my conclusions or those of someone else. As an avenue to evaluation of these group sessions, I will have each student keep a log of activities, which will include a section where the student discusses the significance of each activity he or she has done. This gives me an insight into how well individuals are arriving at proper conclusions.

Small Group, "Post-Organizer" Construction

This activity follows many of the lines drawn in the small group discussion section. Only, here I am asking the students to prepare as a group, in any form they wish (table, graph, outline, summary, pictures, cartoon sequence, etc.) a "post-organizer." I want a complete analysis of the conclusions that they have drawn from the reading selection exemplified in a group effort. This allows me to see if they are developing the right conclusions, and it allows students the benefits of group interactions. Many times misconceptions are cleared up simply by talking over the issue at hand.

Films and Various Other Media Presentations

These activities are optional, but those students who choose this as one of their activities will be required to complete the same procedure as is used for the small group discussion. This is done so that each student has an opportunity to discuss those things which he or she has learned. The use of small group interactions in this instance helps many of the slower students by giving them more of a chance to become involved in the discussion.

Laboratory Activities

Each lab activity will be carried out on an individual or small group (2 students) basis. I will give students the reference for the activity and the resources needed to complete the lab. This type of activity is designed to facilitate personal development of the concepts, because lab activities seem to go better when students work alone. This promotes complete understanding of the purposes and procedures, and prevents other students from free-loading on another's efforts. Each student will again be required to assimilate his or her conclusions and present them in the form of a written lab report.

Extra Readings

Again, most readings require a short summary or some type of R-R activity as dictated by the activity key.

Research Paper

Research papers are a means by which those students who have an interest above and beyond that covered by the regular class material can explore the subject in greater detail. It is used on an individual basis as it is seen to be needed by each individual student.

The overall emphasis of my approach to the above activities is to satisfy as many means of learning as possible according to each individual's own ability level. I am trying to individualize my approach so that each student may come to grips with each concept in the way that is easiest for him or her.

A CONTENT READING LESSON

  I. Conceptual Objectives
     1. Genetic information is stored in the molecule DNA.
     2. Molecules of DNA make up the chromosomes.
     3. Molecules of DNA are replicated during mitosis and meiosis.
  II. This lesson will involve all three stages of the content reading lesson: motivation, interaction, and synthesis. The motivational aspect will consist of the following types of introductory questions.

What is DNA?

What do you think DNA does in the cell?

What do you know about DNA?

What do you think a reading selection on DNA will tell you?

What do you expect to learn about DNA?

What would you want to learn about DNA?

What type of experiments might be involved in DNA research?

What are the names of famous people who worked on DNA?

Etc.

By asking these questions, you are in effect organizing and building the student's awareness of the topic of the reading selection. By asking these questions, you also generate motivation through curiosity. The students pose things they feel the article will deal with, and are curious to see if those things they did mention are in fact included within the reading selection.

Interaction is accomplished with the reading material itself. By engaging the students in short segments rather than the whole article, the students are more likely to retain the information. After each segment, I will ask questions like:

What did you find out about DNA?

Did you find out anything that you thought would be present in the article?

After reading this segment, what else do you expect to find in this reading selection?

I will, one by one, cross off those things which we have found in the article, as predicted by the students. I will also add others as they come up in the discussions. By writing these things on the board, the students and the teacher will have a better recall and understanding of the things they have talked about. In effect, by having the students recall information about the article as compared to those things they predicted, the students must actually think about the reading selection, which by definition is interacting with the reading material.

Synthesis is accomplished through reflection and reaction to the material the students have learned. To reflect requires understanding and to react to a subject requires the formation of an opinion. All of these activities require the student to think, which was our original goal. Continued application includes extension activities. Some for this unit are:

Build a model of a DNA molecule.

Draw the molecular structure of a DNA molecule, and compare its properties to those which were predicted by Watson & Crick.

How might mutations occur in the DNA molecule? (a mechanism)

Do a lab activity isolating for DNA, and testing for nucleoproteins, sugars, phosphorus compounds, etc.

Read Watson and Crick's original experiments on DNA.

Through lab activities, compare the relative amounts of DNA present in different organisms.

All of these activities will reinforce and motivate a greater understanding of the function of DNA in the cell.

Reading selection: Oram, Hummer, Smoot. *Biology: Living Systems*, pp. 181–183; 184–187.

THREE LEVEL STUDY GUIDE

(For "Biology Compounds," *Biology: Living Systems*, 52–57.)

Conceptual Objectives

1. Cells function on a molecular level.
2. All biological compounds contain the element carbon, thus living systems are made up of organic compounds.

Study Guide—Biological Chemistry

I.
1. Why aren't atoms like arsenic and lead used in living systems?
2. Since carbohydrate is an energy source, what types of foods might contain molecules of glucose, galactose, or mannose?
3. In what different parts of the cell might carbon compounds like carbohydrates, proteins, lipids, and nucleic acids be found?

II.
1. What is the difference between saturated and unsaturated fats?
2. What occurs when carbohydrates are metabolized in the cell?
3. What gives a protein characteristic properties?

III.
1. What are the building blocks of carbohydrates?
2. What is the difference between a disaccharide and a polysaccharide? Give examples of each.
3. What are lipids used for in the cell?
4. How is a fat molecule formed?
5. What are the building blocks of proteins?

6. What element makes proteins different from lipids and carbohydrates?
7. What are two important nucleic acids?

COMBINATION STUDY GUIDE

(For "Inside the Cell," *Biology: Living Systems*, 63–71.)

I. Conceptual Objectives
1. The cell is made up of organelles, each of which has a specific function within each cell.
2. The organelles function together to regulate the cell's metabolism.
II. Study Guide—Cell Structures: Functions
1. As you read pages 63–71 of the text, place the correct word from the list below in the proper blank of each statement.

cytoplasm	lysosomes
ribosomes	plastids
centrioles	endoplasmic reticulum
nucleus	Golgi bodies
nucleoplasm	vacuoles
mitochondria	nucleoli

1. The _____ is the protoplasm inside the nucleus.

2. _____ is protoplasm outside the nucleus.

3. _____ are the sites of energy release.

4. The _____ transports materials within cells.

5. _____ are mainly composed of RNA and are the site of protein synthesis.

6. _____ are thought to be involved in producing and storing cellular secretions.

7. _____ are fluid-filled sacs used for storage of food and minerals.

8. _____ contain the hydrolytic enzymes produced by the ribosomes.

9. The _____ are the structures from which spindle fibers arise during cell division.

10. _____ contain chlorophyll which is necessary for photosynthesis.

11. The _____ is the control center of the cell.

12. _____ within the nucleus are responsible for ribosome production.

2. Categorize each organelle under the cellular process in which it is involved.

Energy Production	Cell Division	Protein Synthesis	Food Digestion	Food Synthesis	Chromosome Duplication

3. For each of the cellular processes, briefly discuss how each organelle might function in relation to the process in which it participates.

III. Read "Inside the Living Cell," pages 63–71 in *Biology: Living Systems*, Oram, Hummer, Smoot.

Following this reading selection, I will hold an open discussion to talk about the interrelatedness of the functions of the different cellular structures. After this discussion the students will be doing some microscope work on various plant and animal tissues, identifying the type of cell, with the types of organelles present. I want them to see the division of labor among cells in terms of function. For example, those cells which respire heavily have a lot of mitochondria.

A REFLECTIVE REACTION ACTIVITY

I. Conceptual Objectives
1. Cellular organelles function together in response to the specialization of that cell to a tissue.
2. The specialization and diversity of cell types is in response to the function that the cell serves.
3. In multicellular organisms, groups of cells differentiate to function together for a specific purpose.

II. Reflective-Reaction: Organelle Functions—Interrelatedness
1. Prepare and stain for observation the following tissue samples: (a) frog heart muscle, leg muscle, and a mesentery tissue. Stain with Janus Green B* for mitochondria. (b) Observe chloroplasts in Elodea leaves and Euglena. (c) Stain protozoa with Janus Green B* for Golgi Apparatus, also stain frog intestinal cells. (d) Stain protozoa with Nile

Blue sulfate* for food vacuoles. (e) Stain cells of an onion root, and cells from the root tip with aceto-orcein.* Observe the nucleus. *(See instructor for exact procedure on staining.)

2. Record your observations. (You might want to note things like the number of mitochondria in certain cell types, or the relative size of the organelles in different tissues.)

3. Meet in small groups for discussion of the results of the observations you made.

III. This activity will succeed a reading assignment and study guide on cell organelles and the functions they perform in different cell types.

IV. This R-R activity is designed to enhance the idea that cellular organelles function together in cells, to the purpose that the tissue serves in the organism. This activity is also a P-A activity for the next unit on differentiation and specialization of cell types as to function.

V. This activity fits the theoretical criterion of R-R by stimulating the students to draw conclusions from the previous reading selection and apply them to explain the phenomenon observed in the examples of nature displayed in the laboratory activity. By observing that muscle tissues have more mitochondria than mesentery tissue, this activity stimulates the student to rationalize that muscle tissue uses more energy and that the mitochondria are the principal organelle of function in muscle tissue. Therefore, the basic metabolism of muscle cells is in the role of energy production. Many such conclusions can be drawn from the R-R activity, and it reinforces those things learned in the reading selection.

A Unit of Study in Social Studies

THE AMERICAN LEGAL SYSTEM*

Introduction

The following unit has been designed for use in a learning disabled resource room class with approximately ten to fifteen 10th and 11th grade students. This unit is part of an American Government class. American Government is a required course and part of the graduation requirement.

Reading materials were collected in order to cover readability levels ranging from 4th to the 8th grade levels. Activities were planned that take into consideration these students' low reading levels, low motivation, and their difficulties with completing assignments independently.

These students have demonstrated very little understanding of the American legal system even though many of them have been involved with the juvenile court system.

*Prepared by Ms. Margaret Greenfield and reproduced here with her permission.

Materials and Resource Key

OBJECTIVES

Listed by their #'s from List.	A	B	C	D	E	F	G	H
1.	X	X	X				X	X
2.						X		
3.			X					
4.			X			X		
5.						X		
6.	X	X	X					
7.	X	X	X					
8.		X					X	X
9.				X		X		
10.	X				X			
11.	X	X	X					
12.	X	X		X	X		X	
13.	X	X					X	
14.						X	X	
15.							X	
16.						X		
17.					X		X	X
18.		X					X	
19.				X	X			
20.					X	X	X	X
21.						X		

Activities Key

	OBJECTIVES							
	A	B	C	D	E	F	G	H
1. Cloze Test			X					
2. Maze Test	X	X	X					
3. Activity #4 Filmstrip	X	X	X					
4. Speaker—Legal Aid Lawyer		X			X		X	X
5. Film/"With Liberty & Justice for All."	X	X	X					
6. "The Constitution in American Society," Reading & Study Guide.	X	X	X	X	X		X	X
7. "Elijah P. Lovejoy" Reading & Study Guide.		X			X			
8. Field Trip/Newspaper Office.		X				X		
9. Answers & List Sharing from Field Trip.		X				X		
10. Congress & Supreme Court Worksheet Activity.		X			X			
11. Gault Case Reading & Study Guide.				X	X	X		X
12. Recording of Ex-convict & Activity #15.			X			X		
13. Reading "This Court Finds You . . ." & Comp. Check.					X	X		
14. Speaker—Juvenile Probation Officer.						X		
15. Filmstrip/Law & the Youthful Offender & Activity #18.					X	X	X	X
16. Debate/Resolved that juvenile offenders should be treated just the same as adult offenders.						X	X	
17. Recording/"Case of the Missing Step" with Activity #20.					X			
18. Field Trip to County Courthouse.				X	X		X	X

Name: _____ Date: _____

Instructions: I would like to know your true feelings on each of the following items. Place a check in the box that best represents your agreement with the corresponding statement.

SA = Strongly Agree   D = Disagree
A = Agree   SD = Strongly Disagree
U = Undecided

	SA	A	U	D	SD
1. The law protects property rights, but not human rights.					
2. On the whole, judges are honest.					
3. A person should obey only those laws that seem right.					
4. On the whole, policemen are honest.					
5. In the courts, a poor man will receive as fair treatment as a millionaire.					
6. It's okay to break the law if you can get away with it.					
7. All laws should be strictly obeyed because they are laws.					
8. A hungry man has a right to steal.					
9. Past court decisions are an important part of our present legal system.					
10. A person who commits a crime should still be guaranteed his constitutional rights.					
11. Most things which get teenagers in trouble with the law don't hurt anyone.					
12. To get what you want in this world, you have to do some things which are against the law.					
13. The Bill of Rights are an important part of the U.S. Constitution.					
14. A teenager who commits murder should be treated differently than an adult who commits murder.					
15. States should have youthful-offender laws.					

	SA	A	U	D	SD
16. Most public officials (people in public offices) are not interested in the problems of the average man.					
17. People who are poor should be appointed a lawyer through the courts.					
18. It is all right to avoid the law if you don't actually violate it.					
19. The sentences of judges in court are based on their prejudices.					
20. Juries don't understand a case well enough to make a just decision.					

Topic: The American Legal System

Our legal system, Constitutional law, juvenile law, and judicial procedures are the four sections that this unit was designed to cover. The unit sections were chosen to help students to understand the American legal system and how this system stems from the Constitution of the United States.

Unit Length

The unit was designed to cover a period of five weeks. Each of the four sections will last one week except the Constitutional law section, which will last two weeks. This will allow for an intense study of the American Constitution and its most important parts.

Grading

Grading will be based on (A) individual participation and (B) completion of in-class assignments.

Conceptual Objectives

A. The United States Constitution gives us the basic principles by which our legal system works.
B. The first ten Amendments to the U.S. Constitution are the Bill of Rights which protect the civil rights of all citizens.
C. The American legal system operates on three levels: local, state, and federal.

D. In the American legal system, court decisions made in the past play an important part in the decisions that courts make today.
E. Any action that violates the laws in the Constitution or the Bill of Rights can be stopped by the courts.
F. Juvenile courts have a responsibility to use due process of law rights guaranteed under the Constitution.

Performance Objectives

G. Describe the basic civil rights protected in the United States Constitution.
H. Analyze different laws and court cases and state which ones might involve a violation of rights set forth in the Bill of Rights.

Resources

The following is a list of materials and resources to be used in this unit. The ways they are to be used are indicated in the activity key.

Books (*All books have been tested for readabililty using the SMOG Formula.)

1. *Our Legal Heritage.* Textbook. Silver Burdett Co., 1978. 6th.*
2. *Getting It Together: A Reading Series About People.* SRA, Inc., 1973. 6th.*
3. *Careers in the Legal Profession.* By Elinor Porter Swiger. 6th.*
4. *Local Government.* By James A. Eichner. 7th.*
5. *Youth and the Law: Rights, Privileges, and Obligations.* By Irving J. Sloan. 8th.*
6. *Essentials of American Democracy.* By Carr, Bernstein, Murphy, and Danielson. 8th.*
7. *Our Federal Government: How It Works: An Introduction to the United States Government.* By Patricia C. Acheson. 6th.*
8. *The Bill of Rights.* By E. B. Fincher. 7th.*
9. *Young People and the Law: What the Courts Have Had to Say.* Published by Youth Liberation, 2007 Washington Ave., Ann Arbor, MI 48104. 7th.*
10. *The Supreme Court in America's Story.* By Helen Peterson. 6th.*
11. *Justice in America: Law, Order, and the Courts.* By William P. Lineberry. 8th.*

Films

1. "With Liberty and Justice for All," 60 min. Shows how certain individuals have fought to preserve their constitutional rights and describes the

vital role that the nation's courts play in insuring liberty and justice for all.

2. "The Constitution—Guardian of Liberty." Discusses the Constitution and its content.

Filmstrips

1. "Law and the Youthful Offender." Doubleday Multimedia. (Part of kit from EMC-FSAL 3468/73.)
2. "Law and the Individual." Doubleday Multimedia. (Part of kit from EMC-FSAL 3468/73.)

Records

1. Recording of ex-convict. Part of *Citizenship: Rights and Responsibilities* multimedia kit from EMC-FSAL 2007.
2. Recording of "The Case of the Missing Step: Flora Dora, Plaintiff v. Romeo Grant, Defendant." Part of *Citizenship: Rights and Responsibilities* multimedia kit from EMC-FSAL 2007.

Field Trips

1. Newspaper office (of local newspaper).
2. County courthouse.

Guest Speakers

1. Lawyer from legal aid office.
2. Juvenile probation officer.

Lesson Plans (Overview)

1st Week—Our Legal System

Mon. Administer Attitude Scale to all the students.

Tue. Students read pgs. 3–5 of *Our Federal Government: How it Works* and complete Cloze worksheet (Why Have a Government?).

Wed. Students read pgs. 1–10 of *Our Legal Heritage* and complete Maze worksheet (Our Legal System). Class discussion of material. Do exercises (vocabulary) on pg. 11 with class.

Thurs. Students view filmstrip "Law and the Individual."

Fri. Guest speaker comes to class. A lawyer from legal aide will speak to class about his or her role and interesting cases that relate to civil rights. Students will be encouraged to ask questions and will be required to write two paragraphs about what was said when it is over.

2nd Week—Constitutional Law

Mon. Film, "With Liberty and Justice for All." Class discussion.
Tue. Students read in groups "The Constitution in American Society," pgs.
Fri. 60–120 in *Our Legal Heritage* and complete study guide.

3rd Week—Constitutional Law

Mon. "Elijah P. Lovejoy" reading. See detailed lesson plan. Parts II and III of lesson plan.
Tue. "Elijah P. Lovejoy" reading continued. Part IV, A.
Wed. Field trip to newspaper office to talk with the editor about freedom of speech and press rights. Part IV, B, from Lovejoy study guide lesson plan. Students ask questions.
Thurs. Answers and lists developed by students from field trip shared in the group. Class discussion.
Fri. Congress and the Supreme Court activity and worksheet. Students complete worksheets in small groups and share answers in larger group.

4th Week—Juvenile Law

Mon. Gault case—reading and study guide.
Tue. Post reading activities on Gault case lesson plan.
Wed. Students listen to recording of ex-convict and complete Activity #15
Thurs. Students read "This Court Finds You. . . ." individually and complete comprehension check questions. Answers discussed in large group.
Fri. Guest speaker comes to class. Juvenile probation officer will speak to the class regarding the manner in which juvenile offenders are treated. The talk will be followed by a question and answer period.

5th Week—Judicial Procedures

Mon. Filmstrip: "Law and the Youthful Offender." Complete Activity #18.
Tues. Debate presented on the topic: Resolved that juvenile offenders should be treated just the same as adult offenders (from Activity #18). Following the debate, class members should be encouraged to express their own opinions on the topic.
Wed. Students listen to recording of "Case of the Missing Step." Complete Activity #20.
Thurs. Field trip to county courthouse to sit in on court proceeding and to speak to judge afterwards. Judge will talk about his or her role and different court cases and procedures.
Fri. Re-administer Attitude Scale to all students.

A CONTENT READING LESSON

(For use with resource class unit on government.)

Text: "Elijah P. Lovejoy," a story in *The Bill of Rights* by E. B. Fincher.

I. *Objectives:*
   A. Students will define the four basic rights which are guaranteed in the First Amendment.
   B. Students will identify incidents in which First Amendment rights of persons have been violated.
   C. Students will examine the conditions in the early 1800s under which newspapers exercised their right of freedom of press as compared to present day conditions.

II. *Pre-Reading Anticipation:*
   Procedures:
   A. Teacher asks the following questions. All responses of students are written on the board under each question.
      1. What does freedom of speech mean to you? (List responses.)
      2. What does the freedom of press mean to you?
      3. What does freedom of religion mean to you?
      4. What does freedom of assembly mean to you?

      Teacher lists all responses under each question. Group then votes on one best definition for each question. Group is divided into four subgroups. Each subgroup is assigned one of the four questions with the chosen definition. Each group is given 15 minutes to come up with and write down ways in which they enjoy that freedom in their lives today. After 15 minutes, the whole group gets back together and each group selects a spokesperson to relate to the rest of the group what they came up with. All ideas are listed on the board under the appropriate question.

      Teacher then asks question: Have Americans always had these freedoms (Idea should be brought out in the discussion that these freedoms are guaranteed in the 1st Amendment—previously taught to them.)

III. *Information Search:*
   Procedures:
   A. Teacher introduces title of selection as "Elijah P. Lovejoy." Teacher states that this story is about a young man who lived in Illinois in the 1800s. Have students read to the end of the third paragraph.
   B. Stop them and have them turn stories over and then look up at the four questions, answers, and examples on the board from the Pre-Reading Anticipation exercises. Ask students which of the four freedoms on the board is Elijah attempting to exercise? Discuss answers with the group. Have students finish the rest of the story.

C. Hand out the three-level study guide before they finish reading the rest of the story after the stop. Tell them to complete this when they are through with the reading. They can refer back to the selection as they are attempting to fill it out.

IV. *Reflective Reaction:*

Procedures:

A. Students get back into a group when all of them have finished reading the selection and completed the study guide. Go over all of the questions as a group and have students discuss answers in the group.

B. As an *extension activity*, group will visit a local newspaper office and meet with the editor of the paper. Students will prepare questions to ask him or her before going on the trip. These questions will be prepared as a group and each student will be given a question to ask.

After the field trip, students will be divided into groups and each group will be asked to make a list of how conditions under which the press exercises its freedom of press and speech rights are different than they were in Elijah P. Lovejoy's time.

Answers and lists will be shared in the group.

Another possible extension activity would be to have the group start a newspaper. One person could serve as an editor and the students would be encouraged to write controversial articles which express strong opinions. Group discussions would occur regularly to discuss the reactions that some of these articles caused.

V. *Bibliography:*

A. *Our Legal Heritage*, textbook.
B. *The Bill of Rights* by E. B. Fincher.
C. *Essentials of American Democracy*, 7th Edition, textbook.
D. Editor of local newspaper.

References

Adler, M. J., and Van Doren, C. 1940/1972. *How to read a book.* New York: Simon & Schuster.

Alexander, J. E., and Filler, R. C. 1976. *Attitudes and reading.* Newark, Del.: International Reading Association.

Anderson, R. C., and Freebody, P. 1979. *Vocabulary knowledge* (Tech. Rep. No. 136). Champaign: University of Illinois, Center for the Study of Reading.

Anderson, R. C.; Reynolds, R. E.; Schallert, D. L.; and Goetz, E. T. 1977. Frameworks for comprehending discourse. *American Educational Research Journal* 14: 367–381.

Antonnen, R. G. 1968. *An examination into the stability of mathematics attitude and its relationship to mathematics achievement from elementary to secondary school level.* Ph.D. diss., University of Minnesota. Ann Arbor, Mich.: University Microfilms, No. 68-01528.

Ausubel, D. P. 1968. *Educational psychology: A cognitive view.* New York: Holt, Rinehart, Winston.

Ausubel, D. P.; Novak, J. D.; and Hanesian, H. 1978. *Educational psychology: A cognitive view.* 2d ed. New York: Holt, Rinehart, Winston.

Banan, J. M. 1972. Negative human interaction. *Journal of Counseling Psychology* 19: 81–82.

Barron, R. F. 1969. The use of vocabulary as an advance organizer. In *Research in reading in the content areas: First year report,* edited by H. L. Herber & P. L. Sanders, 29–39. Syracuse, N.Y.: Syracuse University Reading and Language Arts Center.

Barron, R. F., & Stone, V. F. 1974. The effect of student-constructed graphic post

323

organizers upon learning vocabulary relationships. In *Twenty-third yearbook of the national reading conference*, edited by P. L. Nacke, 172–175. Clemson, S.C.: National Reading Conference.

Barron, R. F. 1979. Research for the classroom teacher: Recent developments on the structured overview as an advance organizer. In *Research in reading in the content areas: The fourth report*, edited by H. L. Herber and J. D. Riley, 171–177. Syracuse, N.Y.: Syracuse University Reading and Language Art Center.

Bormuth, J. 1966. Readability: A new approach. *Reading Research Quarterly 1:* 79–132.

Bormuth, J. 1968. *Readability in 1968.* New York: National Conference on Research in English.

Buros, O. K. 1938 and subsequent editions. *Mental measurements yearbooks.* Highland Park, N.J.: Gryphon.

————. 1968. *Reading: Tests and reviews.* Highland Park, N.J.: Gryphon.

————. 1974. *Tests in print.* Highland Park, N.J.: Gryphon.

Combs, A. W. 1971. *Helping relationships: Basic concepts for the helping professions.* Boston: Allyn and Bacon.

Dale, E., and Chall, J. A. 1948. *A formula for predicting readability.* Columbus: Ohio State University Educational Research Bull. *XXVII.*

Dewey, J. 1902, 1959. *The child and the curriculum.* Chicago: University of Chicago Press. (Reprinted in Dworkin, M. S., *Dewey on education.* New York: Teachers College Press, 1959.)

DeWitz, P.; Henning, M. J.; and Patberg, J. P. 1982. The effects of content area reading instruction on teacher behavior. In *Reading in the content areas: Application of a concept*, edited by J. P. Patberg, 11–39. Toledo: University of Toledo College of Education.

Dulin, K. L., and Chester, R. D. 1974. A validation of the Estes Attitude Scale. *Journal of Reading 18:* 56–69.

Earle, R. A. 1969. Use of the structured overview in mathematics classes. In *Research in reading in the content areas: First year report*, edited by H. L. Herber and P. L. Sanders. Syracuse: Syracuse University Reading & Language Arts Center.

Earle, R. A. 1976. *Teaching reading and mathematics.* Newark, Del.: International Reading Association.

Edwards, A. L. 1957. *Techniques of attitude scale construction.* New York: Appleton-Century-Crofts.

Elam, S. 1970. The age of accountability dawns in Texarkana. *Phi Delta Kappan 10:* 59.

Elkind, D. 1983. *The hurried child.* Reading, Mass.: Addison-Wesley.

Estes, T. H.; Estes, J. J.; Richards, H. C.; and Roettger, D. M. 1981. *Estes Attitude Scales: Measures of attitudes toward school subjects.* Austin, Tex.: ProEd.

Fader, D. 1973. *The Naked Children.* New York: Macmillan.

Fish, S. 1978. Normal circumstances, literal language, direct speech acts, the ordinary, the everyday, the obvious, what goes without saying, and other special cases. *Critical Inquiry:* 625–644.

Fry, E. 1977. Fry's readability graph: Clarifications, validity, and extension to level 17. *Journal of Reading 21:* 242–252.

Gates, A. T., & MacGinitie, W. H. 1965, 1972. *Gates-MacGinitie reading tests.* New York: Teachers College Press, Columbia University.

Goodlad, John I. 1983. A study of schooling: Some findings and hypotheses. *Phi Delta Kappan 64:* 465–470, 552–558.

Goodman, Y. M. 1978. Kid watching: An alternative to testing. *The National Elementary Principal 57:* 41–45.

Goodman, Y. M., and Burke, C. L. 1972. *Reading miscue inventory.* New York: Macmillan.

Harman, D. 1975. Reading tests. *The National Elementary Principal 54:* 81–87.

Herber, H. L. 1970. *Teaching reading in content areas.* Englewood Cliffs, N.J.: Prentice-Hall.

Herber, H. L. 1978. *Teaching reading in content areas.* 2d ed. Englewood Cliffs, N.J.: Prentice-Hall.

Hoffman, B. 1964. *The tyranny of testing.* New York: Collier.

Homans, G. 1965. Group factors in worker productivity. In *Basic studies in social psychology,* edited by H. Proshansky and B. Slidenberg, 592–604. New York: Holt, Rinehart & Winston.

Irwin, J. W., & Davis, C. A. 1980. Assessing readability: The checklist approach. *Journal of Reading 24:* 124–130.

Iser, W. 1978. *The act of reading: A theory of aesthetic response.* Baltimore: Johns Hopkins University Press.

Johnstone, J. P. 1974. Convergent and discriminant validity of a scale to measure attitudes toward school subjects. Ph.D diss. University of Virginia. Ann Arbor, Mich.: University Microfilms, No. 73–32.

Klare, G. 1974. Assessing readability. *Reading Research Quarterly 10:* 62–102.

Klare, G. 1982. Readability. In *Encyclopedia of educational research,* edited by H. E. Mitzel. 5th ed. New York: Free Press.

Kohlberg, J. W., and Mayer, R. 1972. Development as the aim of education. *Harvard Educational Review 42:* 449–496.

Kohn, S. D. 1975. The numbers game: How the test industry operates. *The National Elementary Principal 54:* 6, 11–23.

Langer, J. A. 1981. From theory to practice: A pre-reading plan. *Journal of Reading 25:* 152–156.

Langer, J. A., and Nicolich, M. 1981. Prior knowledge and its effect on comprehension. *Journal of Reading Behavior 13:* 373–379.

Likert, R. S. 1932. A technique for the measurement of attitudes. *Archives of Psychology 140.*

Lyman, H. B. 1963. *Test scores and what they mean.* Englewood Cliffs, N.J.: Prentice-Hall.

Mager, R. F. 1962. *Preparing instructional objectives.* Palo Alto, Cal.: Fearon Publishers.

Manzo, A. V. 1969. ReQuest procedure. *Journal of Reading 13:* 123–126.

McLaughlin, G. H. 1969. SMOG grading—a new readability formula. *Journal of Reading 12:* 639–646.

Miller, G. A. 1956. The magical number seven, plus or minus two: Some limits on our capacity for processing information. *Psychological Review 63:* 81–97.

Miller, G. R., and Coleman, E. B. 1967. A set of 36 prose passages calibrated for complexity. *Journal of Reading Behavior 6:* 851–854.

Minsky, M. 1975. Framework for representing knowledge. In *The psychology of computer vision,* edited by P. H. Winston, 211–276. New York: McGraw-Hill.

Neale, D. C. 1969. The role of attitudes in learning mathematics. *The Arithmetic Teacher 16:* 631–640.

Neisser, U. 1976. *Cognition and reality.* San Francisco: W. H. Freeman.

Niles, O. S. 1964. Developing basic comprehension skills. In *Speaking of reading,* edited by J. K. Shert, Jr., 631–640. Syracuse, N.Y.: Syracuse University School of Education.

OEO's performance experiments will test seven instructional approaches. 1970. *The Nation's Schools 9:* 55.

Ogden, C. K., and Richards, I. A. 1923. *The meaning of meaning.* New York: Harcourt, Brace & World.

Payne, D. A. 1977. Reviews: Estes Attitude Scales. *Journal of Educational Measurement, 14,* 291–293.

Preston, R. C., and Botel, M. 1967. *Study habits inventory.* Chicago: Science Research Associates.

Rakes, T. A., and McWilliams, L. 1981. Assessing reading skills in the content areas. In E. K. Dishner, T. W. Bean, and J. E. Readence (Eds.) *Reading in the content areas: Improving classroom instruction.* Dubuque, Iowa: Kendall Hunt.

Richards, H. C., and Clark, D. S. 1983. Factor-analytic replications of the Estes attitude scales. *Journal of Psychoeducational Assessment 1:* 387–394.

Robinson, R. D. 1971. *An introduction to the cloze procedure.* Newark, Del.: International Reading Association.

Rogers, C. R. 1969. *Freedom to learn.* Columbus, Ohio: Merrill.

Rogers, C. R. 1982. *Freedom to learn in the 80s.* Columbus, Ohio: Merrill.

Rosenblatt, L. M. 1978. *The reader, the text, the poem.* Carbondale: University of Southern Illinois Press.

Ruddell, R. A. 1964. A study of the cloze comprehension technique in relation to structurally controlled reading material. *Proceedings of the international reading association 9:* 298–303.

Sanders, N. M. 1966. *Classroom questions: What kinds?* New York: Harper & Row.

Shaw, M. E., and Wright, J. M. 1967. *Scales for the measurement of attitudes.* New York: McGraw-Hill.

Shepherd, D. 1978. *Comprehensive high school reading methods.* 2d ed. Columbus, Ohio: Merrill.

Smith, F. 1982. *Understanding reading* 3d. ed. New York: Holt, Rinehart, Winston.

Smith, F. 1973. Twelve easy ways to make learning to read difficult. In *Psycholinguistics and reading,* edited by F. Smith, 183–196. New York: Holt, Rinehart, Winston.

Smith, F. 1975. *Comprehension and learning.* New York: Holt, Rinehart, Winston.

Spache, G. D. 1960. *Good reading for poor readers.* Champaign, Ill.: Garrard Press.

Spache, G. D., and Spache, E. B. 1977. *Reading in the elementary school,* 4th ed. Boston: Allyn and Bacon.

Stauffer, R. G. 1975. *Directing the reading-thinking process.* New York: Harper & Row.

Summers, E. G. 1977. Instruments for assessing reading attitudes: A review of research and bibliography. *Journal of Reading Behavior, IX,* 2, 137–155.

Taylor, W. 1953. Cloze procedure: A new tool for measuring readability. *Journalism Quarterly 30:* 415–433.

Thomas, E. L., and Robinson, H. A. 1981. *Improving reading in every class: A source book for teachers,* 3d. ed. Boston: Allyn and Bacon.

Thorndike, E. L. 1917. Reading as reasoning: A study of mistakes in paragraph reading. *Journal of Education Psychology 8:* 323–332.

Vacca, R. T. 1981. *Content area reading.* Boston: Little, Brown.

Valmont, W. J. 1972. Creating questions for informal reading inventories. *The Reading Teacher 25:* 509–512.

Vaughan, J. L. 1977. A scale to measure attitudes toward teaching reading in content classrooms. *Journal of Reading 20:* 605–609.

Vaughan, J. L. 1980. Affective measurement instruments: An issue of validity. *Journal of Reading, 24:* 16–19.

Vaughan, J. L., and Gans, P. J. 1978. Secondary reading inventory: A modest proposal. *Journal of Reading, 21:* 716–720.

Vaughan, J. L., and Sabers, D. 1977. Factors in validating affective scales: An applied study. *Journal of Reading Behavior 9:* 253–258.

Warmke, R. F.; Wyllie, E. D.; and Sellars, B. E. 1977. *Consumer decision making: Guides to better living.* Dallas: Southwestern.

Weber, G. 1974. *Uses and abuses of standardized testing in the schools.* Occasional Papers No. 22, Washington: Council for Basic Education.

Wigginton, E., ed. 1972. *The foxfire book.* New York: Doubleday.

Wigginton, E., ed. 1973. *Foxfire 2.* New York: Doubleday.

Wigginton, E., ed. 1975. *Foxfire 3.* New York: Doubleday.

Wigginton, E. 1975. *Moments: The foxfire experience.* Available from IDEAS, Magnolia Star Route, Nederland, CO., 80466.

Williams, M. 1958. *The velveteen rabbit.* New York: Doubleday.

Wolf, A., and Greenewald, J. 1980. Frequency of reading in secondary content areas: A follow-up observation study. Paper presented at National Reading Conference convention, San Diego.

Index